Competition and Regulation in the Airline Industry

Puppets in chaos

Steven Truxal

Routledge
Taylor & Francis Group

LONDON AND NEW YORK

First published 2012
by Routledge
2 Park Square, Milton Park, Abingdon, Oxon OX14 4RN

Simultaneously published in the USA and Canada
by Routledge
711 Third Avenue, New York, NY 10017

Routledge is an imprint of the Taylor & Francis Group, an informa business

British Library Cataloguing in Publication Data
A catalogue record for this book is available from the British Library

Library of Congress Cataloguing in Publication Data
Truxal, Steven.
   Competition and regulation in the airline industry : puppets in chaos / Steven Truxal.
   p. cm. — (Routledge research in competition law)
   ISBN 978–0–415–67196–5 (hardback) — ISBN 978-0-203-11946-4 (e-book) 1. Aeronautics,
Commercial—Law and legislation. 2. Aeronautics, Commercial—Deregulation.
3. Airlines—Deregulation. 4. Airlines—Mergers. 5. Competition, International. I. Title.
   K4095.T78 2012
   387.7'1—dc23
   2011045352

ISBN 978–0–415–67196–5(hbk)
ISBN 978–0–415–71854–7(pbk)

Typeset in Garamond
by Swales & Willis Ltd, Exeter, Devon

Competition and Regulation
in the Airline Industry

An examination of the relationship between competition and the deregulation and liberalization of the US and European air transport sectors reveals that the structure of the air transport sector has undergone a number of significant changes. A growing number of airlines are entering into horizontal and vertical cooperative arrangements and integration including franchising, codeshare agreements, alliances, 'virtual mergers' and in some cases, mergers with other airlines, groups of airlines or other complementary lines of business such as airports.

This book considers the current legal issues affecting the air transport sector incorporating recent developments in the industry, including the end of certain exemptions from EU competition rules, the effect of the EU–US Open Skies Agreement, the accession of new EU Member States and the Lisbon Treaty. The book explores the differing European and US regulatory approaches to the changes in the industry and examines how airlines have remained economically efficient in what is perceived as a complex and confused regulatory environment. Competition and Regulation in the Airline Industry will be of particular interest to academics and students of competition law as well as EU law.

Steven Truxal is Visiting Professor of English Law at Humboldt University, Berlin.

Routledge Research in Competition Law

Available titles in this series include:

The Internationalisation of Competition Rules
Brendan J. Sweeney

Antitrust Federalism in the EU and the US
Firat Cengiz

Competition and Regulation in the Airline Industry
Puppets in chaos
Steven Truxal

Forthcoming titles in this series include:

Merger Control in Post-Communist Countries
EC merger regulation in small market economies
Jurgita Malinauskaite

Merger Control in Europe
The gap in the ECMR and national merger legislations
Ioannis Kokkoris

Contents

Tables

Table of cases, decisions and legislation

EU case law and Commission decisions

Aer Lingus and Sabena [1989] OJ C204/11.

Air France and Alitalia [1989] OJ C 204/5.

Air France and Brymon [1989] OJ C 204/6.

Air France and Iberia [1989] OJ C 204/4.

Air France and NFD Luftverkehrs AG [1989] OJ C 204/3.

Air France and Sabena [1989] OJ C 204/7, 8 and 10.

Austrian Airlines–Lufthansa [2002] OJ L 242/25, [2003] 4 CMLR 252.

Austrian–Lufthansa [2002] OJ L 242/25, [2003] 4 CMLR 252.

British Airways–Air Liberté Commission Decision of 28 February 1997, Case IV/M.857.

British Airways–TAT (II) Commission Decision of 26 August 1996, Case IV/M.806.

British Midland v Aer Lingus Commission Decision of 26 Feburary1992, Case IV/33.544, [1992] OJ L 96, 10 April 1992.

Case 322/81, *NV Nederlandsche Banden Industrie Michelin v Commission* [1983] ECR 3461.

Case 40/73, *Suiker Unie v EC Commission* [1975] ECR 1663, [1976] 1 CMLR 295.

Case 56/65, *Société Technique Minière v Maschinenbau Ulm GmbH* [1966] ECR 234, 249, [1966] 1 CMLR 357.

Case 66/86, *Ahmed Saeed Flugreisen and Silver Line Reisebüro GmbH v Zentrale zur Bekämpfung unlauteren Wettbewerbs E.V.* [1989] ECR 803, [1990] 4 CMLR 102.

Case 85/76, *Hoffmann-La Roche v Commission* [1979] ECR 461, [1979] 3 CMLR 211.

Case C-38/2010 (ex NN 69/2010 CP 63/2010), Malév Hungarian Airlines, Negative decision and recovery, 09 January 2012.

Case C-169/08, *Presidente del Consiglio dei Ministri v Regione Sardegna* [2010] OJ C24/6, 30 January 2010

Case C-244/94, *Fédération Française des Sociétés d'Assurance and Others v Ministère de L'Agriculture et de la Pêche* [1995] ECR I-4013, [1996] 4 CMLR 536.

Case C-333/94, *Tetra Pak v Commission* (Tetra Pak II) [1996] ECR I-5951.

Case C-35/96, *Italy v Commission* [1998] ECR I-3851, [1998] 5 CMLR 889.

Case C-364/92, *SAT Fluggesellschaft v Eurocontrol,* [1994] ECR I-43, [1994] 5 CMLR 208.

Case T-203/01, *Manufacture française des pneumatiques Michelin v Commission* [2003] ECJ CELEX LEXIS 489.

Case T-219/99, *British Airways Plc v Commission* [2003] ECR 242.

Case T-342/07, *Ryanair Holdings Plc v European Commission (Ireland, intervening)* [2011] 4 CMLR 4.

Case T-342/99, *Airtours v Commission; Airtours–First Choice* [2000] OJ L 93/1.

Case T-83/91, *Tetra Pak International SA v Commission* [1994] ECJ CELEX LEXIS 6909.

Cases 48, 49, 51–7/69, *ICI v Commission* [1972] ECR 619, [1972] CMLR 557.

Cases T-68, 77 and 78/89, *Società Italiana Vetro v Commission* [1992] ECR 11-1403, [1992] 5 CMLR 302.

Commission Decision 94/118/EC of 21 December 1993 concerning aid to be provided by the Irish government to the Aer Lingus group [1994] OJ L 54/30, 25 February 1994.

Commission Decision 94/653/EC concerning the notified capital increase of Air France, 27 July 1994.

Commission Decision 94/696/EC regarding Olympic Airways and its subsidiaries, 7 October 1994.

Commission Decision 94/698/EC concerning increase in capital, credit guarantees and tax in favour of TAP Air Portugal, 6 July 1994.

Commission Decision 95/404/EC of 19 July 2005 on a procedure relating to the application of Council Regulation (EEC) No 2407/92 (Swissair–Sabena), [1995] OJ L 239/19–28, 7 October 1995.

Commission Decision of 16 January 1996, Case IV/25.545 – *Lufthansa–SAS* [1996] OJ L 54, 5 March 1996.

Commission Decision of 20 July 1995 concerning *Swissair–Sabena* Case IV/M.616.

Commission Decision of 7 March 2007 regarding state aid case C 10/06 (ex N555/05) – *Cyprus Airways Public Ltd's restructuring plan*, [2008] OJ L 49/51, 22 February 2008.

Commission Decision of 28 August 2009 declaring a concentration to be compatible with the common market and the EEA Agreement. Online. Available at <http://ec.europa.eu/competition/mergers/cases/decisions/m5440_20090828_20600_en.pdf> (accessed 27 July 2011).

EBU, [1993] OJ L 179/23, [1995] 4 CMLR 177.

Eurostar Case No. IV/M.1305 (19 December 1998).

Film Purchases by German Television Stations [1989] OJ L 284/96, [1990] 4 CMLR 841.

Höfner and Elser v Macrotron, [1991] ECR I-1979, [1993] 4 CMLR 306.

IAZ International Belgium NV v Commission, [1983] ECR 3369, [1984] 3 CMLR 276.

KLM–Air UK Case No. IV/M.967 (22 September 1997).

KLM–Alitalia Commission Decision of 11 August 1999, Case M/JV-19.

London City Airways and Sabena [1989] OJ C 204/12.

Lufthansa–SAS [1996] OJ L 54/28, [1996] 4 CMLR 845, (1998) 19 ECLR 116.

Marine-Wendel–SairGroup–AOM Commission Decision of 3 August 1999, Case IV/M.1494.

Olympic Airways [2003] OJ L 132/1, Decision 2003/372/EC of 11 December 2002.

Polypropylene, [1986] OJ L 230/1, [1988] 4 CMLR 347.

Ryanair/Aer Lingus [2008] OJ C 47/7, 'Final report of the Hearing Official in Case COMP/M.4439- *Ryanair/Aer Lingus*', 20 Febrary 2008.

Saachi, Case 155/73, [1974] ECR 409, [1974] 2 CMLR 177.

Sabena [1991] OJ L 300/48, 31 October 2001.

SAS v Community T-241/01 [2001] OJ L 265/15.

SAS–Maersk Air [2001] OJ L 265/15, [2001] 5 CMLR 1119.

Spanish Courier Services [1990] OJ L 233/19, [1991] 4 CMLR 560.

The Distribution of Package Tours During the 1990 World Cup [1992] L326/31, [1994] 5 CMLR 253.

United Airlines–US Airways Commission Decision of 12.1.2001, Case COMP/M.2041.

Virgin Atlantic/British Airways Commission Decision 2000/74 of 14 April 1999, OJ L30/1, 4 February 2004.

Völk v Vervaecke, Case 5/69, [1969] ECR 295.

Volkswagen, [1998] OJ L 124/60, [1998] 5 CMLR 33.

EU/EC/EEC legislation

Commission Regulation (EC) No 793/2004 of 21 April 2004 on common rules for the allocation of slots at Community airports [2004] OJ L 138, 30 April 2004.

Commission Regulation (EC) No 2790/1999 of 22 December 1999 on the application of Article 81(3) of the Treaty to categories of vertical agreements and concerted practices [1999] OJ L 336/21 of 29 December 1999.

Commission Regulation (EC) No 323/1999 of 8 February 1999 amending Regulation (EEC) 2299/89 on a code of conduct for computer reservations systems (CRSs) [1999] OJ L 40/1–8, 13 February 1999.

Commission Regulation (EC) No 868/2004 of 21 April 2004 concerning protection against subsidisation and unfair pricing practices causing injury to Community air carriers in the supply of air services from countries not members of the European Community [2004] OJ L 162, 30 April 2004.

Commission Regulation (EEC) No 1617/93 of 25 June 1993 on the application of Article 85 (3) of the Treaty to certain categories of agreements and concerted practices concerning joint planning and coordination of schedules, joint operations, consultations on passenger and cargo tariffs on scheduled air services and slot allocation at airports, [1993] OJ L 155/18 of 26 June 1993, [1988] OJ L 239/9.

Commission Regulation (EEC) No 2407/92 of 23 July 1992 on licensing of air carriers [1992] OJ L 240 of 24 August 1992.

Commission Regulation (EEC) No 2409/92 of 23 July 1992 on passenger fares and air cargo rates [1992] OJ L 240 of 24 August 1992.

Commission Regulation (EC) No 1105/2002 of 22 June 2002 on consultations on passenger tariffs and slot allocations at airports [2002] OJ L 167, 26 June 2002.

Council Regulation (EC) No 1/2003 of 16 December 2002 on the implementation of the on competition laid down in Articles 81 and 82 of the Treaty [2003] OJ L 1/1, 4 January 2003.

Council Regulation (EC) No 193/2004 of 20 January 2004 on the control of

US case law

Acknowledgements

I am indebted to Professor Jason Chuah for his eternal optimism, Rupert Dunbar for his eye for detail and Vincent Nichol for his sound research assistance on this book.

This book is dedicated to Christian and my parents for their unwavering support and encouragement.

Abbreviations

Airline abbreviations

AA	American Airlines
AC	Air Canada
AF	Air France
AM	Air Malta
AQ	Aloha Airlines (defunct)
AT	American Trans Air (defunct)
AWA	America West Airlines Inc.
AWAC	Air Wisconsin Airlines Corp.
AY	Finnair
AZ	Alitalia
BA	British Airways
BEA	British European Airlines (now BA)
BD	British Midland
BMED	British Mediterranean Airlines
CO	Continental Airlines (merged with United Airlines)
CX	Cathay Pacific
DL	Delta Air Lines
EA	Eastern Air Lines (defunct)
EI	Aer Lingus
F9	Frontier Airlines
FR	Ryanair
GB	GB Airways (defunct)
IB	Iberia
IJ	TAT European Airlines
JL	Japan Airlines
KL	KLM Royal Dutch Airlines (merged with Air France)
LA	Lan Chile
LH	Lufthansa German Airlines
LX	Swiss International Airlines
MG	Champion Air (defunct)
NH	All Nippon Airways

NW	Northwest Airlines (merged with Delta Air Lines)
OA	Olympic Airlines
OS	Austrian Airlines
OZ	Ozark Air Lines (defunct)
PA	Pan American Airlines (defunct)
PE	People Express Airlines
QF	Quantas Airways
QR	Qatar Airways
RW	Republic Airlines (defunct)
SB	Sabena (defunct)
SK	SAS Scandinavian Airlines System International
SQ	Singapore Airlines
SX	Skybus Airlines (defunct)
TG	Thai Airways
TP	TAP Air Portugal
TWA	Trans World Airlines (defunct)
TZ	Texas Air (defunct)
UA	United Airlines
VS	Virgin Atlantic Airlines

Airport abbreviations

AMS	Amsterdam Schipol (Netherlands)
ATL	Atlanta Hartsfield (US)
BOS	Boston Logan (US)
CDG	Paris Charles de Gaule (France)
CRL	Brussels-South Charleroi Airport (Belgium)
CVG	Cincinnati/Northern Kentucky (US)
DCA	Washington Regan National (US)
DEN	Denver Stapleton (US)
DFW	Dallas-Ft Worth (US)
DTW	Detroit Metro (US)
DUB	Dublin (Ireland)
EDI	Edinburgh
EWR	Newark (US)
FRA	Frankfurt am Main (Germany)
GLA	Glasgow
HHN	Hahn (Germany)
JFK	New York John F Kennedy (US)
LAX	Los Angeles Airport (US)
LCY	London City
LGA	New York LaGuardia (US)
LGW	London Gatwick
LHR	London Heathrow
LON	London (all airports)

LTN	Luton
MEL	Melbourne (Australia)
MIA	Miami (US)
MSP	Minneapolis-St Paul (US)
MUC	Munich (Germany)
MXP	Milan (Italy)
NYC	New York City (all airports) (US)
ORD	Chicago O'Hare (US)
ORY	Paris Orly (France)
STL	St Louis Lambert (US)
STN	London Stansted
SYD	Sydney (Australia)
ZRH	Zurich (Switzerland)

Other abbreviations

ADA	US Airline Deregulation Act
AFL-CIO	American Federation of Labor and Congress of Industrial Organizations
APEC	Asia-Pacific Economic Cooperation
ASEAN	Association of South East Asian Nations
ATA	Air Transport Association of America (now Airlines for America)
BSA	bilateral air service agreement
CAA	UK Civil Aviation Authority
CAB	US Civil Aeronautics Board (defunct)
CFI	European Court of First Instance (now General Court of the European Union)
CJEU	Court of Justice of the European Union (formerly European Court of justice)
CRS	computer reservations system
DB	Deutsche Bahn (German Rail)
DG	EU Energy and Transport Directorate General
ECMR	European Community Merger Regulation
ECN	European Competition Network
EEA	European Economic Area
EPP	employee protection programme
ETS	EU Emissions Trading Scheme
FAA	US Federal Aviation Administration
FARs	US Federal Aviation Regulations
FFP	frequent flyer programme
FTC	US Federal Trade Commission
GATS	General Agreement on Tariffs in Services
GCEU	General Court of the European Union
GDP	gross domestic product
GDS	global distribution system
IATA	International Air Transport Association

ICAO	International Civil Aviation Organization
LCC	low-cost carrier
MFN	most-favoured nation
MMC	UK Monopolies and Mergers Commission
MNC	multinational corporation
NAFTA	North American Free Trade Agreement
OECD	Organisation for Economic Cooperation and Development
OFT	UK Office of Fair Trading
OLC	open liberalization club
PSO	public service obligation
R&D	research and development
SNCF	*Société Nationale des Chemins de fer français* [National Corporation of French Railways]
SME	small and medium size enterprise
TFC	EC Temporary Framework Communication
US CAA	US Civil Aeronautics Administration (defunct)
US DoJ	US Department of Justice
US DoT	US Department of Transport
VAT	value-added tax
WTO	World Trade Organization

1 Introduction

Airlines operate within what is often perceived as a complex and confused regulatory environment. Despite the difficult competitive atmosphere in the sector, many US and European airlines have remained 'economically efficient'[1] or at least 'survived'. The remarkable level of innovative strategies devised and adopted by airlines, particularly through multilateral cooperation within the air transport sector and with firms in sectors complementary to air transport, is supporting evidence of this. Whilst the perceived impetus for this strategizing is that airlines are finding a way to 'cope' in a difficult regulatory environment, the actual impetus is a result of the combination of the industry's current structure as influenced or restricted by the respective regulatory regimes and the creative adaptation of the law to these business strategies, wedged within the confines of the current regulations.

Analysis of the US and European regulatory environments, in the international context and comparatively, reveals confusion – due to different approaches and rules – which, in addition to a number of separate theories that support cooperation and the inherently complex competitive markets, encourage private ordering through integrated business strategies. Through these, airlines are able in effect to utilize the law on liberalization and deregulation to achieve a competitive advantage, notwithstanding that the practices do at times skirt along the edges of competition rules. Thus, airline sector deregulation has impacted on and implicated airlines in the context of 'workable competition' which, taking the orthodox, Chicago School of economics view on market regulation, public ordering should produce. Despite the uncertainties of liberalization and deregulation as economic principles, the advent by airlines of market and non-market strategies has yielded a 'successful' sector. In other words, the examples of airline innovation provided in this book demonstrate workable business strategies for the sector; whether these are survival or success strategies remains to be determined.

The purpose of this book is to evaluate whether the state of intense industry cooperation and apparent innovation through tactical and strategic cooperation, which

---

1 The phrase 'economically efficient' is of course subject to various interpretations. Although it is not the aim of this book to theorize on what constitutes economic efficiency, a consensus view must be accepted to demonstrate how airlines have remained economically efficient.

most would consider to have been ushered in by deregulation and liberalization[2] as economic policies and air transport sector re-regulation, are a welcome outcome to what was envisaged by the neoclassical ideals of deregulation and liberalization as economic principles.[3] This book will demonstrate that the lack of certainty over deregulation and liberalization ideals and objectives has produced ineffectual deregulation and liberalization policies. This has resulted in poorly constructed regulatory frameworks that have brought about policy confusion and, at times, the risk that policymakers protect competitors rather than competition.[4] A level of complex and stated confusion by the industry of the regulatory frameworks, which are coincidental and consistent with policymakers, has reflected market innovation. However, the degree to which the innovation is a welcome policy outcome varies.

This book posits that, while there is a difference in approach in that the European Union (EU) system forces fair and transparent competition and the United States (US) system catches proven anti-competitive behaviour, market innovation is global. Despite the aforementioned complex and confused regulatory environment, airlines have demonstrated innovation through the conception of a myriad of economic efficiency-seeking commercial practices.[5] Thus, whilst the environment is perceived as difficult in terms of competitiveness, airlines appear in fact to be quite able to manoeuvre successfully within or along the edge of the competition rules to achieve efficiencies. It is clear that, before deregulation, regulators were puppets and their strings were pulled by airlines under regulatory capture. Now, post-deregulation, it remains unclear whether the regulators, as one might expect, or the airlines are pulling the strings. It is possible that the lessons learnt in the case of the airline industry should guide future regulators towards drafting more coherent policies, taking into account the significance of the market environment, with a greater emphasis on

2 *See* A.E. Kahn, 'Surprises from Deregulation', *AEA Papers and Proceedings*, 78, 1988, 316–317, generally and as a starting point on the experience of deregulation in the US; S. Morrison and C. Winston, 'The Remaining Role for Government Policy in the Deregulated Airline Industry', in S. Peltzman and C. Winston (eds), *Deregulation of Network Industries: What's Next?* (Washington: Brookings Institution Press, 2000), pp. 1–40; *and generally* S. Morrison and C. Winston, *The Economic Effects of Airline Deregulation* (Washington: Brookings Institution Press, 1986), on the positive effects of deregulation in the US; M. Franke, 'Innovation: The Winning Formula to Regain Profitability in Aviation?' *Journal of Air Transport Management*, 13, 2007, pp. 23–30, on devising new business models and differentiated products as an innovative approach to profitability; V. Inglada, B. Rey, A. Rodríguez-Alvarez and P. Coto-Millan, 'Liberalization and Efficiency in International Air Transport', *Transportation Research Part A*, 40,2006, 95–105, for an empirical approach to measuring efficiency post-deregulation in the US and liberalization in Europe.
3 At this stage deregulation and liberalization are applied as economic concepts rather than policies.
4 A policy risk is to confuse antitrust's objectives through the exercise of power through antitrust law to protect firms rather than balance this with the interests of the consumer–public and general competition. *See* S.G. Breyer, 'Regulation and Deregulation in the United States: Airlines, Telecommunications and Antitrust', in G. Majone (ed.), *Deregulation or Re-Regulation: Regulatory Reform in Europe and the United States* (New York: St. Martins Press, 1990), p. 34; this is discussed further below in Chapter 2 'The Evolution of Air Transport' and Chapter 4 under 'American and European Legislative Perspectives' in the context of constraints on regulatory authorities and the corresponding legal constraints on airlines.
5 These practices are detailed below in Chapter 5 'The Development of Tactical and Strategic Alliances' and include cost-saving and information-gathering alliances.

achieving a compromise between policy and the ideal industry situation, rather than adapting to the market-consequential behaviour of the industry.

Although on a fundamental level European competition law and American antitrust law agree in their definition of 'efficiency' as enhancing consumer welfare, their interpretations of 'consumer welfare' are divergent. The European approach recognizes efficiencies under Article 101(3) of the Treaty on the Functioning of the European Union (TFEU),[6] e.g. public service obligations and a history of block exemptions from the provisions of Articles 101 and 102 TFEU[7] as well as provisions on certain types of state aid under Articles 107 to 109 TFEU. American antitrust enforcers consider the key statutory 'rule of reason'[8] in the Sherman Antitrust Act,[9] e.g. where a combination or agreement between two firms unreasonably constrains trade.

The aim of the European competition rules is 'workable competition' in oligopolistic industries and therefore practices which European competition law deems procompetitive are evidence of this. On the other hand, the American antitrust law adopts an allocative efficiency[10] model, which is supply and demand-driven. Unsurprisingly then, the two respective policy methodologies are also dissimilar.

The European definition of 'economic efficiency' is adopted in this book in the context of these business practices. Rather than falling foul of Articles 101 and 102 TFEU, these business practices are evidence of 'workable competition' and are therefore 'efficient'. This takes into account efficiencies recognized by competition law under Article 101(3) TFEU with respect to enhancing consumer welfare such as public service obligations as qualifying exemptions from the competition rules.[11] The rationale for this methodology is that the EU system of competition law forces fair competition and operates alongside sector-specific market regulation, whereas the US antitrust system is concerned with anti-competitive behaviour that can be proved to have caused loss. Veljanovski sums up the positions:

> Competition law seeks to support the market and differs from the *ex ante* rules and standards which characterise much of economic and social regulation by being reactive, or as is often termed *ex post* regulation . . . However, generally

6 OJ C115/47, 9 May 2008.

7 These provisions will be discussed further below in Chapter 4.

8 As applied in *Standard Oil Co. v United States*, 221 U.S. 1, 66 (1911); *See also* R.A. Posner, 'The Rule of Reason and the Economic Approach: Reflections on the *Sylvania* Decision', *The University of Chicago Law Review*, 45(1), Fall 1977, 1–20; F.H. Easterbrook, 'Vertical Arrangements and the Rule of Reason', 53 *Antitrust LJ*, 1985, 135–174.

9 15 U.S.C. §1; The Act will be discussed in greater detail below in Chapter 4.

10 The allocative efficiency model suggests that a limited number of resources are allocated to consumers according to their desires under a system of supply and demand.

11 It should be noted here that American antitrust law also recognizes efficiencies under the Sherman Act's 'rule of reason'. In other words, only concentrations that unreasonably restrict trade are subject to antitrust actions. In *National Society of Professional Engineers v United States*, 435 U.S. 679 (1978), the US Supreme Court confirmed its landmark decision in *Standard Oil Co of New Jersey v United States*, 221 U.S. 1 (1911), that the 'rule of reason' analysis should focus on the economic and not social consequences of a restraint.

ex post competition law stands in contrast to statutory regulation which is typically a prescriptive *ex ante* approach.[12]

There are always two systems of competition legislation impacting on the transatlantic sector. Again, despite the complex and confused regulatory environment, the advent of non-market and market strategies has yielded a successful sector. This study argues that this 'efficiency' is achieved in the air transport sector through this innovation and cooperation.

It is put forward in this book that many of the business practices devised by airlines in the deregulated and liberalized sectors are innovative. The presumption is that the innovation and cooperation through tactical and strategic alliances and other commercial manoeuvring is evidence of healthy competitive behaviour. It is accepted that some practices may not be 'workable', notwithstanding whether the practices are discriminatory. Thus the contractual collaboration between airlines and with firms in industries complementary to air transport is innovative in the deregulatory context. If the practices are not discriminatory under applicable competition rules, then they are *prima facie* evidence of workable competition and are therefore efficient in the European context.[13]

The complexities surrounding the regulatory environment in which airlines operate comprise economic, social and political elements. The influence of economic theory on the development of competition policies and regulations varies by jurisdiction, creating disparity in the interpretation of competitive behaviour. The sector also has a significant 'public interest' character, as it exists within the public domain and is influenced to a certain extent by 'legacy' flag carriers through national identity, which evidently carries political weight. The degree to which this public interest rhetoric (on social welfare) influences regulators towards domestic competition policies impacts on the air transport sector.[14]

As pioneers of deregulation and privatization of the airline industries and on the basis of the magnitude of the transatlantic market, the EU and US are the most appropriate forums, as they provide an appropriate model from which to examine the two approaches to *market regulation*. First, a distinction must be made between the deregulatory policy approach taken in the US – as in the removal of government regulation – in the late 1970s and the liberalization – in the sense of relaxation of government restrictions – of the European market a decade later. It should be remembered that the situations in the respective markets were very different at the start of the deregulation and liberalization processes. This shaped the measures taken subsequently in the respective sectors. Although classically the economic concepts of deregulation and

---

12 C. Veljanovski 'Economic Approaches to Regulation', in R. Baldwin, M. Cave and M. Lodge (eds), *The Oxford Handbook of Regulation* (Oxford: Oxford University Press, 2010), pp. 18–19.

13 In Chapter 4, this regular and necessary interaction between firms implementing new strategies and the competition regulator leads to a quasi-fine tuning of the competition rules on terms of economic efficiency, which is made apparent with reference to Case T-219/99, *British Airways Plc v Commission* [2003] ECR 242.

14 The public interest aspect of air transport will be further examined in Chapter 2.

liberalization have similar objectives, they should not be regarded in the present study as a single deregulation–liberalization concept.[15]

In the US, deregulation meant a relatively swift withdrawal of governmental micromanagement of the industry, replaced by a market system policed by antitrust laws applied, for the most part, similarly across industries. European liberalization took the shape of a process with several steps, accounting for the unification of several national markets into a single market under the competition rules set out in Articles 101 and 102 TFEU. The application of competition rules in the EU takes a more direct approach, as they are often tailored to specific industries.[16] The general 'blanket' approach of US antitrust law, on the other hand, is slightly more comprehensive in the broad sense, which is likely a product of robust consumerism and capitalism at play in the American markets.

This study approaches certain aspects of the law from public and private[17] perspectives, including deregulation and liberalization as economic concepts applied to markets through policy, competition rules and antitrust, the socio-political concept of public utility, and economic theories on efficiency. The trend, or for now 'phenomenon',[18] in the airline sector is towards consolidation and commercial manoeuvring through various business strategies, which leads one to question 'what is the relief airlines seek' within what they perceive as a difficult regulatory environment under current European and US regulatory regimes?

To begin, this study recognizes that deregulation engenders autonomy. Airlines operating in a deregulated sector enjoy a level of freedom to manoeuvre in their quest for acquiring greater market share. Within this environment, airlines may devise what they perceive as a 'competitive strategy'.[19] What is phenomenal in the airline industry is the level of intense cooperation often between what formerly were rivals or competitor firms through a range of contractual arrangements, each with a varying degree of integration.

Though not a central theme, this book does consider the behaviours of individuals[20] who, within this 'free space', take strategic actions on behalf of a firm towards

---

15 The legal tapestry required for a balanced view on the varied approaches to the application of antitrust and competition law as mentioned here is offered in Chapter 4.

16 The EU and US regulatory approaches to competition are markedly different. The statutory language (Articles 101 and 102 TFEU and §§1 and 2, Sherman Act, respectively) and the application of these principles to anti-competitive behaviour will be examined in Chapter 4.

17 This intimates the aspect of private (contract) law (e.g. agreements airlines form with other airlines and with firms in sectors complementary to air transport) rather than private aspects of air transport (e.g. passengers).

18 This refers to the state of intense air transport industry-level cooperation and apparent innovation.

19 M.E. Porter, *Competitive Strategy: Techniques for Analyzing Industries and Competitors* (New York: Free Press, 1980).

20 A detailed analysis of the behaviours of individuals is outside the scope of this study. However, this perspective is necessary to mention in light of network theory and corporate governance issues as a 'legal' constraint on airlines; *See* B. Kleymann and H. Seristö, 'Challenges to Federation Governance', in *Managing Strategic Airline Alliances* (Aldershot: Ashgate, 2004), pp. 155–177.

group forming. Organizational behaviour theory[21] asserts that this is a natural tendency. Individuals responsible for the management of airlines' business strategies may exhibit behaviour that is based not necessarily on laws or cost-benefits, but on instinct. Other relationships may develop inorganically, through the active strategies that managers and directors devise and implement as influenced by business needs or desires, which are ultimately founded on the firm's survival.

When one adjusts the unit of analysis from the individual to the organization (airline), what is to observe is that airlines collaborate and form either tactical or strategic alliances. Network theory[22] *vis-à-vis* the creation of strategic alliances through repeated inter-firm cooperation and collaboration towards innovation and efficiencies, offers a second layer to the foundations of organizational behaviour theory to explain the new, flexible form of economic organization, applied to the air transport sector as strategic or global alliances, towards higher levels of network integration.

Next, situational[23] and contingency[24] theories suggest that airlines will adapt to their regulatory environment. Because agreements underpin the functionality of alliances and establish the inter-firm relationship, it is essential first to identify the contract as the key mechanism governing the terms of the integration arrangement and the pre-formation dialogue of such a contract. Contract theory recognizes the contract as of central importance to the law. In the classical sense, contract theory holds that the contract represents an expression of the will of the contracting parties, and for that reason should be respected and enforced by the courts. It follows, however, that although the associated principles of contract law are seen as objective and neutral, based on voluntary choices by the concerned parties, many of the problems contract law must deal with arise as a result of what parties have disagreed about, rather than what they have expressly agreed. Nonetheless, it is the contract that backs the market, which by its nature provides safeguards to the transacting parties.

Once an alliance[25] contract is agreed, relevant contributions made and standards are met, the alliance may finally begin operation.[26] As with the operation of any ven-

---

21 *See generally* H. Mintzberg, *The Rise and Fall of Strategic Planning* (Hemel Hempstead: Prentice Hall, 1994); J.B. Quinn, *Strategies for Change: Logical Incrementalism* (Homewood, IL: Irwin, 1980); and J. Child, D. Faulkner and S. Tallman, *Cooperative Strategy: Managing Alliances, Networks, and Joint Ventures*, 2nd ed. (Oxford: Oxford University Press, 2005).

22 R. Cowan, N. Jonard and J.B. Zimmermann, 'Bilateral Collaboration and the Emergence of Innovation Networks', *Management Science*, 57(7), 2007, 1051–1067; D. Lavie and L. Rosenkopf, 'Balancing Exploration and Exploitation in Alliance Formation', *Academy of Management Journal*, 49(4), 2006, 797–818.

23 For background on situational theory, *see* J. Barwise (ed.), *Situation Theory and Its Applications* (Stanford, CA: Center for the Study of Language and Information, 1991); and K. Devlin, *Logic and Information* (Cambridge: Cambridge University Press, 1991).

24 *See* M.A. Ketokivi and R.G. Schroeder, 'Strategic, Structural Contingency and Institutional Explanations in the Adoption of Innovative Manufacturing Practices', *Journal of Operations Management*, 22, 2004, 63–89.

25 This concept will be discussed in the context of tactical and strategic alliances below in Chapter 6.

26 This is at least in most domestic cases. In the event of an international (cross-border) alliance, questions might arise about the competitiveness of the agreement, which will be fielded by the concerned competition authorities in the respective jurisdictions.

ture involving more than one corporation, the alliance must ensure that the commitment of senior management is addressed, as well as general fiduciary matters, such as the linking of budgets and resources with strategic priorities, and measuring and rewarding alliance performance.

To clarify, there are different types of contracts: the classical sales contract (generally short-term or instantaneous), the complex market contract (more long-term in nature, such as those establishing franchises and joint ventures), and the social contract (in terms of public services and governance and the power to make law or enforce contracts). The circumstances of each transaction scenario determine the appropriate contract type. Each type of contract-based cooperation currently utilized in the airline industry merits discussion.

So, the contract plays a central and fundamental role not only in guiding the rules of engagement, but also as a protection against associated risks. One of these risks not yet accounted for is that which might arise in response to the law. Competition laws in both the EU and US prohibit trusts and cartels by strict definition of distorting competition. Thus the contract governing the cooperative relationship between airlines also brings with it added protection against being labelled a 'cartel' by competition authorities. This is under the assumption, however, that the agreed terms of the cooperative venture do not stretch far enough to include the collusion of misconduct by way of fraudulent trading.

Short of an 'actual' joint venture, where two companies typically pool resources in creating a separate entity, a 'tactical' or 'strategic' alliance is a mutually beneficial long-term formal relationship formed between two or more parties to pursue a set of agreed goals or to meet a critical business need while remaining independent organisations. The most typical types of contractual strategic alliances include licensing and cross-licensing, franchising, joint research and development (R&D), management contracts and 'turnkey' projects.[27]

When two parties begin working together with a common goal, this relationship might be construed as a *de facto* partnership. In common law, if the two entities are cooperating with a view to making a profit, this is a partnership. Up until the point of being an 'actual' joint venture, any cooperation, including those conducted under R&D-type motivations, should be outlined in a memorandum of association to avoid misunderstandings with one another and the law.

The responsiveness of airlines to this autonomy is evidenced by contractual (cooperative) relationships working towards economic efficiencies, including adaptation to the environment, which this study recognizes relates to situational and contingency theories, but does not aim to capture concretely within its scope. It is clear nonetheless that the level of adaptation depends on an array of situational factors, and therefore there is no 'single solution'. This study discusses the situational fators surrounding law and policy, rather than say, pure economics. However, an

---

27 In a 'turnkey' project, each entity is separately responsible for setting up a new business venture/factory and bringing it into full operation. This is generally done by bids made to the project management company under a procurement process.

examination of competition requires some introspect into economic and market regulation theories. Airlines form groups, which impact upon the global market and state of competition, which in the case of air transport is an oligarchic environment as oligopoly theory[28] advances. These groups also stimulate the interworking of the industry through private ordering[29] and rapport between airlines through their strategic moves, which game theory[30] generally seeks to explain. Thus the contract supports cooperative arrangements through private ordering in a regulatory space where public ordering appears to fail.[31]

Since airlines in a deregulated sector are exposed to strong, dynamic market forces, the contract mechanism therefore becomes paramount to a competitive sector in a deregulated market in relation to the operation of the sector in providing fundamental market stability. Airlines develop faith in the market, which, backed by contracts, provides safeguards to the transacting parties. The experience of intense cooperation between airlines globally, predominantly on the transatlantic sector, evidences the significance of organizational behaviour through cooperative manoeuvring and of the contract itself. So the contract is, from the perspective of legal positivism as adopted in this book, central to the bilateral and multilateral nature of cooperation through partnerships and strategic alliances in the air transport sector.

It must also be noted that air transport has a unique economic structure.[32] The fact that its very operation calls for the close involvement of governments in the business practice of route planning through bilateral and multilateral agreements on air services owing to the sovereignty issue surrounding national airspace distinguishes air transport from other industries through a system of public ordering.[33] The system of reliance on governments may be further influenced by or interpreted as economic protectionism. Although the air transport industry is global by nature, national air transport sectors are generally regulated on a bilateral basis, and as the demand for air transport increases and new airlines come to the market or existing airlines offer new routes or frequencies, this necessitates continuous, open negotiations between governments on behalf of airlines to secure reciprocal traffic rights. 'It is ironic that

---

28 *See* J. Friedman, *Oligopoly Theory* (Cambridge: Cambridge University Press, 1983); and M. Olson, *The Logic of Collective Action*, (Cambridge, MA: Harvard University Press, 1965).

29 *See* M.J. Trebilcock, *The Limits of Freedom of Contract* (Cambridge, MA: Harvard University Press, 1997); and S.L. Schwarcz, 'Private Ordering', *Northwestern University Law Review*, 97, Fall 2002, 319–350.

30 *See* T.C. Schelling, *The Strategy of Conflict* (Cambridge, MA: Harvard University Press, 2007); D. Fundenberg and J. Tirole, *Game Theory* (Boston, MA: MIT Press, 1991); and W.J. Baumol, *Economic Theory and Operations Analysis* (Englewood Cliffs, NJ: Prentice-Hall, 1965).

31 *See generally* P.A. Bolton and M.A. Dewatripont, *Contract Theory* (Cambridge, CA: MIT Press, 2005); S.A. Smith, *Contract Theory* (Oxford: Oxford University Press, 2004); and M.C. Keeley, *A Social-Contract Theory of Organizations* (Notre Dame, IN: University of Notre Dame Press, 1988).

32 The economics of the airline industry are characterized on three levels: (1) by its (political) dependence on governments to secure traffic rights; (2) its network structure (R.A. Posner, *Economic Analysis of Law*, 7th ed., Austin, TX: Wolters-Kluwer, 2007), which effects scheduling, traffic and aircraft size (J. Brueckner, 'Network Structure and Airline Scheduling', *Journal of Industrial Economics*, 52(2), 2004, 291–312); and (3) its cost structure, including tax, fees, exchange rate risk and product differentiation.

33 This concept will be discussed in further detail in Chapter 3 under 'Public ordering'.

government intervention has rendered air travel – an industry that should naturally be more global than most – far less global in its operations than virtually any other large industry'.[34]

The growing global trend is towards the negotiation of air traffic rights on a regional or multilateral basis. Despite this, a fundamental dialogue through airline dependence on governments to negotiate these rights on their behalf between industry and regulator remains paramount to the operation of the industry. The culmination of this is the EU–US Air Transport Agreement,[35] first implemented provisionally in March 2008, which sparked what is undoubtedly the biggest regulatory development in the industry for 30 years and affects directly economic and operational decisions and structures.[36] 'The agreement . . . is estimated to have an impact of over 12 billion dollars per year.'[37] Under the first phase of the working agreement, previous limits imposed on flights between specific EU and US airports through bilateral agreements were removed.[38] Any airline that is registered in a Member State of the EU or in the US may now fly to any airport within the other's borders, subject to the availability of take-off and landing slots at both ends of the proposed route.[39] Thus there does remain a 'layer' of regulatory control.[40]

34 B. Vasigh, K. Fleming, and T. Tacker, *Introduction to Air Transport Economics* (Farnham: Ashgate, 2008), p. 138.
35 The agreement was originally referred to as the EU–US Open Skies Agreement. *See* Decision 2007/337/ EC of the Council and the Representatives of the Governments of the Member States of the European Union, meeting within the Council of 25 April 2007, on the signature and provisional application of the Air Transport Agreement between the European Community and its Member States and the United States of America, OJ L134/1, 25 May 2007; *See also* Protocol to Amend the Air Transport Agreement between the United States of America and the European Community and its Member States, signed on April 25 and 30, 207. Online. Available HTTP: <http://ec.europa.eu/transport/air/international_avi-ation/country_index/doc/2010_03_25_us_protocol_attach_b.pdf> (accessed 12 March 2011). The Council of Transport ministers adopted the Second Stage Agreement (Protocol amending the First Stage Agreement) on 24 June 2010.
36 An example of this elsewhere is the Multilateral Agreement for the Liberalization of International Air Transport (MALIAT), or 'Kona Agreement', between APEC nations. More recently, regional coop-eration within African states has been in the press (D. Semberya, 'Kikwete Advises on Air Transport Investment', *East African Business Week*, 5 September 2011. Online. Available HTTP: <http://www.busiweek.com/11/news/tanzania?start=5> (accessed 13 September 2011)). *See also* R. Doganis, *The Airline Business in the 21st Century*, 2nd ed. (London: Routledge, 2006), pp. 59–62.
37 Vasigh, Fleming and Tacker, *Introduction to Air Transport Economics*, p. 160 citing E. Alford and R. Cham-pley, 'The Impact of the 2007 US–EU Open Skies Air Transport Agreement', *International Trade Admin-istration: US Department of Commerce*, ITA Occasional Paper no. 07–001(2007).
38 This includes the former bilateral 'Bermuda II Agreement' between the UK and US, which will be discussed in further detail in Chapter 6.
39 Open skies agreements are not exclusively found in the EU and US. *See for instance* T.H. Oum and K. Yamaguchi, 'Asia's tangled skies', *Far Eastern Economic Review*, January–February 2006, as cited in Vasigh, Fleming and Tacker, *Introduction to Air Transport Economics*, p. 164 for a study on Australia–New Zealand; and L. Francis, 'Singapore–China "Open Skies" has Restriction on LCCs', *Air Transport Intel-ligence News*, February 2005, as cited in Vasigh, Fleming and Tacker, *Introduction to Air Transport Economics*, p. 165.
40 It was hoped that a Trans-Atlantic Common Aviation Area would be created, moving from 'open skies' to 'clear skies', but this is yet to be achieved fully. *See* Doganis, *The Airline Business*, pp. 59–66.

It followed that British Airways (BA)[41] formed a new airline, registered under the name 'Open Skies', which came into operation in June 2008. The airline flies from Paris base at ORY to Newark (EWR)[42] and Washington, DC–Dulles (IAD).[43] Air France (AF) made a similar move in collaboration with Delta Airlines (DL), expanding its services to include London Heathrow (LHR) to Los Angeles, beginning of the provisional implementation of the EU–US Air Transport Agreement in 2008.[44] These examples represent EU freedom of establishment meeting true freedom of the (open) air.[45]

Commonly held views on 'regulating' international aviation may be taken to include a wide range of aspects, including government aviation administrations and international conventions.[46] Whilst it is accepted that general and even market 'regulation' impacts on the way airlines deliver services (e.g. the aspects in which airlines interact with passengers), this study recognizes that although there is a myriad of regulatory instruments[47] (such as conventions and antitrust), there is no unified system of international economic market control for aviation. Indeed, even after the Chicago Convention introduced nine so-called 'freedoms of the air' in 1944, which were subsequently adopted as express terms in most bilateral air service agreements,[48] the former Bermuda I and II Agreements between the US and UK, for instance, did set out which airlines could access which airports and with what frequency.[49]

It is considered that airlines are subject to diverse and complex national market regulatory regimes, each with varying degrees of formalization, which in the light of the global nature of air transport[50] means that an airline operating on an international route is likely to encounter two different, overlapping policy-based systems of *economic and market regulation*.[51] The situation is further hurdled by policy considerations for

---

41 Airline abbreviations are based on the two letter IATA airline designator codes, with one exception, 'US Airways' is written out as 'US' denotes the United States.

42 Airport abbreviations are based on the three letter IATA airport designator codes.

43 *See* the airline's website at <http://www.flyopenskies.com> (accessed 15 August 2011).

44 Air France cancelled the route seven months later ('Air France Cancel London – LA from 26 October 2008', *Airline Route*. Online. Available HTTP: <http://airlineroute.net/2008/10/08/air-france-cancel-london-la-from-26oct08/> (accessed 5 July 2011).

45 *See* B.F. Havel, *Beyond Open Skies: A New Regime for International Aviation* (The Netherlands: Kluwer Law International, 2009).

46 The Warsaw, Chicago and Montreal Conventions are the most notable examples.

47 *See* S.G. Breyer, 'Analyzing Regulatory Failure: Mismatches, Less Restrictive Alternatives, and Reform', *Harvard Law Review*, 92, 1979, 549–609; *Regulation and Its Reform* (Cambridge, MA: Harvard University Press, 1982).

48 *See* ICAO, Doc 9626, Part 4. Online. Available HTTP: <http://www.icao.int/icao/en/trivia/freedoms_air.htm> (accessed 10 May 2011). *See* Table 1.1.

49 The Bermuda II Agreement was formerly the 'traditional' bilateral air services arrangement between the US and UK governments, which was in place until the Air Transport Agreement with the US was provisionally implemented in March 2008. Signed in 1977, the Bermuda II amended the previous 1946 Bermuda I agreement. The highly restrictive agreement outlined which airlines were permitted to fly, for instance, to London's Heath row *versus* Gatwick airports from designated US cities.

50 Examples of regional agreements are the European Union (EU) and Asia-Pacific Economic Cooperation (APEC) arrangements.

51 It is emphasized here that the focus of this study is on economic and market regulation rather than other forms of regulation. This concept will be explored further in Chapters 3 and 4.

Table 1.1 Freedoms of the air[a]

Freedom	Rights
1st	To fly across the territory of either states without landing
2nd	To land in either state for non-traffic purposes, e.g. refuelling without boarding or deplaning passengers
3rd	To land in the territory of the first state and board passengers coming from the home state of the airline
4th	To land in the territory of the first state and board passengers travelling to the home state of the airline
5th	To land in the territory of the first state and board passengers travelling on to a third state where the passengers deplane (beyond rights)
6th	To transport passengers moving between two other states via the home state of the airline
7th	To transport passengers between the territory of the granting state and any third state without going via the home state of the airline[b]
8th	To transport cabotage traffic between two points in the territory of the granting state on a service which originates or terminates in the home state of the foreign carrier or outside the territory of the granting state (consecutive cabotage)
9th	To transport cabotage traffic of the granting state on a service performed entirely within the territory of the granting state (stand alone cabotage)

a Only the first five 'freedoms' have been officially recognized in international treaties, therefore the remaining four 'freedoms' are considered 'so-called' by the ICAO (ICAO, Doc 9626, Part 4. Online. Available HTTP: <http://www.icao.int/icao/en/trivia/freedoms_air.htm> (accessed 12 June 2011)).

b *See* P. Forsyth, 'The Economics of 7th Freedom' in J.F. O'Connell and G. Williams (eds), *Air Transport in the 21st Century: Key Strategic Developments* (Farnham: Ashgate, 2011), pp. 211–233.

environmental[52] and safety[53] concerns, and consumer regulation,[54] in that each impacts on economic regulation and thus implies that organizations within the industry should behave accordingly. An airline might develop an innovative business strategy, either in response to a policy or of its own accord, which causes a certain repercussion in the sector. According to Porter, a firm or group of firms might be able to apply its

52 *See* on the EU Emissions Trading Scheme (ETS), the European Parliament Legislative Observatory for Directive 2008/101/EC of 19 November 2008 amending Directive 2003/87/EC so as to include aviation activities in the scheme for greenhouse gas emission allowance trading within the Community [2009] OJ L8/3 (ETS Directive). Online. Available HTTP: <http://www.europarl.europa.eu/oeil/file.jsp?id=5428942> accessed 12 March 2011. A challenge was brought against the expansion of the ETS scheme to aviation and the 'legality' of the ETS legislation before the UK High Court, which made a reference for a preliminary ruling to the CJEU. See Case C-366/10 *Air Transport Association of America, American, Continental and United Airlines v Secretary of State for Energy and Climate Change* (2011), available at <http://curia.europa.eu>(accessed 5 January 2012).

53 The International Civil Aviation Organization (ICAO) is mandated by the Chicago Convention to oversee international safety standards. *See* 'Convention on International Civil Aviation, 9th ed., Doc. 7300/9, 2006' (Chicago Convention 1944). Online. Available HTTP: <www.icao.int/icaonet/arch/doc/7300/7300_9ed.pdf> (accessed 12 May 2011).

54 *See for instance* Regulation (EC) No 261/2004 establishing common rules on compensation and assistance to passengers in the event of denied boarding and of cancellation or long delay of flights, and repealing Regulation (EEC) No 295/91, [2004] OJ L46/1; Bill HR 729, 112th US Congress, 1st Session, 15.02.2011.

business model and, although profitability is low, individual airlines have been able to make a return in excess of the industry average by applying unique business models.[55] This action might be evidence of a workable business strategy. Therefore at some stage that economic regulation will impact on the structure of the market: either defining directly this structure *vis-à-vis* explicit rules, such as in the EU; guiding indirectly the structure by law through policy, an optimal situation where airlines and regulators respond to one another; or a less 'hands-on', more *ex post* approach that provides airlines with autonomy required for an entrepreneurial spirit to flourish.

The complexity of the environment as characterized by potential conflicts presents a difficult competitive situation for airlines, *sine qua non*. These conflicts might include the national *versus* regional *versus* supranational approaches to regulate; regional *versus* national market control; as well as market and non-regulatory operational *versus* regulatory influences. While it is neither the purpose of this introductory chapter nor the book to discourse on the general concept of regulation or regulation theory,[56] some discussion is required on how the accepted knowledge of regulation might be applied to the context of air transport deregulation. This book focuses on the regulation of markets, rather than the regulation of the operations of the airline industry, e.g. safety and the environment.[57] The aim is not to assess directly whether or not deregulation and liberalization were 'good' ideas, nor is it to debate whether they were the appropriate remedies to the long experience of gross inefficiencies of the air transport industry. Nonetheless, the impact of market deregulation and liberalization on airlines will be evaluated, thereby indirectly addressing the efficacy of these movements in the context of air transport. Supreme Court Justice Breyer argues that deregulation has been accomplished, to the extent that the US sector is in fact 'deregulated' in the classical sense.[58] Thus, both deregulation and liberalization are accepted as achieved in terms of implementation and, consequently, that is the starting point for this study.

Although the study is posited against the backdrop of a deregulated[59] air transport sector, it will be essential first to provide an industry 'snapshot' of the situations in the US and EU at the moment of deregulation and liberalization to serve as a template comprising the original objectives and notions of deregulation of the US and EU air transport sectors from both a historical and legal perspective. Once the study defines the deregulation and liberalization policy approaches and objectives, the template

---

55 Porter, *Competitive Strategy*.

56 *See* H.M. Bernstein, *Regulating Business by Independent Commission* (Princeton, NJ: Princeton University Press, 1955); C. Findlay and D. Round, 'The "Three Pillars of Stagnation": Challenges for Air Transport Reform', *World Trade Review*, 5(2),2006, 251–270; R. Baldwin, and M. Cave, *Understanding Regulation: Theory, Strategy, and Practice* (Oxford: Oxford University Press, 1990).

57 While the author accepts that issues relating to the environment and safety are important to many discussions on the operation of the airline industry, these do not feature in the current study for reasons of maintaining a manageable scope.

58 Breyer, 'Regulation and Deregulation'.

59 Both the US and European air transport sectors are accepted as 'deregulated' in the classical sense: that is, 'free' of government controls on market entry and pricing, and from state aid. The process of deregulating the sectors is discussed in further detail below, where a distinction is made between steps taken to *deregulate* the US sector *versus* to *liberalize* the EU sector.

will be used to assess whether the policy through law followed by policy industry responses lead to achievement of the original policy objectives.

This book examines the relationships between competition, deregulation and liberalization, which reveals that the structure of the air transport sector is undergoing a number of significant changes: a growing number of airlines are entering into cooperative horizontal and vertical arrangements and integration including interlining, franchising, code share agreements, tactical and strategic alliances, 'virtual mergers' and in some cases, mergers with or acquisitions of other airlines, groups of airlines and other complementary lines of business such as airports, catering and ground handling. These cooperative strategies may be evidence of an accelerated continuation of the consolidation movement that kicked off in the US industry in the 1980s, motivated by any number of factors, from 'survival' to 'joint marketing strategy'. To date, the European experience has been consolidation of former flag carriers into 'pan-European' carriers and the procurement success of low-cost carriers (LCCs) of lucrative relationships with smaller, regional airports throughout Europe. The historical development of LCCs in the US and EU must first be distinguished. In the US, many LCCs entered the deregulated market and quickly exited to be replaced by stronger LCCs, however, 'LCCs quickly appeared in Europe following deregulation, opening new markets and entering established intra-EU markets of the legacy carriers . . . [thus] the stability of LCCs in Europe was more firmly established from the beginning'.[60] Again, since European and US airlines have led the movement, the respective air transport sectors serve as unparalleled platforms from which to examine the multitude of factors influencing cooperation within the industry, owing to the sheer amount of cooperative manoeuvring in these markets.[61]

Sector deregulation introduces a number of risks that challenge the new system.[62] The conflicting economic and social influences[63] over the deregulatory policy approach produce an at times confused hybrid system in the case of the air transport sector. Furthermore, the lack of certainty over deregulation and liberalization objectives, particularly in the EU where Member States already suffer from a certain lack of certainty, has produced confused deregulation and liberalization policies. The poorly

60 European Commission and US Department of Transportation (ECDOT), 'Transatlantic Airline Alliances: Competitive Issues and Regulatory Approaches' (2010), p. 2. Online. Available HTTP: <ec.europa.eu/competition/sectors/transport/reports/joint_alliance_report.pdf> (accessed 23 July 2011); *see also* M. Reisinger, 'Why Do Low Cost Carriers Arise and How Can They Survive the Competitive Responses of Established Airlines? A Theoretical Explanation', in P. Forsyth *et al.* (eds.), *Competition versus Predation in Aviation Markets: A Survey of Experience in North America, Europe and Australia* (Aldershot: Ashgate, 2005) pp. 269–287; *see* on the impact of low cost carriers in Europe, G. Williams *Airline Competition: Deregulation's Mixed Legacy* (Aldershot: Ashgate, 2002) pp. 87–121.

61 The author accepts that whilst there are instances of cooperation in sectors outside of the EU and US, and that a similar study on command or mixed economies merits research, these are declined in the current study for reasons of manageability.

62 E.g. public policy and interest debates, environmental considerations and legal efficacy. These will be discussed below.

63 This refers to the economic regulation of an industry that is in the public domain, insofar as it is scrutinized by the public who influence regulators to create certain policies, or for some reason leave regulators hesitant to act.

constructed regulatory framework brings about confusion and the risk of regulators protecting competitors rather than competition. Confusion over unclear objectives has led to transport and competition policies and laws, which should encourage innovation and economic efficiency, but in fact confuse the already complex competitive environment so much so that airlines resort to private ordering and to an extent self-regulation to drive industry innovation. The objectives of deregulation and liberalization are thus achieved, but if regulators were more concerned with outcomes, it is argued that a more symbiotic, interdependent dialogue with private orderings would be evidence of 'good regulatory policy'.

European Commission regulations and to some extent the Court of Justice of the European Union (CJEU) decisions are evidence of liberalization of the sector towards European 'antitrust' and away from the Chicago School of market regulation, where practices are 'forbidden unless expressly allowed'. For instance, the 'U-turn' from the previous prohibition of the larger European incumbent carriers from merging in the early 1990s, according to Williams, was a policy reaction to the increasing number of US megacarriers.[64]

Schwarcz puts forward that a seemingly more efficient, quasi-self-regulation is evident in the airline sector; airlines have to some degree corrected the failures of lawmakers and avoided using interest groups to assert pressure.[65] According to Ayres and Braithwaite, private ordering may be categorized as self-regulation, enforced self-regulation, or command regulation with discretionary punishment.[66] Assisted by the empirical foundation of Rose-Ackerman's analysis, these theories reveal that good regulatory policy is acceptance of an inevitability of some symbiosis existing between public and private orderings.[67] These interdependent dialogues between the state regulation, private orderings, industries and regulators are referred to as 'the code'.

This book critiques the actions taken by airlines to determine whether they are purely innovative (autonomous); or are taken in response to regulation supported by law[68]; or if they are a reaction to internal changes in the industry, market or market structure, and thus evidence of independent or entrepreneurial market innovation. Although deregulation and liberalization were paramount as neoclassical economic ideals to the production of policies and provide airlines with the autonomy necessary to manoeuvre

---

64 Williams, *Airline Competition*.

65 Schwarcz, 'Private Ordering', pp. 319–350.

66 I. Ayres, and J. Braithwaite, *Responsive Regulation: Transcending the Deregulation Debate* (Oxford: Oxford University Press, 1992).

67 S. Rose-Ackerman, 'Progressive Law and Economics – and the New Administrative Law', *Yale Law Journal*, 98, 1988, 341–368.

68 For example, in 2007, BA admitted collusion over the price of long-haul passenger fuel surcharges resulting in a cartel. Set independently, fuel surcharges do not constitute a cartel. It was fined £121.5m by the Office of Fair Trading (OFT) for the infringement of competition law. Virgin Atlantic was not fined, in accordance with the OFT's leniency policy, which provides immunity to the firm who participates in but first notifies the OFT of the prohibited activity. The OFT is currently conducting a criminal investigation into whether the actions of the individuals responsible at BA were in breach of the Enterprise Act 2002. ('British Airways to pay record £121.5m penalty in price fixing investigation' *OFT*. Online. Available HTTP <www.oft.gov.uk/news/press/2007/113–07> (accessed 10 March 2011)).

commercially, neither the principles alone nor policymakers should be given all the credit for the innovation. There are other influencing factors afoot in the airline sector's 'rationalization' of the situation, including the creative, non-conservative character of the airlines, the continuous development of technology, globalization and growing populations and economies.

Of course the lessons learnt from the 'airline experience' should guide future regulators towards drafting clearer policies, taking into account the significance of the market environment, to achieve a policy–industry equilibrium: one that is more linear or causal. Policymakers in a deregulated and liberalized air transport sector otherwise will have little impact on the state of market innovation and level of economic efficiency. To add to the 'chaos', the complex system of bilateral air service agreements that is already compounded by differing regulatory and policy approaches, are being replaced slowly by multilateral arrangements. The industry is on the verge of new challenges, however, such as climate change and environmental protection as prompted by the inclusion of aviation in 2012 in the EU Emissions Trading Scheme (ETS). It is unforeseeable whether the chaos will ever really subside: 'One of the most unique features of the aviation industry is the unprecedented amount of regulatory and operational control that the industry is subject to.'[69]

A comparative look at the EU and US approaches to airline deregulation and re-regulation through competition rules and antitrust offers the reader two instances of market regulation along a regulatory spectrum. At one end is the explicit rules-based approach that forces or defines the market structure and in an *ex ante* fashion, and at the other end is the far less interventionist model where firms act more autonomously and the 'rule' is applied more *ex post*. Recent developments in more interdependent dialogue between EU and US competition authorities and with representatives from the airline industry evidence progress towards the industry–policy equilibrium and an opportunity for airlines to restructure while policymakers develop and adapt more befitting remedies, and less 'puppeteering'.

---

69 Vasigh, Fleming and Tacker, *Introduction to Air Transport Economics*, p. 107.

2 The evolution of air transport

Introduction: the regulation era (1914–1978)

The air transport industry has radically transformed since the first scheduled commercial airline took to flight in 1914.[1] In 1926, the US Congress passed the Air Commerce Act,[2] which assigned the US Department of Commerce a number of regulatory tasks associated with civil air transport. This was headed under the Aeronautics Branch of the Commerce Department, which was later named the Bureau of Air Commerce. Under the Civil Aeronautics Act of 1938,[3] responsibility for civil aviation was transferred from the Bureau of Air Commerce to a new, independent agency, the Civil Aeronautics Administration (US CAA). The governing body for this new administration was the Civil Aeronautics Board (CAB).[4]

John Robson, Chairman of the CAB in the years leading up to deregulation (1975–77), said the CAB was created to

> protect the public and maintain order in the rapidly growing field of commercial aviation, the CAB was also launched with the blessing of the existing carriers that, in the immortal 1938 comment to Congress of one airline executive, wanted protection from 'destructive competition'.[5]

What ensued was a highly bureaucratic regulation of the domestic air transport sector, most notably inefficient in the CAB's dealing with requests from both incumbent and new airlines to operate on new routes or increase frequencies on existing routes. The Federal Aviation Act of 1958[6] established the Federal Aviation Administration (FAA)

---

1 For a detailed examination of the evolution of international aviation beginning with Orville Wright taking to the sky in 1903, *see* D.L. Rhoades, *Evolution of International Aviation: Phoenix Rising*, 2nd ed. (Aldershot: Ashgate, 2008).

2 Ch. 344, §10, 44 Stat. 568, 20 May 1926.

3 52 Stat. 973, 23 June 1938.

4 The incremental deregulation and the effects of deregulation are discussed below in the context of US antitrust.

5 J.E. Robson, 'Airline Deregulation: Twenty Years of Success and Counting', *Regulation*, Spring 1988, 17.

6 49 U.S.C. §1382.

to replace the US CAA. The CAB retained the 'regulatory' authority to determine which routes airlines could fly and oversee the fares they charged, but its authority to set aviation regulations was subsequently transferred to the FAA. Section 414 of the Federal Aviation Act required the CAB to immunize from antitrust laws transactions specifically approved or necessarily contemplated by an order of approval under section 412,[7] provided the immunity was found to be in line with public interest. The immunity would attach automatically upon approval. The CAB was thusly required to approve any agreement by air carriers it did not find 'adverse to public interest'[8] or 'in violation of the Act'.[9] In addition, the Federal Aviation Act grants sole responsibility to the FAA for US civil and military systems of air navigation and air traffic control. The relevant aviation regulations are known as the Federal Aviation Regulations (FARs).[10] Airlines were effectively protected from market forces, governed instead according to 'internal regulatory politics', a regulatory process, which 'provided little incentive for airline executives to seek better, less costly ways to serve consumers'.[11] Robson recalls the end of that era of state regulation:

> The watershed reform came in April 1976 when the CAB unanimously announced its support for deregulation, becoming the first regulatory agency to acknowledge the fundamental deficiencies of the regulatory system it administered, thereby triggering its own abolition. The CAB's reputation as a first class, non-political, impartial regulator, and the respect it enjoyed for its expertise in commercial aviation, made its embrace of deregulation a politically powerful statement for a major policy change. In a 180–degree turnaround, policymakers came to agree that the airlines could serve consumers better if the intrusive regulatory structure were dismantled, thereby replacing government regulators with market forces as the arbiter of fares and service.[12]

The CAB tightly regulated the US air transport industry until 1978. During this tenure, private interests influenced licensing and regulatory capture was evident. Until 1978, the FAA also assured airlines of an orderly and profitable division of routes, without the opportunity for new entrants to disrupt things. In 1975, the issues surrounding this were raised in the Senate and from 1976–78, the air transport industry benefitted from intense media coverage, thereby serving to remove gradually the regulatory capture. This was a turning point for regulators – from puppets to puppeteers.

In 1978, the US Congress passed the US Airline Deregulation Act[13] (ADA). Its directive was to remove government control from commercial aviation and expose the passenger airline industry to market forces, bringing about a major change to the

---

7 *Turicentro v American Airlines, Inc* 303 F. 3d 293; 2002 US App. LEXIS 18467.
8 This language seems to put public welfare on par with the objective of antitrust policies.
9 49 U.S.C. §1382 at §412(b).
10 *FAA*. Online. HTTP available: <http://www.faa.gov> (accessed 11 July 2011).
11 Ibid., p. 18.
12 Ibid.
13 US Public Law 95–504, passed and signed 24 October 1978.

industry's structure. As a result, US airlines were given the freedom to enter into any interstate city-pair market, without prior permission of the CAB and accordingly, carriers were left to defend their own market territory and economic integrity.

Within the first three years of the Act's implementation, the 'previously strong financial position of nearly all US carriers rapidly transformed into one of heavy losses'.[14] Indeed, the consensus view at the time was that, 'the US airline industry (and, to a certain extent, the global airline industry) [had] been characterized by volatility. Periods of high revenues are followed by periods of economic drought'.[15]

Strong market forces gave way to consolidation by way of numerous mergers, bankruptcies and successive acquisitions by the dominant carriers. The principal strategy of the stronger carriers was to develop hub-and-spoke[16] flight networks. In order to maintain a position of dominance at hubs, the relevant state regulatory authority imposed restrictions on market entry. By 1984, the larger carriers began forming so-called 'codeshare'[17] partnerships as tactical alliances with smaller commuter airlines in a mutually beneficial quest for improved connectivity and overall efficiency.[18] Thus economic regulation of the deregulated US aviation market is managed through antitrust principles.

According to William Brock, Secretary[19] of the US Department of Labor:

> After 40 years of extensive regulation of the commercial-airline industry by the CAB, Congress in 1978 decided to make 'a major change and fundamental redirection as to the manner of regulation of interstate and overseas air transportation so as to place primary emphasis on *competition*'.[20]

The ADA[21] was signed into law on 28 October 1978, before which the industry was heavily regulated, with permission to fly particular routes and approve fares held exclusively by the CAB. Following the ADA, the US air transport industry has certainly become what policymakers, and in part even the industry[22] itself, had hoped

---

14 G. Williams, *The Airline Industry and the Impact of Deregulation* (Aldershot: Ashgate, 1993), p. 49.

15 B. Vasigh, K. Fleming and T. Tacker, *Introduction to Air Transport Economics* (Farnham: Ashgate, 2008), p. 1. This also serves as evidence of the cyclical nature of the industry, which is detailed in Chapter 3.

16 The hub-and-spoke model, also known as the spoke-hub distribution paradigm, derives its name from a bicycle wheel, which consists of a number of spokes jutting outward from a central hub.

17 This business term refers to a practice where a flight operated by an airline is jointly marketed as a flight for one or more other airlines.

18 Vasigh, Fleming and Tacker, *Introduction to Air Transport Economics*, pp. 166–171, give a comprehensive review of early international airline alliances. *See also* T.H. Oum, J.H. Park, and A. Zhang, *Globalization and Strategic Alliances: The Case of the Airline Industry* (Oxford: Elsevier, 2000); C. Baker, 'The Global Groupings', *Airline Business* (July 2001); C. Baker, 'Back to the Table', *Airline Business*, (September 2006).

19 Between 1985–87.

20 S. Rep. No. 95–631, p. 52 (1978, *emphasis added*); *Alaska Airlines v Brock* 480 U.S. 678 (1987) at 681.

21 Amending the Federal Aviation Act 1958 to encourage, develop, and attain an air transport system which relies on competitive market forces to determine quality, variety, and price of air services, and for other purposes, PL 95–504, 92 Stat. 1705, 28 October 1978.

22 Although the major trunk carriers in the US had a stronghold influence on policymakers in the 1970s, it is curious that there was such a strong push for deregulation of the industry. Perhaps a struggle for autonomy was the defining point.

for: a market-driven industry, in which consumer demand determines the level of output in the form of air service products and price.

Initially, Congress freed airlines from the CAB's protection and exposed them to market forces. However, this was only one segment of the air transport sector. Congress failed to free up the complementary and essential infrastructure in airports and air traffic control systems, which remained government-controlled and government-owned. 'Not surprisingly, problems emerged when a consumer-responsive airline industry placed demands on an infrastructure still bureaucratically controlled.'[23] A number of waves ensued in the decade that followed.[24] The first was a move from pre-deregulation point-to-point to more efficient hub-and-spoke route systems. This structural change is discussed elsewhere in this book, but it is noted that the origins of such a change are in the US deregulation. On the other hand, by the time of liberalization of the market European airlines had developed strong hub-and-spoke systems on the basis that a flag carrier could only establish a hub within its own state.

The next by-product of deregulation was the advent of LCCs, most notably the success of Southwest Airlines in the early 1990s to present. Aside from the Laker experience in the late 1970s, discussed below, the origins of the successful LCC were in deregulation. Finally, the demand for short-haul travel in early years of deregulation contributed to the invention of the smaller, regional jet.[25]

Deregulation is not without regulation; some areas of air transport do continue to be regulated. The CAB's erstwhile authority was in effect shifted to a number of different government agencies. The first of these is international travel. Air traffic agreements between the US and foreign countries are known as 'bilaterals', or bilateral service agreements (BSAs).[26]

In Hanlon's view:

> Co-operation with other airlines is a means of tapping into worldwide traffic flows and enhancing the 'global reach' of a carrier's network, which might otherwise be limited by the traffic rights which its national government has been able to negotiate.[27]

As early as 1960, on this side of the Atlantic, UK regulators began making various attempts to introduce head-to-head competition on domestic routes through licensing policies implemented by the UK Civil Aviation Authority (UK CAA)[28], although

---

23 R.E. Poole Jr and V. Butler, 'Airline Deregulation: The Unfinished Revolution', *Regulation*, 22(1), 1999, 44.

24 As discussed by Poole and Butler, ibid., pp. 44–51.

25 *See for instance* A. Dobson, *Globalization and Regional Integration* (London: Routledge, 2007).

26 *See* R. Doganis, *The Airline Business in the 21st Century* (London: Routledge, 2001), pp. 28–32.

27 J.P. Hanlon, *Global Airlines: Competition in a Transnational Industry*, (Oxford: Butterworth-Heinemann, 1996), p. 210. An alternative to government's unwillingness or failure to negotiate a BSA, airlines must pay royalties in the form of revenue compensation to purchase traffic rights from the incumbent airlines, where permitted. *See* R. Doganis, *Flying Off Course: The Economics of International Airlines*, 4th ed. (London: Routledge, 2010), pp. 32–33.

28 P.S. Johnson, *The Structure of British Industry*, (London: Routledge, 1988), pp. 293–294.

'it has been only since the 1980s that the avoidance of any harmful effects to the national airline has not been the predominant factor in such decision making'.[29] This will be explored further below.

More recently in the EU, the approach has been to harmonize and liberalize previously restrictive national policies on international aviation. Although reluctant to relinquish control of their mostly state-owned, virtually monopolistic flag carriers,[30] which had long been important instruments of public policy, Member States began liberalization efforts in the mid-1980s. While the two situations were in many ways different, the lessons learnt from US carriers, a decade ahead in progress, 'exerted a strong influence on the strategic behaviour of both airlines and regulators'.[31]

The pre-liberalization aims of the regulatory regimes within Europe were to 'protect their scheduled, mostly publicly owned, flag carrying airlines from competition', which restricted market entry on both domestic and international routes, and provided flag carriers with virtual monopoly power.[32]

Under the charge of the European Commission, the first round of liberalization measures were implemented throughout the EU in 1987, in accordance with the competition rules of the TFEU. The EU liberalization programme, the 'Single European Aviation Market', was fully realized in 1993.[33] Much like the new rights offered under the US ADA, the Single European Market facilitates EU carriers to enter without restriction into any intra-EU market. However, as anti-competitive agreements,[34] decisions and concerted practices,[35] as well as the use of a dominant position[36] to affect interstate trade, are expressly prohibited, a certain level of regulation remains under the TFEU.

The strict regulatory regimes throughout Europe and in the US prior to liberalization and deregulation were heavily criticized for hampering industry efficacy where the industry structure was held as 'sufficiently competitive'. Economic regulation was

---

29 Williams, *The Airline Industry and the Impact of Deregulation*, p. 71.

30 *See* S.D. Barrett, *Deregulation and the Airline Business in Europe: Selected Readings* (London: Routledge, 2009), pp. 104–119.

31 Williams, *The Airline Industry and the Impact of Deregulation*, p. 71.

32 Ibid., p. 67.

33 Although the market was liberalized in 1993, it is discussed elsewhere in the book that the *actual* turning point was either in 2002, following EU competency on negotiating multilateral agreements, or in 2004, when European Commission obtained jurisdiction on all competition matters, bringing an end to special treatment of airlines.

34 Article 85 of the TEC: 25 March 1957 (now Article 105 TFEU).

35 Revenue pooling, limiting of capacities and agreed tariffs are regular practice and although they constitute clear breaches, airlines had been issued block exemptions where applicable. The Commission reviewed and renewed a series of (revised) block exemptions for airlines in October 2006 under Block Exemption Regulation (EC) No 1459/2006, showing signs of a reduction in exemptions. (IP/06/1294 'Competition: Commission revises Block Exemption for IATA passenger tariff conferences', 2 October 2006, Brussels); however, the Commission elected not to renew the block exemptions, which expired on 30 June 2007 for routes between the EU and the US or Australia, and 31 October 2007 for routes between the EU and third countries. As a result, IATA and individual carriers must now ensure that their agreements are compatible with the EU competition rules. (IP/07/973 'Competition: Commission ends block exemption for IATA passenger tariff conferences for routes between the EU and non-EU countries', 29 June 2007, Brussels).

36 Article 86 of the TEC: 25 March 1957 (now Article 106 TFEU).

'regarded as too blunt and intrusive an instrument of public policy; one that had been ineffective and often counter-productive, acting against the best interests of consumers. Hence [there was] attraction for removing all such controls'.[37]

> Economic regulation is based on the principle that industries with inherent market defects require government intervention to control prices and entry to ensure stability and longevity, for the benefit of the public. Thus, a critical issue is how, if at all, the regulator can best induce the regulated firm to employ its privileged information to further the broad interests of society, rather than to pursue its own interests.[38]

The point above raises the public policy and interest issue which risks contention between the encouragement by regulators through law and policy, the reactions of and effects on the industry, and the actual benefits to consumers.[39]

1978: US industry 'snapshot'

In the case of the United States, the CAB regulated the air transport sector throughout the 1970s, despite no apparent market defect. This 'economic' regulation prevented price competition and allowed new entry to the market only if approved by the CAB, which was rarely the case. The industry experienced gross inefficiencies with under-sold flights operating at unnecessary frequencies and at high prices. Economic theory would suggest that because regulation in this instance prevented competition, it should be removed (de-regulated) or reworked (re-regulated). Again, the sector underwent formal deregulation in 1978 and there were two aspects to this deregulation: administrative and legal. The first called for dissolution of the CAB and the second for the provision of a legal structure to ensure fair play between firms in the industry through the application of antitrust laws. Dismantling the CAB was a non-issue, whereas the many unique characteristics of the air transport industry presented significant challenges for the existing legal framework. When assessing the impact of a free market for air transport, consideration must be given to the interests that exist within the public domain, e.g. safety, the environment, public service obligations, landing rights and slots.

On drafting the ADA, the primary objective of deregulators was to limit or remove government control of prices and entry to encourage economic efficiency, while leaving intact government authority of, and thus responsibility for, issues surrounding safety.[40] In some cases[41] the reduction of government control *vis-à-vis* deregulation

---

37 Williams, *The Airline Industry and the Impact of Deregulation*, p. 123.

38 M. Armstrong, and D. Sappington, 'Recent Developments in the Theory of Regulation', in M. Armstrong and R.H. Porter (eds) *Handbook of Industrial Organization* (Oxford: North-Holland, 2007), p. 3.

39 The issues surrounding the 'public utility' aspect of air transport will be consolidated in Chapter 3.

40 S.G. Breyer, 'Regulation and Deregulation in the United States: Airlines, Telecommunications and Antitrust' in G. Majone (ed.), *Deregulation or Re-Regulation: Regulatory Reform in Europe and the United States* (New York: St. Martins Press, 1990).

41 The best example of this was the application for US antitrust immunity with the Netherlands (between the concerned parties, NW and KLM). Another application was lodged for a similar provision between the US and UK, with the support of AA and BA, but this was rejected by US regulators.

meant sanctioning special treatment of the air transport industry by legislators and competition authorities. As a matter of public policy, a distinction must be made between deregulated and never-regulated industries: the former ought to be treated differently from the latter.

If an industry is already 'structurally competitive', the objectives may be met through regulatory reform. To achieve workable competition, the courts may be used to enforce antitrust policies indirectly or competition rules or an adversarial process may be employed directly as a form of economic regulation.[42] For instance, if a monopoly or concentration is unjustifiable, courts may require a firm to restructure[43] or divest[44] with a view to promoting competition for its welfare benefits. An administrative economic regulation sets rules or orders for determining a regulated firm's prices and thereby incentivizing it to innovate towards production efficiency.[45]

The classical approach to deregulation proposes that 'Decentralized individual decisions made in a workably competitive marketplace . . . [are more favourable than] centralized, bureaucratic decisions of the economic regulator',[46] and that regulation can subsequently correct defects in the market as supplement or even substitute. Antitrust can thus be viewed as an alternative to regulation, rather than a form of regulation, that can be used to promote competition in industries where inherent features may prevent competition from working properly.[47] Therefore, government policymakers should look first to the marketplace to promote efficiency and encourage more desirable innovation to protect consumers, and then antitrust, if required.

There is a risk that 'government policy-makers will protect competitors instead of competition . . . when regulators or antitrust enforcers confuse means with ends . . .'[48] The conflict here is whether policymakers follow, aim for and achieve the objectives of individual firms or the industry, or are better balanced towards the promotion of adequate competition, benefiting consumers, while ensuring a healthy industry. 'Virtually all economists see substantial problems with at least some aspects of antitrust regulation, and some even maintain that the costs of these regulations clearly exceed the benefits and that they should be completely abolished.'[49] According to Breyer, one 'special policy risk of deregulation is that government policymakers will protect consumers instead of protecting competition . . . when regulators or antitrust enforcers confuse means with ends by thinking that the object of law is to protect

---

42 Mainly to control fares and freight tariffs, flight frequencies and capacities.
43 The corporate restructuring may take the shape of adapting the proposed merger to consider effects on market share and dominance (and any follow-on potential for distortion of competition).
44 In the air transport sector, an example of this was the EC Decision in 1996 to require Lufthansa and SAS to divest in slots on affected markets between Scandinavia and Germany following their proposed block space, codeshare and joint marketing agreements, thereby freeing up market share (freezing capacity) on the routes to allow for new entry and increased competition.
45 Breyer, 'Regulation and Deregulation'.
46 Ibid., p. 20.
47 Ibid.
48 Ibid., p. 28.
49 Vasigh, Fleming and Tacker, *Introduction to Air Transport Economics*, p. 222.

individual firms from business risks rather than to bring consumers the price and production benefits that typically arise from the competitive process'.[50]

In the case of the air transport sector, the public service obligation as a social welfare issue and to some degree the now fading concept of the flag carrier may contribute to a protectionist regulatory mind-set. On the other side of the equation are the individual firms. Neoclassical theory has it that in a firm the owners' preferences are the priority, with wealth–profit maximization for the owners–shareholders. In the context of the remaining state-owned airlines in the EU, this naturally means politicians.

As mentioned earlier, prior to deregulation excessive competition and predatory pricing were not evident in the air transport industry.[51] Arguments for the industry's ability to support competition were strong and regulatory justification weak. Presentations were made to the US Congress, based on empirical evidence gathered from tests in California and Texas, as well as initial results on deregulation from then-Chairman[52] of the CAB, Alfred Kahn's work at the time.[53] Despite strong misgivings by most of the industry, Kahn's predictions of what deregulation would offer were optimistic and influential.[54]

Classical thinking suggests that 'antitrust can adequately replace regulatory efforts to provide economic protection for the public'.[55] The risk to the public is of course that reformers are wrong in thinking newly deregulated markets are structurally competitive. For the air transport industry, low prices with high seat availability, flight frequencies and miles flown would demonstrate that its structure would support 'workable competition'. In an Air Transport Association (ATA) report, there were 173 million passengers in the US in 1971 (comprising 49 per cent of the population), which increased to 457 million (72 per cent) by 1987.[56] The market saw a change from a surplus of seats to a better-matched supply and demand curve. The effect was driven-down prices and increased efficiency, which naturally better matched consumer preferences.

50 S.G. Breyer, 'Antitrust, Deregulation, and the Newly Liberated Marketplace', *California Law Review*, 75(3), May 1987, 1018.

51 *See* A. Lall, 'Predatory Pricing: Still a Rare Occurrence?', in P. Forsyth, D.W. Gillen, O.E. Mayer and H-M. Niemeier (eds), *Competition versus Predation in Aviation Markets: A Survey of Experience in North America, Europe and Australia* (Aldershot: Ashgate, 2005), pp. 37–56.

52 Alfred E. Kahn was Chairman for the Civil Aeronautics Board from 1977–78.

53 *See* A.E. Kahn, 'The Changing Environment of International Air Commerce,' *Air Law*, (Netherlands Journal), Vol. 3, No. 3, 1978a; A.E. Kahn, 'Deregulation of Air Transportation – Getting from Here to There,' *Regulating Business: The Search for an Optimum* (Institute for Contemporary Studies, San Francisco, CA, 1978b), pp. 37–63.

54 *See* Statement of A.E. Kahn before the Aviation Subcommittee of the House Public Works and Transportation Committee on H.R. 11145, 95th Cong. 2d Sess. 8 (6 March 1978); Aviation Regulatory Reform, Hearings before the Subcommittee on Aviation of the House Committee on Public Works and Transportation, 95th Cong. 2d Sess. 124 (1978c); and A.E. Kahn, 'Surprises from Deregulation', *AEA Papers and Proceedings*, 78, 1988, 316–317.

55 Breyer, 'Regulation and Deregulation', p. 22.

56 Air Transport Annual Report 1972. Online. Available HTTP: <http://www.airlines.org/Economics/Review Outlook/Documents/1972 Annual Report.pdf> (accessed 5 May 2011), as cited Ibid.

However, owing to the protective spirit towards firms in a regulated industry, it is clear that at the moment of deregulation, some firms would automatically be labelled by competition policy as (natural) 'monopolies'. Upon closer investigation, while the firms do fit policy's definition of anti-competitive, it should be borne in mind that they have not ever been exposed to a pro-competitive environment. Once new firms are free to enter the market with relatively little restriction, economic 'free market' principles should prevail and force these incumbent firms with large market shares to enter into fare wars with one another as well as feel the effects of the new entrant. If an airline is unable to compete under the new conditions, and does not benefit from some continued government protection, it will be forced to bow out. This raises the issue of mergers and acquisitions, necessitating the first sizeable response by regulators since the moment of deregulation. This remains an important topic today.

Breyer[57] argues contrarily that, in a newly deregulated market, new entrants may require some direct protection,[58] but it may be that this protection has the potential to create a market distortion, however, which risks the stability of the market. There is no reason to keep this protection indefinitely and thus 'it is fair to count a policy of protecting competitors, rather than competition, as one of the policy risks facing the newly deregulated world'.[59]

1987: EU industry 'snapshot'

Liberalization of the European air transport industry has been very different in terms of its evolution when compared with the earlier period of deregulation of the American market; however, 'similar competitive dynamics on both sides of the Atlantic have led to remarkably similar competitive structures'.[60] The process of EU liberalization brought together under one market a number of distinct national markets, which were previously linked through several bilateral air service agreements. Prior to passage of the EU's Single Market Act 1986,[61] domestic air services were governed by national competition rules including licensing controls and the regulation of fares

---

57 Breyer, 'Regulation and Deregulation'.
58 It is clear that incumbents who were accustomed to a protected monopoly guaranteed by regulators in the regulated market may too seek to extend these anti-competitive benefits in the newly deregulated market. This may be achieved through intense lobbying or coordinated action between incumbents. (*See* R. Pitofsky, 'Competition Policy in Communications Industries: New Antitrust Approaches', *US Federal Trade Commission Speeches* (1997). Online. Available HTTP: <http://www.ftc.gov/speeches/pitofsky/newcomm.shtm> (accessed 8 August 2011); *See* K. Küschelrath, 'Strategic Behaviour of Incumbents: Rationality, Welfare and Antitrust Policy', in P. Forsyth, D.W. Gillen, O.E. Mayer and H-M. Niemeier (eds), *Competition versus Predation in Aviation Markets: A Survey of Experience in North America, Europe and Australia* (Aldershot: Ashgate, 2005), pp. 3–36.
59 Breyer, 'Regulation and Deregulation', p. 34.
60 European Commission and US Department of Transportation (ECDOT), 'Transatlantic Airline Alliances: Competitive Issues and Regulatory Approaches', A report by the European Commission and the United States Department of Transportation (16 November 2010), p. 2. Online. Available HTTP: <http://ec.europa.eu/competition/sectors/transport/reports/joint_alliance_report.pdf> (accessed 2 August 2011).
61 The objective of the Act was to unify Member States under a single Community market by 1992.

by national governments and/or under the charge of the International Air Transport Association (IATA),[62] which meant that at the moment the first liberalization package was implemented, there were varied levels of 'workable competition' from state to state. When the regulatory reforms were introduced in 1987, the situation of the European air transport sector was grim: actual or impending recession, high costs of major flag carriers mixed with pre-existing dominance in home markets, and growing congestion at a number of key EU airports.[63]

Unlike at the comparable juncture in US airline history, the steps taken to liberalize the European sector were calculated and long negotiated. Rather than attempting to abolish national markets in a single move, the three so-called 'liberalization packages' ensured a slow, managed transition to liberalization in stages. The primary concerns that arose in the course of liberalization in Europe included ensuring that the levels of air service were preserved and the national industry remained as healthy as possible.[64] Following liberalization of the EU market, 'the European industry quickly evolved to closely resemble the US industry in several key respects. Both EU and US industries are largely divided[65] into: pre-deregulation legacy or full-service network carriers, on the one hand, and post-deregulation no-frills or hybrid low-fare carriers, on the other hand'.[66]

The Organisation for Economic Cooperation and Development (OECD) argue that, 'the removal of restrictions on market entry, capacity, frequency and pricing resulted in greater emphasis being placed on the use of normal competition law to safeguard against anti-competitive behaviour and abuse of market power',[67] as now seen in Articles 101 and 102 TFEU. The OECD found that, post-liberalization European flag carriers restructured in some cases with the help of their respective governments, and the majority have survived and prospered in the liberalized environment. The European experience demonstrates that overall employment in the industry has increased through incumbents cutting costs and the introduction of new, low-cost airlines[68]; and generally that 'it is possible for an airline to find its

---

62 IATA, Doganis argues, is itself an example of tight cartelization, one that was excepted in the EU, but for the recent removal of block exemption and allegations of the IATA system serving as a platform to the international fuel surcharge cartel between 2002 and 2006. IATA and individual carriers are now under increased scrutiny to ensure that their agreements are compatible with the EU competition rules (Doganis, *Flying Off Course*, pp. 23–24).

63 Organisation for Economic Cooperation and Development (OECD), *Deregulation and Airline Competition* (Washington, DC: OECD Publications, 1988), p. 3.

64 Ibid., p. 1.

65 ECDOT, *Transatlantic Airline Alliances*, p. 2.

66 Pre-liberalization, '"legacy" carriers in the EU, most of which were state-owned, achieved substantial cost efficiencies as they were privatized and moved rapidly to restructure their businesses by adopting a more comprehensive hub-and-spoke model designed not only to connect national and European feeder networks to intercontinental flights, but also to more effectively connect passengers on intra-Europe journeys' (ECDOT, *Transatlantic Airline Alliances*, p. 2).

67 OECD, *Deregulation and Airline Competition*, p. 4.

68 On the Ryanair story, *see* S.D. Barrett, 'Ryanair and the Low-Cost Revolution', in J.F. O'Connell and G. Williams (eds), *Air Transport in the 21st Century: Key Strategic Developments* (Farnham: Ashgate, 2011), pp. 113–127; *and* Barrett, *Deregulation and the Airline Business*.

niche in a liberalized environment without regulatory protection and to be a success-ful business'.[69]

The UK experience

A more focused look at the regulatory environment in the UK at the moment of lib-eralization of the Union air transport sector provides insight into the deregulation and privatization that occurred within an individual Member State's air transport sector prior to the Union-wide liberalization.

The UK domestic air transport market was partially deregulated over the period 1976–86. The UK CAA is in charge of route licensing. BA was seen as withdrawing from some domestic routes and decreasing market share on some competitive routes. An OECD study[70] showed that during the deregulation period under the CAA,

> for the majority of routes an airline that is performing reasonably well will be protected from the threat of substitution. For routes that sustain two or more carriers limited forms of price competition may be possible under the terms of the regulations.[71]

The first step towards deregulation of the UK domestic market was taken on a bilat-eral basis with the Netherlands in 1984.[72] The British and Irish markets were deregu-lated in the broader sense in 1986. The UK competition legislation is applied generally to air transport, but some aspects of the sector are either excluded or exempted from the rules. International airline services are exempted from the Competition Act 1998[73] and the monopoly provisions of the Fair Trading Act 1973.[74] Complaints about anti-competitive behaviour have been directed first to the UK CAA, with the support of the Director General of Fair Trading since 1985. In 1986, the UK CAA heard an application by Britannia Airways to place restrictions on BA in the short-haul leisure market with its subsidiary, British Airtours. The UK CAA did not find evidence that BA's behaviour was contrary to the Civil Aviation Act.

---

69 Ibid, p. 2. It is accepted that such a statement may be dated, particularly when it is brought into the context of the current global financial crisis and mounting recession.

70 Barnes also pointed out that whilst the CAA went back on its entry liberalization Decision of 1984, entry controls were eased on the basis that an adverse effect on an incumbent airline's profits was not grounds to refuse granting a licence to a competitor. (K. Button and D. Swann, 'European Community Airlines – Deregulation and Its Problems', *Journal of Common Market Studies*, 27(4), 1989, 259–282.)

71 OECD, *Deregulation and Airline Competition*.

72 The UK-Netherlands Agreement 1984.

73 Amending the Competition Act 1980.

74 Schedule 1, Anti-Competitive Practices (Exclusions) Order 1980, as amended by the Anti-Competi-tive Practices (Exclusions) (Amendments) Order 1984; Schedule 7, Restrictive Trade Practices Act 1973, as amended by the Monopoly References (Alteration of Exclusions) Order 1984. The UK Com-petition Commission is currently consulting new merger guidelines on remedies such as divestiture, prohibition and behavioural measures, taking into account the Commission's experiences in imple-menting the Enterprise Act 2002.

Already in 1966, the late Sir Fredrick Alfred Laker, better known as Sir Freddie Laker, created Laker Airways in the UK. Laker was committed to making air transport affordable and was one of the first airline owners to adopt a low-cost pricing and operational structure. He made an application to the British Air Transport Licensing Board in 1973 for permission to fly his transatlantic 'Skytrain' service between the UK and US. Four years later he received a licence to do so. In September 1977, the Skytrain service between London and New York went into operation as the first deregulated international airline. Laker Airways was successful in the short-term, increasing services to Miami and Los Angeles from London's Gatwick Airport (LGW). Laker campaigned for approval to expand Laker Airways operations to Australia and Hong Kong, but was refused. Laker did secure licences from Gatwick, Manchester and Prestwick to Chicago, Detroit, San Francisco, Seattle and Washington, DC under the Bermuda II Agreement, but suffered financial difficulties which prevented the airline from acquiring additional required aircraft. In addition, competitors at the time, such as British Airways, Pan American Airlines and TWA dropped their prices below Laker's already low fares and paid secret commissions to travel agents to divert business from Laker Airways.

Despite Laker's attempts at rescuing the airline, it was forced into bankruptcy in 1982; however, the experience proved that a privately owned airline could successfully combat incumbents including state-owned airlines as well as manoeuvre existing regulations and bureaucracy to gain access to the lucrative transatlantic markets. Indeed, Sir Freddie Laker's legacy is not for the failed attempt but for the success of change he brought about which has provided lessons for subsequent entrepreneurial success such as, on the one hand Sir Richard Branson's Virgin Atlantic, and on the other Michael O'Leary's Ryanair and Stelios Haji-Ioannou's EasyJet. It has often been argued that Laker peaked too soon, which begs some curiosity as to the likelihood of his success if he had created the Skytrain a few years later, particularly if there had been a few years' experience of deregulation of the American sector in the equation.

Five years later, the Secretary of State for Trade and Industry referred the proposed merger of BA and British Caledonian Group plc (BCAL) to the Monopolies and Mergers Commission (MMC).[75] BA made a proposal to return all of BCAL's licences and slots on all its domestic routes to the CAA, not to oppose any application made by carriers wishing to compete on routes with the new merged airline, to surrender a minimum of 5,000 routes at LGW, and to merge to charter the activities of British Airtours with the small remaining operations of BCAL under the latter's name.[76] On weighing the benefits and risks associated with the proposed merger, the MMC cleared BA's bid. It should be noted that this was a controversial decision that was said to have 'shocked the nation', and that if it were put forward again, the MMC would likely have responded with amended conditions.

Until the Competition Act 1980 came into force, the UK regulatory position on mergers was not entirely straightforward: proposed mergers and acquisitions were

---

75 It should be noted that the merger provisions of the Fair Trading Act 1973, which has now been repealed by the Enterprise Act 2002 and Communications Act 2003, did not apply to the air transport sector in 1987.

76 OECD, *Deregulation and Airline Competition*.

referred to the MMC.[77] The many amendments and respective orders pertaining to concentrations and mergers provided for a confusing state for firms, with particular respect to exclusions. The Competition Act 1998, as well as the Enterprise Act 2002 that followed, have provided some clarification as to the regulatory position on acceptable mergers and cooperative practices. With that said it should be borne in mind that the Competition Act has been subject to a number of exclusion orders on such grounds as public policy, public transport ticketing schemes, land agreements, and financial and personnel services. The Enterprise Act has since been amended to include the European Economic Area (EEA) and insolvency issues. Nonetheless, the multitude of orders, amendments and exclusions to the new legislation may yet again cause a similar state of confusion.

The most significant experience in the UK with respect to airline competition is the sparking of debates over charter and scheduled air services. By design, charter airlines bundle flights and accommodation in a holiday package, whereas traditional airlines sell seats on regularly scheduled routes, independent of any additional services. The distinction is also evident in the application of UK competition rules. Charter services are exempt from the competition rules as applied to air services generally. Between the late 1990s and early 2000s, there were allegations of anti-competitive behaviour by *Airtours*,[78] a charter airline, selling package holidays to consumers who were only using the air services portion of the deal, thereby allowing the charter airline to avoid the more restrictive competition including licensing arrangements. This led to a reinvestigation of the different rules applied to the scheduled and charter segments[79] of the UK air transport sector, treating them as different relevant markets[80] in the context of competition law. The consequence of this is that scheduled and charter airlines are treated as non-competitors on shared routes for the purposes of competition law. This is evidence of the UK competition rules impacting on the structure of the domestic air transport sector.[81]

The UK air transport sector had already been deregulated prior to implementation of the Community-wide liberalization packages. Competition rules in the UK resemble the American legislation on antitrust, both in terms of language and severity of penalties, up

---

77 Since 1999 the Competition Commission.

78 Leading to Case T-342/99 *Airtours v Commission; Airtours/First Choice* [2000] OJ L 93/1, [2002] ECR II-2585 (the CFI decision). In this case, the CFI annulled the Commission's decision on three grounds: although the relevant market definition between short and long-haul was accurate, (1) the finding that major operators had an incentive to stop competing with one another was incorrect; (2) that a dominant oligopoly would ensue was incorrect; and (3) the Commission underestimated the foreseeable collective action of smaller operators.

79 For a more recent view, *see* G. Williams, 'Comparing the Economic and Operating Characteristics of Charter and Low-cost Scheduled Airlines', in J.F. O'Connell and G. Williams (eds), *Air Transport in the 21st Century: Key Strategic Developments* (Farnham: Ashgate, 2011), pp. 185–195.

80 The definition of relevant market in this book is taken from the EU: combining the product market and geographic market as regards 'interchangeability', 'substitutability' where conditions are 'sufficiently homogeneous'. (*See* the European Union website, http://europa.eu/scadplus/leg/en/lvb/l26073.htm for a more detailed definition.)

81 This approach to 'segmenting' for the purposes of determining the relevant market when considering breaches of competition rules is also adopted by the EU in application of Article 102 TFEU.

to and including imprisonment.[82] It might be suggested that market liberalization is an evolved state of deregulation, since the EU competition rules follow, in theory, a different policy-fronted economic principle from deregulation, namely liberalization.[83]

US consolidation movement[84]

Antitrust can have either too strict – leading to potentially missed efficiencies – or too lenient an impact – where a concentration of market share is found to exist – on the outcome of applications for proposed[85] acquisitions[86] or mergers. 'Antitrust rules designed to deal with industry in general may not reflect properly the special features of the airline industry'.[87] A positive shift in antitrust attitude towards mergers suggests that potential competition is as good as actual competition. This can be seen both from the enforcement and market perspectives; the latter represents firms' reactions, up to and including retaliation. 'Congress, as early as 1975, believed that there were enough potential entrants at the low end of cost continuum to keep prices low in particular markets.'[88]

The ordinary travelling consumer must also understand that fares will decrease, or the deregulation policy will lose political support. The US Congress amended the ADA in 1984 by placing airline mergers under the charge of the US Department of Transportation (US DoT). Until this time, all mergers were handled by the US Department of Justice (US DoJ), and this move raised concerns for the inexperienced and possibly less sensitive US DoT's ability to conduct merger applications from airlines.[89] This move provides further evidence of the 'regulatory exception' and 'special treatment' of the air transport sector whereas the US DoJ handles similar matters arising in all other industries, whilst uniquely the US DoT handles airlines under the guise[90] of 'specialization'.

During its administration, the CAB artificially stabilized the air transport market through a mileage-based fare system, adopting the slogan 'equal fares for equal

---

82 In fact, under the Enterprise Act 2002, the Office of Fair Trading Serious Fraud Office investigates breaches and the penalties include a prison sentence of up to five years, an unlimited fine or conviction.

83 For a contrast of 'deregulatory' and 'liberal' competition policies examined through law, *see* Chapter 4 under the heading 'American and European legislative perspectives'.

84 Although they are outside the scope of this book, it is needful to note mergers in other jurisdictions (e.g. Air Canada–Canadian Airlines and Japan Airlines–Japan Air Systems). (Vasigh, Fleming and Tacker, *Introduction to Air Transport Economics*, pp. 14–18).

85 This refers to domestic mergers; cross-border mergers present an altogether more complicated issue: the conflict of national (competition) laws. This subject will be addressed further in Chapter 5.

86 It should be noted that industry consolidation might occur as acquisition followed by absorption, acquisition by continued separation of brand identities, merger amongst true equals or horizontal alliances (S. Holloway, *Straight and Level: Practical Airline Economics,* 3rd ed. (Aldershot: Ashgate 2008), Part 1.

87 Breyer, 'Regulation and Deregulation', p. 24.

88 Ibid., 26.

89 This is the remaining fundamental difference in regulatory approach from the EU approach, which has in recent years broken away from its 'block exemption' policy on giving exceptional treatment to airlines. This will be discussed below in further detail.

90 Particularly as evidenced by the DoT's autonomy in the merger and acquisition approval applications process.

miles'.[91] A more lenient view could be taken to recommend that deregulation upset longstanding patterns of operation; and the resulting free competition forced airlines to experiment with fares and services. Firms were made for the first time to respond to changes in cost and demand; and if they were unable, they ran the risk of failure. This became something of a 'survival of the fittest' situation where 'industry shakedown'[92] has forced industry consolidation. Antitrust policy is supported in this instance in the interest of failing companies and efficiency arguments, as a defence against otherwise unacceptable merging.

In the decades following the 1978 deregulation, the US industry has become far more concentrated through consolidation and mergers. It has been argued that carriers consolidated in the period immediately following deregulation as a way of staving off bankruptcy.[93] Deregulation allowed unrestricted entry as well as exit from the market, which allowed the creation of hub-and-spoke systems. As a result, four US hubs became duopolies (Atlanta Hartsfield (ATL), Chicago O'Hare (ORD), Dallas-Fort Worth International (DFW) and Denver Stapleton (DEN)), whereas the remainder developed into monopolies.[94]

In reflection on US airline deregulation, Goetz and Dempsey found that:

> During the first decade of deregulation, there were more than 50 mergers, acquisitions, and consolidations, the major ones concluded in 1986 and 1987 when the Reagan administration's Transportation Department embraced an exceptionally permissive antitrust policy.[95] Indeed, the Department of Transportation approved each of the 21 mergers submitted to it.[96]

The public interest argument is that 'competition in a free market, policed by a strong anti-merger policy, should provide adequate protection for the public'.[97] The US DoT will apply the statutory public interest test[98] in merger approval

---

91 Breyer, 'Regulation and Deregulation', p. 27.

92 Ibid.

93 P.S. Dempsey and A.R. Goetz, *Airlines Deregulation and Laissez-Faire Mythology* (London: Quorum Books, 1992), p. 13. *See also* Doganis, *The Airline Business*, pp. 110–115) on the less stringent treatment of merger and acquisitions under the 'failing carrier doctrine' in US antitrust law.

94 Where 'a single airline [controlled] more than 60 per cent of the take-offs and landings, gates, and passengers.' (Dempsey and Goetz, *Airlines Deregulation and Laissez-Faire Mythology*, p. 13 citing P.S. Dempsey, *The Social and Economic Consequences of Deregulation* (New York: Quorum Books, 1989).

95 A.R. Goetz, and P.S. Dempsey, 'Airline Deregulation Ten Years After: Something Foul in the Air', *Journal of Air Law and Commerce*, 54, 1989, 927.

96 P.S. Dempsey, 'Antitrust Law and Policy in Transportation: Monopoly I$ the Name of the Game', *Ga. L. Rev.*, 21(505), 1987, 15.

97 Breyer, 'Regulation and Deregulation', p. 28.

98 49 USC §41308, 2003. Under the test, the US DoT must weigh the potential efficiencies or benefits before it can grant antitrust immunity: 'When the Secretary of Transportation decides it is required by the public interest, the Secretary, as part of an order under section 41309 or 42111 of this title, may exempt a person affected by the order from the antitrust laws to the extent necessary to allow the person to proceed with the transaction specifically approved by the order and with any transaction necessarily contemplated by the order.'

decisions: if the anti-competitive effects outweigh the public interest in terms of benefits to welfare, it will be denied. Thus, the application of antitrust policy is weighed against public policy. The US DoJ continues to report on each proposed merger, outlining its recommendation or disapproval. Detailed below are the major acquisitions brought before and approved by the US DoT between 1985–87; the US DoJ opposed three.[99]

United Airlines (UA) offered to buy Pan American (PA) Pacific Division in April 1985.[100] The US DoJ was the first to respond to this, and did so voicing concern about the potential strengthening of the IATA fare cartel between the US west coast and Japan, specifically Tokyo. At the time, there were three carriers offering services to Japan from the west coast: United, Pan Am and Northwest. The proposed merger between United and Pan Am would have left only two carriers and potentially less competition at an increased price to consumers.[101]

The US DoT agreed that there might be a lack of competition, but did not find there to be a great risk of a substantial decrease or distortion of competition on the markets. The US entered into a bilateral agreement with Japan, the terms of which promised additional access to the Pacific market. As a result of this memorandum of understanding (MOU), American Airlines (AA), DL and a new Japanese carrier called ANA were given gateways to Tokyo. This resolved the competition issue, and allowed for the approval of the UA–PA merger.[102]

Northwest Airlines (NW) filed an application with the US DoT in January 1986 and requested permission to merge with Republic Airlines (RW).[103] Both carriers comprehensively served Minneapolis-St Paul Airport (MSP) and they were head-to-head competitors on some 45 city-pair markets. The US DoJ opposed the acquisition on the grounds that competition would likely be reduced on these routes, and that for a new entrant successfully to operate on the concerned markets, it would also need to run an effective hub operation from Minneapolis, too, which was next to impossible. The US DoT disagreed on the basis that the relevant market (MSP) enjoyed sufficient competition through the existence of new entrants and competitors offering sufficient one-stop and connecting services.[104]

---

99 The factual information represented in the following merger examples is taken in the main from the OECD report (OECD, *Deregulation and Airline Competition*).

100 *See generally* F.M. Fisher, 'Pan American to United: The Pacific Division Transfer Case', *RAND Journal of Economics*, 18(4), Winter 1987, 492–508.

101 Doganis, *The Airline Business*; *See also* J.G. Wensveen, *Air Transport: A Management Perspective*, 6th ed., (Aldershot: Ashgate, 2007), pp. 181–184.

102 Ibid.

103 *See generally* S. Borenstein, 'Airline Mergers, Airport Dominance, and Market Power', *American Economic Review*, 80(2), 1990, 400–404, where his case study revealed that the increase in fares from 1985–87 was 9.5 per cent, relative to industry averages across 84 routes from Minneapolis-St Paul, the Northwest/Republic hub and anticipatory increases in prices by the independent carriers before the actual merger; *see also* D. Starkie, *Airports and Airlines and the Role of Competition and Regulation Aviation Markets. Studies in Competition and Regulatory* (Aldershot: Ashgate, 2008), pp. 135–151 for a look at competition and its constraints on market power from the European experience.

104 Doganis, *The Airline Business*; *See also* Wensveen, *Air Transport: A Management Perspective*, pp. 181–184.

Frequent travellers on NW brought an action in June 1997 against Northwest, alleging a violation of Section 7 of the Clayton Act for substantially lessening competition through a 'disproportionate increase in fares, market dominance, and use of entry barriers for new competitors'.[105] The US Court of Appeals reversed and remanded the case to the district court. This demonstrates one of the few occasions on which merger applications were opened to public 'consultation' on the issue of 'public interest'.[106]

Trans World Airlines (TW) and Ozark Air Lines (OZ) applied for leave to merge in March 1986, shortly after the NW–RP application.[107] The competition question was similar in this case to that in NW–RW's merger application, in that both TW and OZ had substantial hub operations at St Louis Airport (STL). The two carriers combined would control 76 per cent of the gates.[108] The US DoJ focused on the non-stop city pairs from the STL hub as the (relevant) city pair markets to analyse the potential post-merger situation in terms of competition issues. Their recommendation was for ten gates to be divested at STL to allow for new entries. The US DoT disagreed and unconditionally approved the merger. In 2001, AA acquired TWA before absorbing it entirely.[109]

Texas Air (TZ) attempted to take over Eastern Airlines (EA) later that year.[110] In this merger application, overlapping hubs was not the issue. This application raised the matter of city-pairs as a relevant market on the Washington DC National (DCA)–New York City LaGuardia (LGA) and LGA–Boston Logan (BOS) routes. New York Air, a subsidiary of TA, and EA serviced these routes by hourly shuttle service mainly used by business travellers. As such, new entry to these markets would require several flights a day at regular intervals. Access to these airports was heavily restricted, owing to their proximity to the cities, requiring the carriers to obtain a licence for the respective slots. TZ offered to sell to PA a number of slots on the routes to ensure competition on the markets. The US DoT found that competition would still be insufficient because the merged airline would still hold too high a share of the market. Once TA offered to sell PA the additional slots, the US DoT approved the merger.

People Express (PE) offered low fares, opening up air transport to a section of the public who, in the early 1980s, might not have chosen to travel by air.[111] It operated from Newark Airport (EWR) near New York City (NYC). Unfortunately, they began

105 *Midwestern Machinery Inc and others v Northwest Airlines Inc* 167 F. 3d 439, 1991–1 Trade Case P 72, 422 (1998).

106 This requirement for successful US merger applications will be discussed in further detail below.

107 *See generally* Borenstein, 'Airline Mergers', pp. 400–404, where he found that there was little evidence of an increase in prices from the TWA/Ozark merger (based on data collected from St Louis, the TWA and Ozark hub) as compared with the Northwest/Republic merger.

108 Doganis, *The Airline Business*; *See also* Wensveen, *Air Transport: A Management Perspective*, pp. 181–184.

109 Holloway, *Straight and Level*, Part 1.

110 *See generally* A. Berenstein, *Grounded: Frank Lorenzo and the Destruction of Eastern Airlines* (Washington, DC: Beard Books, 1999); G.W. Douglas, 'The Importance of Entry Conditions: Texas Air's Acquisition of Eastern Airlines', in J.E. Kwolka, Jr and L.J. White (eds) *The Antitrust Revolution: Economics, Competition, and Policy* (Oxford: Oxford University Press, 1986), pp. 99–102.

111 This demonstrates a step toward the notion put forward in this book of air transport as 'public transport'. *See generally* S.C. Gilson, *Creating Value through Corporate Restructuring: Case Studies in Bankruptcies, Buyouts, and Breakups* (New York: Wiley, 2001), pp. 84–89.

to experience financial difficulties in early 1986 and were offered a buy out by TZ. It was argued by the US DoJ that Newark did not present itself as a potential hub for TZ, who did not already have a hub there, as little traffic was generated from points beyond the hub. A new entrant to the EWR–NYC market would thus not be faced with competing with a true hub-dominating carrier, which gave adequate grounds for approval of this merger. The US DoT agreed and granted the acquisition.

US Air (now US Airways) operated many routes in the US northeast and Piedmont in the southeast.[112] There were some overlapping routes; particularly of interest were LGA and DCA, owing to the already-mentioned capacity restraints and licensing issues for slots. The US DoT administrative law judge disapproved the merger owing to the overlap and potential for significant decreased competition on some routes, but US Air brought their case to the Court of Appeals and won. The two airlines merged successfully in 1987. Interestingly, the Phoenix-based America West Airline (AWA) opposed the merger, as they were seeking slots at LGA and DCA. US Airways and America West were granted the requisite approval and merged in 2005.

On reflection, the rapid consolidation movement from 1985 onwards produced 25 acquisitions by larger US carriers.[113] It appears that the rapid consolidation movement in the US, post-deregulation, was either a natural evolutionary response to the removal of price and capacity controls or a lenient reaction by antitrust regulators. The US DoT's approval of the mergers and acquisitions listed above, despite the disapproval or warning and concern of the US DoJ, is evidence of the view that potential competition[114] in the relevant markets would be sufficient post-merger to allow the merger. In any case, what was remaining of the US air transport industry, once, for argument's sake, the industry was truly deregulated (post-rapid consolidation) in the early 1990s, were a few large trunk carriers: AA, UA, NW, DL, CO and US Airways.

US made a bid to acquire DL in 2006, which was treated as an attempted hostile takeover and therefore opposed by DL. If the US takeover of DL had not failed, the new airline would have led today to the consolidation of the six largest US airlines into three main carriers. This would have resembled the present situation in the EU, which is discussed below. In 2008, there were talks of mergers between four of the largest US carriers: DL with NW[115] and UA[116] or CO with US Airways. Between

---

112 *See generally* S.R. Kole, and K. Lehn, 'Workforce Integration and the Dissipation of Value in Mergers: The Case of US Air's Acquisition of Piedmont Aviation', in S.N. Kaplan (ed.), *Mergers and Productivity: NBER Conference Report Series* (London: University of Chicago Press, 2000), pp. 239–279.

113 G.J. Werden, A.S. Joskow and R.L. Johnson, 'The Effects of Mergers on Price and Output: Two Case Studies from the Airline Industry', *Managerial and Decision Economics*, 12(5), 1991, 341–352.

114 The American approach generally regards potential competition on a market on a par with actual competition for the purposes of forecasting the post merger competitive environment.

115 *See* Case COMP/M. 5181 – *Delta Air Lines/Northwest Airlines,* Commission Decision of 06 August 2008 declaring a concentration to be compatible with the common market (Case No COMP/M.5181 – DELTA AIRLINES / NORTHWEST AIRLINES) according to Council Regulation (EC) No 139/2004, [2008] OJ C281/3, 05 November 2008.

116 A merger proposal between United Airlines and US Airways might prove problematic in terms of antitrust, owing to both carriers dominance on the US eastern coast.

2008–10, DL and NW 'merged' and UA merged with CO.[117] During the same period of time, four smaller US carriers have shut down: Aloha Airlines (AQ), Champion Air (MG), America Trans Air (AT) and Skybus (SX).[118] In May 2011, Southwest Airlines acquired another LCC, Air Tran, and now awaits a 'Single Operating Certificate' from the US FAA, which was approved in October 2008.

European consolidation movement

In the EU, there was some expectation that the conceptual 'EU air carrier', with common licensing criteria and the right of establishment anywhere within the Union, would lead to a consolidation of incumbent large carriers in the market.[119]

> It has long been widely accepted that consolidation will leave Air France/KLM, British Airways, and Lufthansa as the only surviving legacy carriers, alongside residual niche players and a strong low-cost industry dominated by EasyJet, Ryanair, and possibly airberlin.[120]

The European Commission has viewed airline mergers with a healthy amount of suspicion, however, and has often allowed them only in return for legally binding guarantees not to impede competition on particular routes. It could be argued that the merging of AF and KLM Royal Dutch Airlines (KL)[121] in 2005 was the starting point of this movement. The first European hybrid airline has since investigated acquiring Alitalia (AZ). In the same year, Lufthansa German Airlines (LH) acquired Swissair[122] (LX). In June 2008, LH took a strategic equity share in Brussels Airlines.[123] In October 2008, LH bought a 50 per cent share in British Midland Airlines (BD), which at

---

117 *See* Case COMP/M.5889 – *United Air Lines/Continental Airlines,* Commission Decision of 27 July 2010 declaring a concentration to be compatible with the common market (Case No COMP/M.5889 – UNITED AIR LINES / CONTINENTAL AIRLINES) according to Council Regulation (EC) No 139/2004. Online. Available HTTP: <http://ec.europa.eu/competition/mergers/cases/decisions/m3770_20050704_20212_en.pdf>(accessed 1 June 2006).

118 K. Peterson, 'A United-US Airways Merger Could Restrict Competition', *International Herald Tribune,* 2008. Online. Available HTTP: <www.iht.com/articles/2008/05/04/business/rtrdeal05.php> (accessed 12 May 2011).

119 OECD Annual Report (2003), p. 6. Online. Available HTTP: <http://www.oecd.org/dataoecd/45/28/2506789.pdf> (accessed 11 March 2011).

120 Holloway, *Straight and Level,* p. 43.

121 This merger will be examined in full in Chapter 5 under 'Mergers'. *See* Case COMP/M.3280 – KLM/Air France, Commission Decision of 11 February 2004 declaring a concentration to be compatible with the common market (Case No COMP/M.3280 – AIR FRANCE / KLM) according to Council Regulation (EEC) No 4064/89, [2004] OJ C60/5, 05 March 2004.

122 Now 'Swiss International'.

123 Brussels Airlines merged with Virgin Express in 2004. (Lufthansa German Airlines, 'Green light for Lufthansa and Brussels Airlines: the European Commission has approved the merger of the two airlines'. Online. Available HTTP: <http://www.lufthansa.com/ph/en/Lufthansa-and-Brussels-Airlines> (accessed 23 September 2011).

the time was the second-largest airline operating from LHR after BA, adding to its previous 30 per cent minus one shareholding.[124] In December 2008, LH initiated its bid for Austrian Airlines (OS), which was approved in December 2009.[125]

BA and Iberia began merger talks in 2008 to form what is now the biggest airline in Europe,[126] the International Airlines Group (IAG).[127] In October 2009, the Commission sent a statement of objections to the oneworld alliance – specifically on this occasion British Airways, American Airways and Iberia. The result was a number of commitments in relation to six routes, namely London–Dallas, London–Boston, London–Miami, London–Chicago, London–NYC and Madrid–Miami.[128] The three airlines were also required to make slots available to competitors at London airports – LHR, LGW and another airport of the competitor's choice – on the New York, Boston, Miami, and Dallas routes.[129] The following more general commitments were also made:

- *fare combinability agreements*: competitors may fly passengers to a particular location and sell tickets for the return flights with the parties in question. This allows competitors to develop more attractive schedules
- *special pro-rate agreements*: favourable term for connecting short-haul to long haul flights, *e.g.* BA flies the passenger from Manchester to London, and the competitor then flies them to New York
- *frequent flyer programmes*: if flying with a competitor that does not offer similar FFP, they can still redeem those for flights with competitors
- *reporting obligation*: must report on parties' cooperation to the Commission, so that they can effectively monitor the situation.[130]

These commitments will last until 2020–21 and it is expected that this period of time will allow new entrants to be sufficiently secure of market conditions for a sufficiently reasonable time to justify entering a market while recognizing the ever changing face

124 'BMI Being Taken Over by Lufthansa', *BBC News* (29 October 2008). Online. Available HTTP: <http://news.bbc.co.uk/1/hi/business/7697261.stm> (accessed 10 June 2011).
125 Summary of Commission Decision of 28 August 2009 declaring a concentration compatible with the common market and EEA Agreement (Case COMP/M.5440 – Lufthansa/Austrian Airlines), OJ C16/11, 22 January 2010.
126 D. Robertson, 'BA-Iberia Merger Would Create Biggest Airline in Europe', *Times Online* (30 July 2008). Online. Available HTTP: <http://business.timesonline.co.uk/tol/business/industry_sectors/transport/article4426034.ece> (accessed 4 August 2008).
127 They also retain separate brands: <http://www.iairgroup.com/phoenix.zhtml?c=240949&p=about overview> (12 October 2008).
128 CASE COMP/F-1/39.596 – BA/AA/IB Commitments to the European Commission. Online. Available HTTP: <http://ec.europa.eu/competition/antitrust/cases/dec_docs/39596/39596_3244_14.pdf> (accessed 16 July 2011).
129 'Antitrust: British Airways, American Airlines and Iberia Commitments to Ensure Competition on Transatlantic Passenger Air Transport Markets Made Legally Binding – Frequently Asked Questions', *Europa Press Release Rapid* (MEMO /10/330, Brussels, 14 July 2010). Online. Available HTTP: <http://europa.eu/rapid/press Releases Action.do?reference=MEMO/10/330&format=HTML&aged=0&language=EN&guiLanguage=en> (accessed 16 July 2011).
130 Ibid.

of the industry. The Commission will re-assess the situation once these commitments expire, and the commitments will persist even if the parties decide to terminate their alliance. Consumers will benefit as it becomes easier for new competitors to enter the market. The procedures for the enforcement of these rules are detailed in the commitments. Effectively, the Commission allocates the slots through long-term leases.[131] The Commission, as a means of settling any disputes, also appoints an independent monitoring trustee. Competitors are not obliged to pay for the slots, although they are not prohibited from doing so; if several competitors for a slot would offer equal competitive constraints, compensation may be paid for the allocation. The commitments took effect at the beginning of the IATA summer on 27 March 2011.

In the *BA/AA/IB* case, the Commission was satisfied that these commitments would maintain a sufficient level of competition in the market to ensure consumer welfare would not suffer. Conversely in *Ryanair holdings Plc v European Commission (Ireland, intervening)*,[132] commitments offered by Ryanair did not satisfy the Commission in this regard. Ryanair flew to 400 destinations in 40 countries and wanted to buy Aer Lingus, which flew 70 routes between Ireland and other EU member states. The Commission issued its decision,[133] finding the merger to be anti-competitive and incompatible with the common market. In particular, there would be significant overlap in 35 routes to and from Dublin, Shannon, and Cork, creating a dominant position on these routes. The applicant could also potentially subject other routes to a dominant position. Ryanair had proposed several commitments in 2007,[134] but the Commission found these to be unsatisfactory at avoiding anti-competitive practice. Ryanair appealed. Simply having a large market share is not a breach of the rules *per se*; only abuse of such a dominant position is. Market dominance need not necessarily lead to monopolistic, rent seeking behaviour either; Iberia was charged by the new antitrust agency in Spain (National Competition Commission) with anti-competitive practices on its Madrid–Asturias route as it held a monopoly in this market. It was cleared of any wrongdoing when it was found that the prices they charged were comparable to other domestic routes of a similar distance.[135] Ryanair had made an argument that their own and Aer Lingus's services were not close competitors because they offered different price levels and quality of service, but this was rejected by the Commission. Price regression analysis performed by the Commission showed that

---

131 The slots issue is of particular significance in the EU, where space for additional runways and airport expansion is often limited. The US has been more successful at building capacity through infrastructure and with the exception of the FAA's implementation of a slot system in 1969 at New York LGA, New York JFK, Chicago ORD and Washington DCA; the US has little experience with slot controls. (Vasigh, Fleming and Tacker, *Introduction to Air Transport Economics*, p. 192); *See*, on US slot trading, Starkie, *Airports and Airlines*, p. 175–192.

132 Case T-342/07 *Ryanair Holdings Plc v European Commission (Ireland, intervening)* [2011] 4 CMLR 4.

133 C(2007) 3104 in Case COMP/M.4439 (the contested decision).

134 This is based on Art 8(3) of Regulation 139/2004, commonly referred to as the 'Merger Regulation'.

135 R. Miller and J. Chua (eds), *Airlines – 2006 World Wide Competition Law Review*, A Civil Aviation Authority (CAA) policy document. Online. Available HTTP: <www.caa.co.uk/default.aspx?catid=5&pagetype=90&pageid=6264> (accessed 18 July 2011). Contributions on Spain by Dr D.N. Varona (Partner) and L. Moscoso del Prado (Associate).

the two airlines exercised competitive constraints over one another. This complemented qualitative evidence that supported the Commission's decision. Arguments that new entrants had trouble entering the market due to Ryanair's exceptional efficiency were similarly dismissed. Essentially, Ryanair needed to prove that there were efficiencies to be gained from a merger which otherwise could not be realized and that these would somehow be passed on to the consumer.

Commitments made by parties will only justify mergers with an anti-competitive element if the Commission is able to conclude with certainty that they are feasible and endure long enough to ensure that the dominant position or hindrance of competition would not materialize in the near future. Commitments should be submitted to the Commission not more than 65 working days after the initiation of proceedings.[136] This is so that there is sufficient time to investigate the likely effects of the proposed commitments, and that there is sufficient time to consult the Member States concerned. In this case, the Commission found it was impossible for new entrants to enter the route, and merely giving away some slots did not suffice.[137]

Unlike their US counterparts, EU carriers had, by the inception of the liberalization movement, formed efficient hub-and-spoke flight networks, with the hub of flag carriers located within each country's respective borders.[138] The removal of safeguards and other forms of government intervention in the affairs of the industry highlighted flag carriers' dominant positions at their respective hubs and has forced a reconsideration of ideologies: the 'Union's priorities' take precedence over individual 'Member State interests'.

The European Commission carefully evaluated these European airline mergers,[139] such as the recent unions of KL with AF[140] and LH with LX,[141] BD[142] and OS,[143] in terms of the likely impact on intra-European as well as global competition.

136 Art 19(2) of Regulation 139/2004.

137 Case T-342/07, *Ryanair Holdings Plc v European Commission, [2011] 4 CMLR 4*.

138 This yields at least one hub per Member State, and respectively at least one flag carrier per Member State.

139 This is in respect to EC Council Regulation No 139/2004 of 20 January 2004 on the control of concentrations between undertakings, commonly known as the 'EC Merger Regulation', *See* Council Regulation (EC) No 193/2004 of 20.1.2004 on the control of concentrations between undertakings (the EC Merger Regulation), [2004] OJ L 24/1, 29 January 2004.

140 *See* Case COMP/M.3280 – KLM/Air France, Commission Decision of 11 February 2004 declaring a concentration to be compatible with the common market (Case No COMP/M.3280 –AIR FRANCE / KLM) according to Council Regulation (EEC) No 4064/89, [2004] OJ C60/5, 05 March 2004.

141 *See* Case COMP/M.3770 – *Lufthansa/Swiss*, Commission Decision of 04 July 2005 declaring a concentration to be compatible with the common market (Case No COMP/M.3770 – LUFTHANSA / SWISS) according to Council Regulation (EC) No 139/2004. Online. Available HTTP: <http://ec.europa.eu/competition/mergers/cases/decisions/m3770_20050704_20212_en.pdf> (accessed 10 July 2011).

142 *See* Case COMP/M.5403 – *Lufthansa/BMI*, Commission Decision of 14 May 2009 declaring a concentration to be compatible with the common market (Case No COMP/M.5403 – LUFTHANSA / BMI) according to Council Regulation (EC) No 139/2004, [2009] OJ C158/1, 11 July 2009.

143 Case COMP/M.5440–*Lufthansa/Austrian Airlines,* Summary of Commission Decision of 28 August 2009 declaring a concentration compatible with the common market and EEA Agreement (Case COMP/M.5440 – Lufthansa/Austrian Airlines) (notified under document C (2009) 6690 final), [2009] OJ C16/11, 22 January 2010.

Although the KL–AF merger was given the go-ahead in early 2004, the decisions of the European Commission provoked controversy and debate 'given the undoubtedly clear conflict of interest between what the Commission would regard as being best for consumers, namely a strong competitive environment, and that which would serve most the objectives of the flag carriers'.[144] Given the recent Commission decisions with respect to LH's acquisitions, it would appear that the consolidation movement is favourable to consumers, regulators and the individual firms.

European liberalization of air transport began over a decade after American deregulation, but in some aspects, the American experience had a demonstrative effect in Europe. Today, we can view a quasi-reverse demonstrative effect of the 'European product', which is arguably more stability seeking, on the American sector. The consolidation of US carriers, particularly over the decade that followed deregulation, might initially be observed as having a demonstrative effect on Europe's current situation. The consolidation movement in the EU is further characterized, however, by the influence of national governments over 'flag carriers' in terms of public interest, the evolution of stable and considerably lucrative LCCs in the European sector,[145] and the more ethereal, yet regulations-based liberalized environment in Europe, encouraging Union-wide harmonization.

Product differentiation and industry segmentation

Applying economic theory, firms will differentiate to gain some competitive advantage. Investments in research and development (R&D) will produce strategies that are cost-effective and will bring a successful increase market share. If an airline is able to create an altogether new strategy or product, this is likely to place them at a competitive advantage. If what makes a firm truly different is well received by the consumer, it will *prima facie* be market leader. Finding a competitive differentiation is one step closer to 'efficiency' for a firm.

To increase hard and soft values, it is in the best interest of airlines to seek out new technologies continually through R&D. In an effort to achieve the common goal of economic efficiency, which is to maximize profits and cut losses, businesses around the world invest in various forms of strategic R&D. Traditionally, R&D refers to industry innovation, which put simply means conducting research to achieve the ends of technological development, or a better product, whereby overall operational costs are reduced. In the context of commercial arrangements, R&D is understood

---

144 Williams, *The Airline Industry and the Impact of Deregulation*, p. 88.

145 The LCCs challenge legacy carriers with increased competition on short and medium-haul routes, and are therefore 'increasingly dependent on revenues from long-haul international services to sustain the viability of their networks. To remain competitive, the legacy carriers have two main challenges: expanding their networks, which are an important comparative advantage versus LCCs, and making their overall costs more competitive with the growing LCC sector'. In the EU, legacy carriers are also facing more competition from the development of high-speed rail links (ECDOT, *Transatlantic Airline Alliances*, p. 3).

as investing a ratio of revenues to develop strategic, future-oriented activities or ventures, motivated by forecasts of a positive commercial yield. Clearly, pharmaceutical, engineering or high technology companies will tend to spend more than others, but whatever the investment, all firms conducting R&D share a common objective: increased or maintained efficiency through economic growth and stability.

Hagedoorn identified the existence of two broad sets of reasons why firms join alliances: 'motives associated with technology, such as that required for basic or applied research; and the motives concerned with market access and/or with influencing the structure of the market'.[146] It is perhaps necessary to examine both elements of this statement a little further. If joining an alliance is what has evolved as the primary form of collaboration and cooperation within an industry, as it would seem is the case in the airline industry, then the benefits may, in addition to cost-saving and other 'network' synergies, include the incentive to develop the industry in technological terms. Market access is a clear objective but the second part of Hagedoorn's statement above indicates that the industry may, under the auspices of 'economic' cooperation, in fact reshape the structure of the industry and interactions on markets. From the perspective of the airline industry, this might be quite a promising venture, such as consolidation of the transatlantic market. Consumers and regulators might enquire, however, whether this phenomenon is the 'natural' evolution of the industry and market or the 'invisible hand' of industry's self-interest.

Although the scope of technological collaboration in the airline industry is smaller than, say, the automobile industry, there are instances of technological alliances dating back as early as the 1960s.[147] In Hanlon's view:

> The purpose of these alliances was to permit alliances to specialize in certain aspects of maintenance, whether airframes, engines, avionics or landing gear, or to concentrate on particular aircraft types, so that for example, Air France specialized on 747 airframes and landing gear plus GE CF6 engines; Lufthansa on Airbus-300 airframes and landing gear plus JT9D engines; Sabena on A310 engines; and Alitalia on DC-10 airframes.[148]

This technological collaboration in Europe resulted in cost savings of up to 20 per cent.[149] The motives prevalent in the airline industry tend to be associated with 'networking'. An airline's flight network is perhaps its greatest marketable asset to consumers; the more extensive the network, the more attractive it may be.

A good 'soft value' example is Virgin Atlantic (VS), which was the first airline to introduce in-flight, in-seat entertainment systems including video screens, movies and

---

146 *See* J. Hagedoorn, 'Understanding the Rationale of Strategic Technology Partnering: Interorganizational modes of Cooperation and Sectoral Differences', *Strategic Management Journal*, 14, 1993, 371–385, as cited in J.P. Hanlon, *Global Airlines: Competition in a Transnational Industry* (Oxford: Butterworth-Heinemann, 1996), p. 208.

147 Hanlon, *Global Airlines*, p. 208.

148 Ibid., p. 209.

149 Ibid.

games, for passengers in 1989; and in-flight beauty treatment for its Upper Class passengers in 1990, along with a drive-thru check-in facility and limo pick-up service.

In early 2003, LH began to offer wireless Internet services on board its international flights.[150] The competitive advantage enjoyed by LH will most likely soon be compromised, however, as other airlines develop and offer similar services through standardization. In January 2007, United Arab Emirates (UAE)-based Emirates launched mobile phone usage in its planes, making it the first airline to allow passengers to make and receive mobile phone calls on its aircraft.[151] Australian-based Qantas Airlines (QF) trialled a similar service on its aircraft only a few months later.[152]

A differentiated product is likely to create a new segment in the market. For instance, in 2008, Singapore Airlines (SQ) upgraded its aircraft to include an 81 × 25 inch seat[153] in business class, the biggest in the world. In addition, it has begun to offer 'suites', a class above and in addition to first class – a compartment-style cabin with private bed and door. This new, differentiated product sets SQ apart from their competitors. It has or will also develop a new market segment: luxury suites or luxury business travel, to be distinguished, for instance, from first or business class travel on competitor airlines. As the only airline to offer these new types of product segment, SQ is the *de facto* market leader. The future may see competitors 'catching up' in order to compete with SQ on affected routes.

The global air transport industry is fragmented in a number of respects. First, different business philosophies (and nationally or regionally accepted practices) lead some airlines to act differently from others. Some may take risks and differentiate; others may benchmark or behave conservatively. Interestingly, the global air transport industry is lacking in multinational corporate entities, e.g. the typically cited, hypothetical full merger BA–AA. This is usually owing to a combination of foreign ownership restrictions in place by national governments with a view to protecting its home industry or security and the airspace sovereignty issue.

Findlay and Round raised the point that more multinational corporate entities, through mergers and acquisitions, would lead to economies of scale in the air transport industry that are at the moment less apparent.[154] A favourable, relaxed merger and acquisition policy, coupled with a proper supervisory environment, might allow for more multinational corporate (airline) entities. This would reduce the level of fragmentation considerably and might aid the encouragement of further consolidation, wherever efficient.

150　*See* Lufthansa's website. Available HTTP: <http://www.lufthansa.com> (accessed 15 August 2011).
151　J. Wong, 'International Airline to Allow Cell Phone Chatter on Planes', *CNN*, 2006. Online. Available HTTP: <http://www.cnn.com/2006/TECH/12/21/wired.airline/index.html> (accessed 6 January 2007).
152　*Qantas Communications*. Online. Available HTTP: <http://www.qantas.com/info/flying/intheair/communications> (accessed 13 July 2011).
153　*See* Singapore Airlines' website. Available HTTP: <http://www.singaporeair.com/saa/en_UK/content/exp/new/businessclass/seatfeatures.jsp> (accessed 20 June 2011).
154　Except for, arguably, airline alliances that enjoy some benefit of a cross-border merger and thus might be the most achievable strategy presently toward economies of scale. *See* C. Findlay, and D. Round, 'The "Three Pillars of Stagnation": Challenges for Air Transport Reform', *World Trade Review*, 5(2), 2006, 251–270.

Legal response and reflection

The air transport industry comprises many market segments with the continuous addition of new and differentiated features or products. The law distinguishes between firms that add features to an existing product – through innovation or other improvement – and those that create an altogether new product. The former is ordinary business practice and is allowed generally speaking,[155] whereas the latter may raise questions around whether a new corresponding market is also created (on which to offer the new product), and therefore new market regulation is required or must at least be considered. Product differentiation in the air transport industry does not appear to suggest a new product so much as a product that corresponds to a new pricing structure. Thus the normative argument[156] holds that the onus is on the regulators to be aware of developments within the industry, as their original policy objectives may no longer be met when the current law is applied (generically) to the new product–segment.

As firms competing within the same sector, a legacy carrier may be investigated for abuse in a market at the request of an LCC. It could be put forward that the law should recognize a distinction between these products–segments. What may have begun as differentiation by LCC pioneers has now become a standard product, which has for the purposes of a legal response potentially created its own sector rather than relevant market. In the presence of the mixed characteristics of airlines: legacy carrier–LCC, legacy carrier–Charter, and LCC–Charter, however, it is becoming increasingly difficult to determine where these firms are likely to or should fall on the regulatory spectrum, but it is clear that the tide is turning such that the growth and success of LCCs evidences their gaining of increasing competitive advantages.[157]

Nonetheless, it is becoming increasingly difficult to determine this relevant market, particularly with the constantly changing character of airlines and the adaptation of competitor strategies that were formerly reserved for intra-segment competition. Legacy carriers are charging for luggage carried in the hold, exit row seating, food and headsets, which were previously inclusive amenities, so it would at this stage seem unreasonable to begin categorizing firms according to their status; particularly when this 'status' is so blurred. To ascertain the 'relevant market'[158] for air transport, one looks to the supply and demand on the affected route with reference to the price elasticity of demand, or how responsive consumers are to a change in the quantity

---

155 *See* the Microsoft case in Europe as a prime example (Case COMP/C-3/37.792, *Microsoft*, 24 March 2004).

156 'Regulation' is viewed here on the presumption of longer-lasting socio-political and economic compromises, with 'mechanisms of redistribution and social cohesion' implying 'transnational public action' toward global regulation, beyond its simple definition of systems of controls within a normative framework. (P. Hugon, 'Global Public Goods and the Transnational Level of Regulation', *Issues in Regulation Theory* 1–3, 48, April 2004. Online. Available HTTP: <http://web.upmf grenoble.fr/regulation/Issue_Regulation_theory/LR48english.pdf> (accessed 25 March 2011)).

157 *See* A. Gogbashian and T. Lawton, 'Airline Strategy: Keeping the Legacy Carrier Competitive. How Can Mature Airlines Stay Ahead in the Low-fare Airline Era?', in J.F. O'Connell and G. Williams (eds), *Air Transport in the 21st Century: Key Strategic Developments* (Farnham: Ashgate, 2011), pp. 129–144.

158 All references to 'relevant market' in this book relate to either the air transport market as a whole in economic terms or in legal terms for determining competition on city–pair markets.

offered, i.e. seats on the route. Defining the market identifies the 'boundaries of competition between firms'.[159] There is some correlation between the way in which airlines set their price structure and changes the structure of supply as the new low-cost model arguably offers a different product,[160] and therefore this should be a factor in ascertaining the relevant market.

Surely the effect of the current application of the law is accurate in terms of promoting or supporting 'workable competition' in the industry; however, as that 'market' has evolved or become segmented, the law as it is presently applied is no longer an accurate reflection of policy. The law is now responding to industry practices and commercial concepts that exist beyond the original ambit of the policy objectives. The deregulation and liberalization policies through competition and antitrust law-followed responses of the airlines, demonstrate a workable strategy for competition, but are not evidence of the objectives of these policy approaches as an element of extra-legal also exists.

In 2010, the European Commission and US DoT initiated a joint research project[161] with a view to fostering a common understanding of the transatlantic airline industry on which to base future work towards building 'compatible regulatory approaches to competition issues in the airline sector'.[162] On the back of the EU–US Air Transport Agreement in 2008,[163] which provided the legal basis and formalized 'cooperation with respect to competition issues in the air transport industry'[164] between the

---

159 For more information on defining the relevant market in the EU, *see* the Commission Notice on the definition of relevant market for the purposes of Community competition law [1997] OJ C 372/5–13, 09 December 1997.

160 It is accepted that this is highly debatable. European case law does not give a straightforward response. The merger application was denied in *Ryanair/Aer Lingus* and the General Court dismissed the appeal. The *Iberia/Vueling/Clickair* merger, however, was approved, subject to conditions. According to the definitions set out in this book, Aer Lingus would be classified as a low-cost model (legacy) carrier whereas Iberia is a typical legacy carrier. All things being equal, this would appear to suggest that combining two low-cost model airlines would be more likely to create a concentration and potential dominance as in the *Ryanair* case than two LCCs merging with a legacy carrier in the case of *Iberia*, and therefore the price structure bears some significance on the post-merger structure of supply. *See* Judgment of the General Court of 6 July 2010 –Case T-342/07 *Ryanair v Commission*, [2010] OJ C221/35, 14 August 2010; Case COMP/M.5364; IP 09/29, 'Mergers: Commission clears Iberia's proposed acquisition of Vueling and Clickair, subject to conditions', 09 January 2009.

161 ECDOT, 'Transatlantic Airline Alliances'.

162 Ibid.

163 The agreement was originally referred to as the EU–US Open Skies Agreement. *See* Decision 2007/337/EC of the Council and the Representatives of the Governments of the Member States of the European Union, meeting within the Council of 25 April 2007, on the signature and provisional application of the Air Transport Agreement between the European Community and its Member States and the United States of America, OJ L134/1, 25 May 2007; *See also* Protocol to Amend the Air Transport Agreement between the United States of America and the European Community and its Member States, signed on April 25 and 30, 207. Online. Available HTTP: <http://ec.europa.eu/transport/air/international_aviation/country_index/doc/2010_03_25_us_protocol_attach_b.pdf> (accessed 12 March 2011). The Council of Transport ministers adopted the Second Stage Agreement (Protocol amending the First Stage Agreement) on 24 June 2010.

164 Annex 2 of the EU–US Air Transport Agreement, provisionally applied as of March 2008. Under Article 18, a Joint Committee was established to deal with interpretation and application of the Agreement and to review its implementation.

European Commission and the US DoT, this more recent undertaking between the airline industry and regulators – competition regulators and transport policymakers – clearly demonstrates the will of the parties to engage in and deepen their existing discourse[165] towards a more beneficial future. The qualitative[166] and quantitative[167] phases of the report contributed to the following overall conclusion:

> Perhaps the most fundamental conclusion of our inquiry is the remarkable similarities between current competitive structures of the airline industries in Europe and the United States and, even more importantly, the remarkable similarities in the trends that continue to shape them, despite significant differences in their historical development.[168]

Thus, whilst one should not forget the respective differences in evolution of the EU and US sectors, the two sides appear to have at last 'caught up' with one another. This evidences a significant common competitive footing of carriers on the transatlantic market; and while the market regulation and transport policy differs as yet, the legal basis for cooperation and undertaking of a joint research project on transatlantic airline alliances signal the inevitability of future alignment of EU and US approaches to regulating air transport.

---

165 The industry–regulator discourse will be elaborated in Chapter 3.

166 This phase consisted of interviews with a representative sample of allied and non-allied EU and US carriers. The European Commission and US DoT also conducted a review of prominent academic papers to assist in developing an appropriate theoretical framework for their inquiry.

167 Using a 10 per cent sample from survey data collected by the US DoT, an independent firm (Corelim Consultants) conducted an econometric assessment of the passenger origin-destination information.

168 ECDOT, 'Transatlantic Airline Alliances', p.1.

3 Deregulation, liberalization and re-regulation

Introduction

The primary aim of this chapter is to discuss and clarify the concepts of 'deregulation' and 'liberalization'. This will proceed with regard to the influences leading to their construction and to the extent to which they have contributed to the commercial measures taken by airlines from an international perspective, which is essential given the international dimension of the industry. This chapter also details and criticizes the application of competition rules in the EU and US sectors *vis-à-vis* restrictions on foreign ownership, antitrust legislation, concerted practices and collusive activities, price discrimination and the abuse of a dominant position.

The scope of this study is the EU and US air transport sectors. Although it is accepted that many industries have been deregulated, privatized and liberalized[1] worldwide over the past few decades, it is in the airline industry that one observes the unique phenomenon of intense cooperative manoeuvring. As Hanlon remarks:

> One of the most striking results of deregulation is the impetus it gave to the level of activity in airline mergers and acquisitions. The constraints imposed in bilateral agreements and the restrictions placed on foreign ownership meant that most of this activity has taken place within national boundaries.[2]

Alongside the freeing up of markets and reduction of government intervention, there has been a significant trend towards industry-wide cooperation between many firms in the deregulated sectors. This cooperation has generally taken the form of a variety of contractual arrangements to integrate through joint ventures, tactical or strategic alliances and mergers. The rather unique trend in the global air transport sector is the increasingly large-scale, complex series of agreements between carriers to form global

---

1 Note the distinction made earlier between (market) deregulation and liberalization as economic principles, and the corresponding (general) policies. Additionally, the privatization of air transport has been an especially important feature of the European sector with most previously state-owned 'flag carrier' airlines going public. Williams puts forward that Europe is the 'world's first fully deregulated region' (G. Williams, *Airline Competition: Deregulation's Mixed Legacy* (Aldershot: Ashgate, 2002), pp. 123–147).

2 J.P. Hanlon, *Global Airlines: Competition in a Transnational Industry* (Oxford: Butterworth-Heinemann, 1996), p. 187.

alliances while government intervention and a high-level of market price transparency remain 'natural' characteristics in the industry.

Political ideologies

History has seen struggle between Western and Eastern ideologies in politics and economies. These ideologies translate into distinct business philosophies and practices. Perhaps the greatest difference between the West and the East in business philosophies 'is that the West is individualistic and competitive right down to an interpersonal level, whilst the East is collective and cooperative within dense networks of relationships'.[3] Many argue that the East's cooperative 'nature' bears out great strength. If so, the West would be wise to research and incorporate cooperative strategies into business culture and practice. In the case of the air transport sector, the experience of cooperation is already far advanced.

In economic systems driven by Western philosophies, goods and services are traded at a price agreed when a seller's asking price matches a buyer's bid price *ad infinitum*, in what is known as a 'market economy'. In theory, there is no guidance or control of this process, although some organisation does result from the complex interplay of supply and demand variables, along with the influence of prices. From the Eastern perspective, the state takes up planning and management of the 'planned economy'. In this type of economic system, decisions about the production, allocation and consumption of goods and services are planned in advance. These plans and decisions, implemented by command in the most well-known planned economies, led to their being called 'command economies', or more specifically, if the planning is centralized, 'centrally planned economies'; if decentralized, 'participatory economies'.

Since the millennium, 'widespread demonopolisation, liberalisation and privatisation . . . coupled with rapid technological changes and the opening up of international trade have unleashed unprecedentedly powerful economic forces'.[4] Although the consequences of these changes may impact on individuals and societies in different ways, there is 'a growing consensus that, on the whole, markets deliver better outcomes than state planning; and central to the idea of a market is the process of competition'.[5] Indeed, it is accepted that governments and free enterprise are both imperfect. 'Exactly how much free enterprise and government control should be in [the] mix is a matter of controversy.'[6] Political ideologies have influenced the structure of economies, which has invariably encouraged various types of business practice, including intense competition in the West.[7] This is clearly in line with the allocative efficiency model-influenced American system.

3 J. Child, D. Faulkner, and S. Tallman, *Cooperative Strategy: Managing Alliances, Networks, and Joint Ventures*, 2nd ed. (Oxford: Oxford University Press, 2005), p. 5.
4 R. Whish, *Competition Law* (Oxford: Oxford University Press, 2009), p. 3.
5 Ibid.
6 B. Vasigh, K. Fleming and T. Tacker, *Introduction to Air Transport Economics* (Farnham: Ashgate, 2008), p. 45.
7 *See* Department of Trade and Industry, *Productivity and Enterprise: A World Class Competition Regime White Paper*, Cm 5233 (2001), para. 1.1, as quoted ibid., p. 16.

The 'game of regulation'

It has been argued that regulation is a game,[8] with many players imposing as stake-holders their self-interests on each other. A struggle ensues between one who has the most bargaining power and the other who stands the most to lose, typically the end-user, or consumer, but in some instances, the state. This 'game of regulation' according to Baldwin and Cave

> is becoming more complex as economic, political and technical changes force agencies and governments to interact with each other in a host of different ways. Pressures both to compete and to coordinate are imposed on regulators at the domestic and sectoral as well as the international level.[9]

The private sector may apply pressure by lobbying legislators to create additional ancillary regulations and competition rules to protect their market power, or petition regulators to take action against an alleged anti-competitive practice by a competitor, or indeed call for less regulation altogether. This was the case in the US air transport industry in the decade leading up to the 1978 Airline Deregulation Act (ADA). Because US-concentrated business interests were said to have been in control of regulatory developments in the 1970s, one could ask why there was such a strong deregulation movement in the first place.[10] The 1960s gave rise to liberal (political) and thriving public interest movements. 'Regulators and large regulated industries were thought to be in bed with each other.'[11]

In keeping with Horwitz:

> [T]he liberalisation of the legal doctrine of 'standing', that is, who was permitted to bring actions in court and who could argue before regulatory agencies, was a crucial factor in the expansion of participation. In this respect there was a kind of alliance between the courts and the public interest movement in the 1960s.[12]

A 'democratisation of regulation' led to parties using 'the regulatory and legal processes to impose costs on their opponents, including the cost of time it would take to reach a final regulatory decision on any particular issue, known as the "regulatory

---

8 Particularly in the telecommunications sector; *see for instance* S.V. Berg, 'Sustainable Regulatory Systems: Laws, Resources and Values' *Utilities Policy*, 9(4), 2000, 159–170; B. Levy, and P.T. Spiller, 'The Institutional Foundations of Regulatory Commitment: A Comparative Analysis of Telecommunications Regulation', *Journal of Law, Economics and Organization*, 10(2), 1994, 201–246; T. Monasso, and F. Van Leijden, 'Telecommunication Regulation as a Game: Deepening Theoretical Understanding', *SSRN Working Paper Series*, 14. December 2007.

9 R. Baldwin and M. Cave, *Understanding Regulation: Theory, Strategy, and Practice* (Oxford: Oxford University Press, 1990) as cited in J.G. Murphy and J.L. Coleman, (eds) *Philosophy of Law: An Introduction to Jurisprudence* (Boulder, CO: Westview Press, 1990), p. 189.

10 The 'industry snapshots' provided in Chapter 2 highlighted additional rationales behind the deregulation movement.

11 R. Horwitz, 'Deregulation as a Political Process', Unpublished. Online. Available HTTP: <http://www.connect-world.com/Articles/14Deregulation.html> (accessed 10 July 2011).

12 Ibid.

lag"'.[13] In combination with severe inflation, this yielded an all-out industrial counter-attack against regulation – its product: deregulation.

On the other side of the story were the economists, who 'had been criticizing the efficiency of regulated industries for several years',[14] concluding through research 'that regulation was sometimes irrational, that monopolies thought to be "natural" were in fact maintained only through regulation, that regulation stifled innovation, and that regulation often was used as a means of cartel management'.[15] Businesses began to use academic studies to create new business strategies 'to transform the political agenda of government regulation'[16] by blaming it for the high inflation and poor business performance. And ideologically, 'regulation was said to compromise basic freedoms'.[17]

Veljanovski looks at the

> strategic use of regulation by industry and regulators, and the rules and procedures that have been and can be put in place to reduce wasteful attempts to 'game the system' . . . [and points to the] obvious though often neglected fact that firms and regulators not only operate within the 'rules of the game' but can also change those rules.[18]

Describing modern regulation as 'complex interaction between politicians, civil servants, industry, interest groups, regulatory bodies, and occasionally consumers', Veljanovski stresses that 'the terms 'strategic' and 'gaming' are not intended to indicate an abuse of the regulatory process or law. Rather, they are the legitimate pursuit of self-interest in order to maximise beneficial outcomes or minimise potential expected losses.'[19]

Economic arguments for regulation

According to Veljanovski:

> The economics of regulation is a wide and diverse subject. It has normative (what should be) and positive (what is) aspects; provides economic analyses of prices, quality, entry, access, and market structure . . . empirical studies of specific legislation . . . and organisational and legal applications which examine the behaviour of institutions and regulatory agencies, and the development and design of rules, standards, and enforcement procedures.[20]

13 Ibid.
14 Ibid.
15 Ibid.
16 Ibid.
17 Ibid.
18 C. Veljanovski, 'Strategic Use of Regulation', in R. Baldwin, M. Cave and M. Lodge (eds), *The Oxford Handbook of Regulation*, (Oxford: Oxford University Press, 2010), p. 87.
19 Ibid., p. 89.
20 C. Veljanovski, 'Economic.Approaches to Regulation', in R. Baldwin, M. Cave and M. Lodge (eds), *The Oxford Handbook of Regulation*, (Oxford: Oxford University Press, 2010), p. 17.

Doganis suggests three economic arguments for and against regulation. The first is that although there are 'strong oligopolistic tendencies in air transport, absence of any regulation would inevitably lead to wasteful competition' because the product offered in the sector is basically non-differentiated and entry into the deregulated or liberalized industry is not difficult.[21] In addition, economies of scale[22] are not apparent[23] and new entrants to a market will simply offer a lower fare on the route than the incumbent competitors to gain the business, leading to an all-out price war or retaliatory action by those incumbents on that or other common market(s). Thus some regulation, whether it takes the form of regulations or reactive law, would in theory ensure fair competition and a more sustainable industry.

Second, Doganis argues in support of regulation on the public utility aspect of air transport. It is imperative to public welfare that one is able to travel as required, and the most common means of transport are by coach, ferry, rail and air. Given the distances that aircraft may cover over a relatively short period of time, air transport may not always be substituted by the other three.[24] In line with the 'public' considerations, most countries developed (at least) one national carrier with governmental participation. 'It was and is still a natural extension of this point of view to believe that free and unregulated competition on international air routes would endanger national interests because it might adversely affect that national airline.'[25] If questioned today, however, one's answer is likely to be different.

The third argument is that because of the marked increase in the number of non-scheduled, charter air carriers operating routes at a lower risk than scheduled carriers as regards their ability to enter and exit a market and make changes at short notice, some regulation to protect scheduled services on certain routes with 'public service' features should be in place. On these necessary routes, scheduled air carriers may be obliged to operate them, albeit at a significant cost, especially as compared with non-scheduled air carriers, which may enter the market and initiate a price war. After a careful examination of the UK air transport sector in respect of scheduled and non-scheduled services, for example, the Committee of Inquiry[26] decided in 1969 that scheduled air carriers should not be forced to compete with non-scheduled air carriers.[27] For this reason, scheduled and non-scheduled markets in both the EU and US are to be kept completely separate in competition inquiries.

---

21 R. Doganis, *Flying Off Course; Airline Economics and Marketing*, 2nded. (London: Routledge, 1991), p. 46.

22 This economic theory suggests that production at a larger scale (more output) can be achieved at a lower cost.

23 Although in recent years, larger scale aircraft have been developed, culminating with the Airbus A-380 double-decker jumbo predicted to carry more than 800 passengers.

24 Take for instance transatlantic travel between London and New York, a journey by ship would take six *days* and by air six *hours*.

25 Doganis, *Flying Off Course*, p. 47.

26 HMSO, *British Air Transport in the Seventies*, Report of the Committee of Inquiry into Civil Air Transport (London, 1969), Chs 5 and 13.

27 As upheld in Case T-342/99 *Airtours v Commission; Airtours/First Choice* [2000] OJ L 93/1, [2002] ECR II-2585 (the CFI decision). (Doganis, *Flying Off Course*, p. 47). *Also see above* Chapter 2.

Evaluating economic policy

It is appreciated that evaluating the efficiency of economic policy is not a straightforward task as it involves assessing the policy measure on its own and then in terms of how fair and equal it distributes benefits across a population. Whereas the concepts 'fair' and 'equal' are generally quite subjective,[28] given the wide range of population it is tested against, 'efficiency' may be more accurately defined with the help of economic theory.

The five commonly used criteria for efficiency, as discussed by Murphy and Coleman,[29] are the Pareto Optimality and Superiority,[30] Kaldor–Hicks Possibility of Compensation,[31] Coase Theorem[32,33] and Pigouvian Tax Efficiency.[34] These types of efficiency use criteria to compare two states of the world, S and S_1, to determine the parameters of their relationship in terms of relative 'efficiency'.

The application of the Pareto criterion is problematic.[35] 'In everyday life, economic measures always have winners and losers. To get around this problem, the economists Hicks and Kaldor proposed an alternative criterion, namely the *Potential Pareto criterion*',[36] under which gainers from a policy change contribute to the losers and yet remain better off overall. This 'compromise' approach appears to be modelled for the most part on the case of the air transport sector, where the industry–regulator discourse is evident.

---

28 And as such belong more to the realm of political philosophy than economic theory.

29 *See* J. Murphy and J. Coleman, *Philosophy of Law: an Introduction to Jurisprudence*, Revised ed. (Boulder, CO: Westview Press, 1990).

30 S_1 is *Pareto Superior* to S provided no one prefers S to S_1 and at least one person prefers S_1 to S, whereas S_1 is Pareto Optimal provided there is no S_n Pareto Superior to S_1; *See* Veljanovski, 'Economic Approaches to Regulation', in Baldwin, Cave and Lodge (eds), *The Oxford Handbook of Regulation*, p. 20.

31 S_1 is *Kaldor–Hicks (K–H) Efficient* to S provided no one would then prefer S to S_1 and at least one person would prefer S_1 to S. S_1 is *K–H Efficient* to S provided S_1 is *Potential Pareto Superior (P–P–S)* to S; *See* Veljanovski, 'Economic Approaches to Regulation', in Baldwin, Cave and Lodge (eds), *The Oxford Handbook of Regulation*, p. 20.

32 The *Coase Theorem* states that when transactions (involving private *versus* social costs, marginal cost and marginal profit) are costless and individuals act cooperatively, any assignment of legal rights will be efficient; *See* R.H. Coase, 'The Problem of Social Cost', *JL & Econ*, 3, 1960, 1; *See also* C.G. Veljanovski, 'The Coase Theorems and the Economic Theory of Markets and Law', *Kyklos*, 35, 1982, 53–74.

33 The cap-and-trade approach to air pollution adopted in the EU ETS is an articulation of Coasian Theory, at least with respect to the initial allocation of allowances as property rights. See also A.D. Ellerman and B.K. Buchner, 'The European Union Emissions Trading Scheme: Origins, Allocation, and Early Results', *Rev Environ Econ Policy*, 1(1), 2007, 66.

34 *Pigouvian Tax Efficiency* exists only if compensation, measured as the marginal tax set equal to the marginal damage imposed by the offence, is imposed by a civil authority on and paid by an offending party, as a means to 'internalize externalities'.

35 The difficulty in analyzing the 'soft' (qualitative) sociological properties of economic policy through a seemingly quantitative Pareto, Coase, Pigouvian or Kaldor–Hicks model presents a further obstacle in the comparative policy approach of this thesis.

36 L. Immers and J. Stada, 'Basics of Transport Economics', *Faculty of Engineering, Katholieke Universiteit Leuven*, Belgium (2004), p. 6. Online. Available HTTP: <http://www.kuleuven.be/traffic/stats/download.php?id=65> (accessed 5 March 2011).

Industry–regulator discourse

Some academics argue that good policy analysis is not about whether exposure of a firm or an industry to the free market is the better approach.[37] Exposing an industry to the free market may bring about private regulation by cartels,[38] thereby defeating competition[39]; and state regulation may be nothing more than symbolic, with the industry devising strategies to circumvent it. It is implied that 'regulation is not achieved simply by passing a law, but requires detailed knowledge of, and intimate involvement with, the regulated activity.'[40]

Taking Cunningham's view:

> [G]iven the limitations of both compliance and deterrence as 'stand alone' strategies, most contemporary regulatory specialists now argue, on the basis of considerable evidence from both Europe and the USA, that a judicious *mix* of compliance and deterrence is likely to be the optimal regulatory strategy.[41]

Thus, there must be some symbiosis between state regulation and self-regulation[42] through interdependent dialogues, 'regulatory discourse'[43] between state regulation and private orderings, industries and regulators.[44]

Public ordering

State regulation designates public ordering, that is, the setting of rules to the industry at large by government agency or trade association. The public, open dialogue

---

37 *See for instance* I. Ayres, and J. Braithwaite, *Responsive Regulation: Transcending the Deregulation Debate* (Oxford: Oxford University Press, 1992); S. Rose-Ackerman, 'Progressive Law and Economics – and the New Administrative Law', *Yale Law Journal*, 98, 1988, 341–368; and S. Breyer, 'Regulation and Deregulation in the United States: Airlines, Telecommunications and Antitrust', in G. Majone (ed.), *Deregulation or Re-Regulation: Regulatory Reform in Europe and the United States* (New York: St. Martins, 1990).

38 'Cartels provide a good illustration of strategy and gaming, and how these can be used to design regulation. The received theory of cartels is that gaming among the participants is endemic' (Veljanovski, 'Strategic Use of Regulation', in Baldwin, Cave and Lodge (eds), *Oxford Handbook of Regulation*, p. 88, citing C. Veljanovski, 'EC Merger Policy after GE/Honeywell and Airtours', *Antitrust Bulletin*, 49, 2004, 153–193).

39 The risk is defeating the aim with an increased potential for reverse capture.

40 Majone, *Deregulation or Re-Regulation*, p. 2.

41 N. Cunningham, 'Enforcement and Compliance Strategies', in R. Baldwin, M. Cave and M. Lodge (eds), *The Oxford Handbook of Regulation*, (Oxford: Oxford University Press, 2010), p. 125, citing Ayres, and Braithwaite, *Responsive Regulation*; R. Kagan, 'Regulatory Enforcement', in D. Rosenbloom and R. Schwartz, (eds), *Handbook of Regulation and Administrative Law* (New York: Dekker, 1994); M. Wright, S. Marsden and A. Antonelli, *Building an Evidence Base for the Health and Safety Commission Strategy to 2010 and Beyond: A Literature Review of Interventions to Improve Health and Safety Compliance* (Norwich: HSE Books, 2004).

42 Ayres and Braithwaite, *Responsive Regulation*, p. 3; it should be noted that there are varying definitions of 'self' and 'meta' regulation. *See* C. Coglianese and E. Mendelson, 'Meta-Regulation and Self-Regulation', in Baldwin, Cave and Lodge (eds), *Oxford Handbook of Regulation*, pp. 146–168.

43 *See* J. Black, 'Regulatory Conversations', *Journal of Law and Society*, 29(1), 2002, 163–196; R. Baldwin, M. Cave and M. Lodge, 'Introduction: Regulation – The Field and the Developing Agenda' (2010), in Baldwin, Cave and Lodge (eds), *Oxford Handbook of Regulation*, pp. 3–16.

44 Rose-Ackerman, 'Progressive Law and Economics'.

between regulator and industry may produce positive or negative results; however, the interaction is bound to provide a forum within which information flows efficiently. With this information, regulators can make decisions based on the interests of firms, and in turn firms understand the regulations or laws and regulators' rationales better. The risk here is that regulation and industry leaders may become too intimately engaged, risking regulatory capture[45] or losing sight of the 'public interest' elements of commerce or economics.[46] This is particularly relevant in the case of the air transport industry, as it is near the centre of contemporary 'public life'.

The traditions of Plato that describe governmental policymakers as 'public' individuals survive today. In *Theories of Economic Regulation*, Richard Posner describes these individuals as struggling to find the policy choice that is the best for some polity in whose interests they govern.[47] Politicians and bureaucrats may be described as 'public servants' – in the sense of providing a service to the public – or 'civil servants' – as in legally engaged to serve – in the 'public interest'. Regulatory intervention can be seen as the 'necessary exercise of collective power through government in order to cure "market failures", to protect the public from such evils of monopolistic behaviour, "destructive" competition, the abuse of private economic power, or the effects of externalities'.[48] According to Baldwin, Cave and Lodge:

> Traditional functional and 'public interest' accounts of regulation tended to see both the emergence of regulation and regulatory developments as driven by market failures, the nature of the task at hand, and by disinterested actors engaged in the pursuit of some public interest.[49]

This intervention of course, in a deregulated or liberalized sector, takes the shape of antitrust and competition policy, respectively. On the (new) role of regulators in the airline sector, Williams concludes:

> Where market forces have been shown to produce sustainable competitive conditions, regulatory intervention would be clearly counterproductive and as such should be rightly regarded as interference. When situations arise however, in which consumers are faced with high fares and little or no choice, then regulatory intervention should be viewed as being likely to be of benefit in much the same

45 The concept of regulatory capture, as a risk to regulation, is discussed in further detail below.

46 *See* M. Feintuck, 'Regulatory Rationales Beyond the Economic: In Search of the Public Interest', in Baldwin, Cave and Lodge (eds), *Oxford Handbook of Regulation*, pp. 39–63.

47 R.A. Posner, 'Theories of Economic Regulation', NBER Working Papers 0041, National Bureau of Economic Research Inc (US), 1974. Online. Available HTTP: <http://ideas.repec.org/p/nbr/nberwo/0041.html> (accessed 12 June 2011), as cited in M.E. Levine and J.L. Forrence, 'Regulatory Capture, Public Interest, and the Public Agenda: Toward a Synthesis', *Journal of Law, Economics, and Organization*, 6(168), 1990; it should be noted that 'those working in the regulatory field do not regard the capture theory as a good general description of regulation today, which overtly seeks to regulate market power and to foster competition' (Veljanovski, 'Economic Approaches to Regulation', in Baldwin, Cave and Lodge (eds), *Oxford Handbook of Regulation*, p. 27).

48 Levine and Forrence, 'Regulatory Capture', p. 168.

49 Baldwin, Cave, and Lodge, 'Introduction: Regulation', in Baldwin, Cave and Lodge (eds), *Oxford Handbook of Regulation*, p. 10.

way as technical regulations and those governing the flying hours of flight crew are regarded.[50]

Like economics of regulation, classical public interest theory comprises both positive and normative streams on what motivates policymakers and what *should* motivate them.[51] The economic theories of regulation by Stigler,[52] Posner[53] and Peltzman,[54] and also Levine's 'government services theory',[55] suggest that the regulators' conception of the 'public interest' is at times bound by self-interested goals such as re-election, job retention, personal wealth or self-gratification from the exercise of power,[56] or their actions may be influenced by their constituents' or superiors' conception of 'public interest'.

Stigler[57] observed that 'as a rule, regulation is acquired by the industry and is designed and operated primarily for its benefit'.[58] Levine and Forrence make a distinction between regulatory capture theory and public interest accounts of regulation, not only by separating public and private interests, but also 'regulatory policies and practices designed to pursue other-regarding 'public' interests of a general polity and those designed to advance the other-regarding 'public' convictions of the regulators themselves'.[59] Where a regulator is other-regarding, not producing general public support, but for a special section or on behalf of public interests that are self-regarding, their actions are influenced by 'special interest'.[60]

Post-revisionist literature uses agency and information theory as tools of analysis of the mechanism by which voters' concerns are transformed by the political process into policy.[61] This demonstrates a move away from regulatory capture debate towards

---

50 G. Williams, *Airline Competition: Deregulation's Mixed Legacy*, p. 168.

51 *See* A. Mikva, 'Forward, Symposium on the Theory of Public Choice', *Virginia Law Review*, 71, 1988, 167–177; S. Kelman, 'Public Choice and Public Spirit', *Public interest*, 87, 1987, 80–94.

52 *See generally* on the power of interest groups to use regulatory powers of government to shape regulations (regulatory capture) put forward in G.J. Stigler, *The Theory of Price*, 2nd ed., (New York: Macmillan, 1987); G.J. Stigler and D. Irwin, *Production and Distribution Theories* (London: Transaction Publishers, 1994); *and generally*, K.I. Meier, *The Political Economy of Regulation* (New York: State University of New York Press, 1988).

53 *See generally* on reframing Stigler's theory according to economist's take on the 'interest group' in R.A. Posner, *Economic Analysis of Law*, 7th ed., (Austin, TX: Wolters-Kluwer, 2007); Posner, 'Theories of Economic Regulation'.

54 *See generally* on widening Stigler's definition of 'regulator' to 'legislator' whereby accounting for a political equilibrium including electoral motivations to give a regulatory-demand argument in S. Peltzman and C. Winstron, *Deregulation of Network Industries* (Washington, DC: Brookings Institution Press, 2000).

55 On the public interest theory of regulation, *see* M. Levine, 'Revisionism Revised? Airline Deregulation and the Public Interest', *Law and Contemporary Problems*, 44, 1981, 179–195.

56 Ibid.

57 G.J. Stigler, 'The Theory of Economic Regulation', *Bell Journal of Economics and Management Science*, 2, 1971, 3.

58 E. Dal Bó, 'Regulatory Capture: A Review', *Oxford Review of Economic Policy*, 22(2), 2006, 204.

59 Levine and Forrence, 'Regulatory Capture'.

60 *See* Veljanovski, 'Economic Approaches to Regulation', in Baldwin, Cave and Lodge (eds), *Oxford Handbook of Regulation*, pp. 24–27; C. Findlay and D. Round, 'The "Three Pillars of Stagnation": Challenges for Air Transport Reform', *World Trade Review*, 5(2), 2006, 251–270.

61 Fiorina, M. and Noll, R. 'Voters, Bureaucrats and Legislators: A Rational Choice Perspective on the Growth of Bureaucracy', *Journal of Public Economics*, 9, 1978, 239–254; J. Kau, and P. Rubin,

recognizing the latitude, or slack, given to regulators on a scale from the selfless to the self-interested. Regulatory capture is narrowly interpreted as 'the process through which regulated monopolies end up manipulating the state agencies that are supposed to control them'.[62]

Based on prior experience, incumbents will find strategic ways to position themselves around the new rules and once they have done so, they will begin lobbying[63] for gradual adjustments to the rules that will transform them into a barrier to entry for new competitors. This could be evidence of regulatory capture or simply an intimate dialogue between the industry and regulator. The extent of regulatory capture varies between the EU and US. The European regulator appears to be more intimately involved in individual industries, whilst owing to its supra-Member State status, it maintains a significant distance between consumers: the 'public'. The American regulator is at more of a distance from individual industries while consumers' interests appear to be closer. This is of course a significant change to the pre-deregulation days of intense regulatory capture. The effects of this are that the European focuses on the market, whilst the American focuses on the benefit to consumers *vis-à-vis* what is in the best interest of the firms.

The position of the Supreme Court stands in contrast to what classical regulation theorists such as Bernstein[64] argue is the real objective of antitrust law: that the regulatory process usually protects regulated firms from competition and public scrutiny, which might indeed be detrimental to, rather than serving, the public interest. A lengthy debate may be led on the true external influences on policymakers and their actual intentions, but that is not the aim here. It is needful only to draw attention to the 'special interest' rhetoric that may be abused in this and other industries that have an inherent public service element to them, and that there is a high risk of contention between regulators who protect, and therefore appear to favour, the interests of firms, and antitrust law which clearly favours competition. As raised earlier, the risk is that 'government policymakers, in an era of deregulation, will protect competitors instead of competition, thus confusing antitrust's ends with its means'.[65] US antitrust regulators may be at risk of protecting firms, while their European counterparts appear to be focused on protecting the market. Two degrees of regulatory methodology set out by Findlay and Round[66] may be adopted to categorize US and EU approaches to regulating air transport according to their short- and long-term

'Self-Interest, Ideology and Logrolling in Congressional Voting', *Journal of Law and Economics*, 22, 1979, 365–384; B. Weingast, 'Regulation, Reregulation and Deregulation: The Foundation of Agency-Clientele Relationships', *Law and Contemporary Problems*, 44, 1981, 147–177; A. Denzau, and Munger, M. 'Legislators and Interest Groups: How Unorganized Interests Get Represented', *American Political Science Review*, 80, 1986, 89–106; as referred to in Levine and Forrence, 'Regulatory Capture', p. 170.

62 Dal Bó, 'Regulatory Capture', p. 203.

63 For instance, the European Low Fare Airlines Association has a very strong lobbying presence, which might be taken to effectively (further) segment the industry.

64 H.M. Bernstein, *Regulating Business by Independent Commission* (Princeton, NJ: Princeton University Press, 1955).

65 S.G.Breyer, 'Antitrust, Deregulation, and the Newly Liberated Marketplace', *California Law Review*, 75(3), May 1987, 1005.

66 Findlay and Round, '"Three Pillars of Stagnation"'; Veljanovski, in 'Strategic Use of Regulation', in Baldwin, Cave and Lodge (eds), *Oxford Handbook of Regulation*, makes a very similar point.

perspectives: the short-term, static *ex post* approach of the US is highly responsive, immediate and reactionary. By comparison, the *ex ante* EU approach is more long-term, proactive and dynamic.

Private ordering

If the cooperation between airlines can be attributed to innovation or collective industry action, it may be said that airlines achieve efficiency and enhance the market through the process of private ordering or (private) self-regulation.[67] This may exhibit advantages over legislation and other forms of governmental intervention or participation in the market, as firms are more informed and thus able to quasi-self-regulate, to some degree correcting the failures of lawmakers or avoiding the excessive influences on politically influenced policy through interest groups. Public ordering sometimes sets an adequate level of behaviour through law and private ordering simply repeats these rules, which is redundant. Private ordering that creates new rules should be given merit and considered, so long as it does not contradict the law. The theory of public ordering as applied to the air transport industry would suggest that the airlines are devising their own rules of operation in the game. Their collective action is thus simultaneously self- and industry-regarding.

Airlines play an active role in recognizing the problems facing the air transport industry. The constraints to economic efficiency may not always be clear-cut, but airlines are information-seeking and processing organizations. A collection of management theories, including situational[68] and contingency[69] theories, suggest that there is usually more than one 'best way forward', depending on a multitude of contingencies and that there is, according to Porter, a strong correlation between a firm's organizational structure and its performance.[70] If indeed this is the case, elements of the prisoners' dilemma and game theories must also be examined to understand the risks associated with the private interworking of the industry, as well as the corporate governance issues surrounding the actions taken by managers and directors with respect to collective manoeuvres.[71]

---

67 The principle of 'private ordering' is used here in a commercial sense. It is accepted in this study that airlines have or at least are perceived to have 'legitimacy' to share in the regulatory authority under applicable laws. It is simply suggested that airlines may in some cases be better equipped to regulate or at least participate significantly in the regulatory process. *See* S.L. Schwarcz, 'Private Ordering', *Northwestern University Law Review*, 97, Fall 2002, 319–350.

68 For background on situational theory, *see* J. Barwise (ed.), *Situational Theory and Its Applications* (Stanford, CA: Center for the Study of Language and Information, 1991); and K. Devlin, *Logic and Information* (Cambridge: Cambridge University Press, 1991).

69 *See* M.A. Ketokivi, and R.G. Schroeder, 'Strategic, Structural Contingency and Institutional Explanations in the Adoption of Innovative Manufacturing Practices', *Journal of Operations Management*, 22, 2004, 63–89.

70 M.E. Porter, *The Competitive Advantage of Nations* (New York: Free Press, 1990).

71 The connection between private ordering and both corporate governance and game theory, as applied to developing new, internal rules to the game, are examined in Chapter 4. Game theory is revisited below and again in Chapter 4.

Prior to deregulation of the sector, the structure of the air transport industry was relatively stable as firms were barred from autonomous behaviour. Since deregulation of the US sector in 1978 and liberalization of the EU sector by 1993, both the industry and market structures have evolved, shifting the overall and relative strength of competitive forces on both sides of the Atlantic. Structural changes to a market can positively or negatively influence industry profitability, and the industry trends that are most important for strategy are those that affect an industry's structure.[72] Individual firms influence structural change through strategic moves taken autonomously or in response to policy. If a firm's actions can fundamentally (re)shape the industry's structure, it can shift the rules of competition.[73] The goal would appear to be the discovery of a desirable strategic innovation that increases the firm's profitability and thus its position within the industry. Although this may have positive, short-term benefits for that firm (i.e. a low-cost margin, high profitability), it may undercut entry barriers and increase volatility of rivalry, undermining the long-term profitability of the industry.[74]

Applying Porter's theory[75] to the air transport sector, it seems that the *en masse* new entry of low-cost carriers (LCCs) has fundamentally changed the traditional (post-deregulation) industry and market structures. LCCs offer increased capacity,[76] bring resources to the market and have a better chance of achieving cost-leadership than legacy carriers. LCCs undeniably continue to make waves in the air transport sector, particularly in Europe, raising new considerations such as airport and airspace overcapacity. Prior to the arrival of LCCs, capacity was tightly regulated by a series of bilateral agreements between countries and government-regulated slot allocation procedures. The former Bermuda II Agreement between the US and UK, for instance, set out which airlines could access which (main) airports and with what frequency.[77] LCCs have jumped this entry hurdle by choosing to operate from smaller, regional airports, where capacity was not an issue.[78]

Major airlines cooperate consistently based on commitment through long-term contracts and an element of trust towards a common focal point. Schelling[79] uses game theory to suggest that groups will structure sequences of strategic moves towards this

---

72 M.E. Porter, *On Competition* (Cambridge, MA: Harvard University Business Review Series, 1996).

73 Ibid.

74 Ibid.

75 Ibid.

76 This is through the offering of, for instance, new routes or untapped capacities at smaller regional or under-utilized airports.

77 The Bermuda II Agreement was formerly the 'traditional' bilateral air services arrangement between the US and UK governments, which was in place until the Air Transport Agreement with the US was provisionally implemented in March 2008. Signed in 1977, the Bermuda II amended the previous 1946 Bermuda I agreement. The highly restrictive agreement outlined which airlines were permitted to fly, for instance, to London's Heathrow *versus* Gatwick airports from designated US cities.

78 This raises a new debate over capacity optimum and eco-optimum, in particular with increasing social concerns and policy responses to air transport and the environment. *See* S. Truxal, 'Competitive Distortions, Carbon Emissions Efficiencies or the Green Ultimatum?' *International Trade Law and Regulation*, 14(4), 2008, 77–79; 'EU Transport Emissions Compliance Catch-up', *International Trade Law and Regulation*, 14(6), 2008, 117–121; 'At the Sidelines of Implementing the EU ETS: Objections to "Validity"', *International Trade Law and Regulation*, 16(4), 2010, 111–119.

79 *See* T.C. Schelling, *The Strategy of Conflict* (Cambridge, MA: Harvard University Press, 2007).

common goal, making the competition appear to emerge naturally. An industry in which firms cooperate is likely to be a stable one, with true competitive advantages, i.e. firms make accurate forecasts and gain experience and benefits from peers.

In the absence of continuity of interaction between parties with behaviour ranging from lack of communication to defensive or offensive moves,[80] segmentation in the sector will occur. The entry of LCCs to the market is an example of differentiation, but does this constitute segmentation? If the traditional industry and market structure have indeed been so fundamentally affected by the LCC practices, perhaps these are now two different, basic battlegrounds (markets): low-cost and legacy carrier. They may not, however, be quite separate sub-sectors. Taking the UK model with LCCs operating from main airports and legacy carriers taking on LCC-invented cost-savings practices, one is beginning to resemble the other. In the EU and US, legacy carriers have even started up LCC subsidiaries.[81]

There are also examples of cooperation, albeit it in more simplified, less integrated forms, which is less costly than the legacy carrier global strategic alliances model.[82] For instance, JetBlue, a US domestic LCC, has an interline agreement with Aer Lingus (low-cost model legacy carrier based in Ireland), a codeshare agreement with Lufthansa (legacy carrier based in Germany) and an interline agreement with American Airlines.[83] In 2009, a Canadian LCC, WestJet, signed a codeshare agreement with Air France–KLM and another more recently with American Airlines.[84] As such, it is becoming a bit more difficult to draw a clear line between the two. It would appear that LCCs are changing the 'rules of the game' to the extent that they are shifting the existing paradigm to apply competitive pressure on legacy carriers.

Post-deregulation airline economics

Perhaps the most interesting paradox[85] of the airline industry is that although some airlines[86] make good profits, the industry as a whole cannot recover capital costs in an

80 S.H. Hymer, *The International Operations of National Firms: A Study of Direct Foreign Investment* (Cambridge, MA: MIT Press, 1976); M.E. Porter and M.B. Fuller, 'Coalitions and Global Strategy', in M.E. Porter (ed.), *Competition in Global Industries* (Boston, MA: Harvard Business School Press, 1986), pp. 314–344.

81 Although many of these have either been withdrawn or failed, this type of strategy will be detailed in Chapter 5. *See* relevant studies by P. Flint, 'The Leopard Changes Its Spots', *Air Transport World*, 33(11), 1996, 51–54; C. Goldsmith, 'British Airways Launches No-Frills Unit – Move May Risk Diluting Brand Name, Some Say', *Wall Street Journal*, 22 May 1998, 5; G. Dunn, 'KLM Launches Low Cost Airline – Named "Buzz"', *Air Transport Intelligence News*, 22 September 1999; A. Clark, 'EasyJet Lines Up Merger with Go: Shake-Up of Budget Airlines Could Mean Higher Fares', *Guardian*, 04 May 2002, 2; as cited by Vasigh, Fleming and Tacker (eds), *Introduction to Air Transport Economics*, pp. 326–327.

82 European Commission and US Department of Transportation (ECDOT), 'Transatlantic Airline Alliances: Competitive Issues and Regulatory Approaches' (2010), p. 2. Online. Available HTTP: <ec.europa.eu/competition/sectors/transport/reports/joint_alliance_report.pdf> (accessed 23 July 2011), p. 10.

83 Ibid.

84 Ibid.

85 *See* Doganis, *Flying Off Course*, pp. 1–24.

86 Holloway gives the examples of Ryanair and AirAsia (S. Holloway, *Straight and Level: Practical Airline Economics*, 3rd ed. (Aldershot: Ashgate, 2008), Part 1).

economic cycle or single operational cycle[87] of eight to ten years, five 'good' years of low profits followed by five years of comparatively poorer performance, and so on in the cycle.[88] The airline industry has been described thusly as 'inherently turbulent'.[89] 'For the last 50 years [the industry] has been characterized by continued and rapid growth in demand for its services. Yet it has remained only marginally profitable.'[90] Whilst occasionally the cause is attributed to 'human failings', most would argue that there is a more fundamental, structural problem with the sector. Although this book only considers regulation of the operational side of the industry[91] to the extent that it impinges on the aspect of competition within the related markets, it is needful to note that 'various technical standards and safety procedures undoubtedly constrain airline managers and, at the same time, impose cost penalties on airline operations'.[92]

In an attempt to move out of or influence the operational cycle, airlines develop corporate strategies comprising a variety of actions. In general, 'airlines have been successful at increasing revenues by opening up new routes, dropping unprofitable destinations, selecting the most efficient aircraft type, and implementing advanced revenue management practices'[93] and for LCCs in particular, the 'action' has been largely around managing costs. Over the past two decades, the general trend in the sector has been towards aggregation of know-how and away from diversification as a means to achieve competitive advantage. As stated by Holloway:

> [E]mphasis has shifted towards analysis of shared competencies and the search for a better understanding of how it is that aggregating different businesses within the same corporate group actually creates more shareholder value than would be created were each independent; this has contributed to a move away from conglomerate diversification.[94]

In the air transport sector, this has led to the development of three broad models as the source of operating strategy: the single core (e.g. passenger or cargo) business, a 'portfolio of related businesses' (e.g. passenger, cargo, maintenance), and a 'portfolio of unrelated businesses' (e.g. airlines and car hire companies).[95] Since airlines operate in a market of 'derived demand', all these business models are impacted whether the airline has expanded into unrelated industries or not.[96] Most major carriers have both

---

87 Doganis offers a detailed investigation into the performance over the past 30 years of individual airlines, providing evidence of the cyclical nature of the industry. *See* Doganis, *Flying Off Course*, pp. 15–17.

88 Doganis, *Flying Off Course*, pp. 4–5.

89 R. Doganis, 'An Inherently Unstable Industry: Airlines Have Themselves to Blame', in J.F. O'Connell and G. Williams (eds), *Air Transport in the 21st Century: Key Strategic Developments* (Farnham: Ashgate, 2011), pp. 39–42; J.F. O'Connell, 'Airlines: An Inherently Turbulent Industry', in O'Connell and Williams (eds), *Air Transport in the 21st Century*, pp. 59–96.

90 Doganis, *Flying Off Course*, p. 4.

91 Doganis sets out five main categories of non-economic technical and safety regulations. *See* Doganis, *Flying Off Course*, pp. 26–28.

92 Ibid., p. 28.

93 Vasigh, Fleming and Tacker, *Introduction to Air Transport Economics*, p. 78.

94 Holloway, *Straight and Level*, p. 6.

95 Ibid.

96 Doganis, *Flying Off Course*, pp. 23–24

passengers and cargo operations, although these are sometimes split into two separate activities for one reason or another.[97]

In a regulated market, outputs are controlled; in the case of the airline industry these include seats, space, routes and capacities. It follows that there is little to no incentive for airlines to innovate in such a tightly regulated environment as doing so would increase costs but have little impact on prices or in any case revenue earned. In a deregulated sector, however, barriers to market entry are removed and airlines are, as 'free enterprises', so at liberty to expand their networks. Once the 'artificial cap on supply'[98] is removed upon deregulation of the sector, the market is exposed to 'free competition' and so it becomes necessary for airlines to innovate as a means to realize the margins they seek. Alongside other external influences,[99] the introduction of 'real' competition in the deregulated sector has impacted significantly on the evolution of airline 'business models'.

An airline's business model, as Holloway puts it, 'is a description of the value the company delivers to targeted customers, and of how it configures resources internally and externally to achieve this'.[100] Customers, on the other hand, experience different levels of utility, or value, in their purchase and use of a product. Owing to this 'subjectivity of demand', airlines must target customers with increases in value and they must be relevant in their consideration leading to making a decision to purchase.[101] The two business models that emerged in the deregulated market are distinguished according to their revenue and cost structures[102]: full-service, full-revenue legacy carriers on the one hand and 'no-frills' and hybrid low-fare, LCCs on the other.

For airlines, the key determinant of supply and demand is the ticket price, or for cargo the premium on freight, for the 'good' or service.[103] Here it is essential to emphasize the relationship between an airline's cost structure and the number of variables impacting on its profitability.[104] With a view to achieve and maintain profitability, an airline works towards equilibrium between supply and demand, while mindful of the need to reduce costs and manage yields.[105] An alternative measure of profitability commonly used among airlines is the operating ratio, which is the annual operating

97 *See* Ibid., pp. 21–24.

98 Vasigh, Fleming and Tacker provide the United States–China Air Transport Agreement as an example of artificially limiting the supply of air transportation services between the two countries, or an 'artificial cap' (Vasigh, Fleming and Tacker, *Introduction to Air Transport Economics*, p. 71).

99 Two key factors impacting on the development of airlines' business models has been the growth of the Internet, which has provided consumers with ease of booking, transparency of fares, taxes and charges, and technological advancements in aircraft and engine manufacturing. (Holloway, *Straight and Level*, p. 28); *see also* J. Snow, 'Advanced in Transport Aircraft and Engines', in O'Connell and Williams (eds), *Air Transport in the 21st Century*, pp. 295–315.

100 Holloway, *Straight and Level*, p. 25.

101 Ibid., p. 11.

102 Ibid., pp. 32–33, refers to these as 'revenue model' and 'cost model' respectively. The former focuses on for instance product design to realize target revenues while the latter concentrates on the financial consequences of the revenue model.

103 Vasigh, Fleming and Tacker, *Introduction to Air Transport Economics*, p. 69.

104 Ibid., p. 78.

105 *See* Doganis, *The Airline Business*, pp. 272–278.

profit or loss or the net profit or loss, after tax, expressed as a percentage of the total annual revenue.'[106] So, an airline will be profitable when its revenues per unit are higher than the costs for the same unit. It is needful to mention that whilst the product price is critical it is not, however, the only basis on which customers make their decisions,[107] therefore the relationship might be best described as an indifference curve of price against benefits.[108]

One comparison Holloway offers is between the experiences of Debonair and JetBlue. Debonair made some minor cabin service improvements, but customers either did not realize or did not take these into account when making their purchases and subsequently Debonair failed. JetBlue, on the other hand, offered benefits that were both well communicated and relevant to respective customers' purchase decisions.[109] Airlines realize they offer a relatively homogenous product, and therefore one tends to find it difficult to differentiate its product from the product offered by the competition.

An airline's costs are typically categorized into operating and non-operating categories. Operating costs are again divided into two main categories: 'available seat miles' (ASMs) and 'direct operating costs' (DOCs).[110] The most obvious DOCs are employees[111] (flight crew, administration, ground staff,[112] cargo and operations personnel), fuel, aircraft and jet engine maintenance, aircraft (through ownership or leasing) and airport fees (for take-off, landing and parking).[113] DOCs have in recent years become an increasingly important dynamic.[114] Additionally, aircraft hourly productivity 'is calculated by multiplying the maximum payload an aircraft can carry by its average hourly block speed, i.e. the distance it can fly in an hour.'[115] Higher productivity of aircraft means relatively lower DOCs, and therefore lower costs per seat.[116] It should be noted that the technological developments in aircraft and jet engine manufacturing

106 Doganis, *Flying Off Course*, p. 5.

107 A study by Dunleavy and Westerman (2005) showed that 30 per cent of customers do not choose the least expensive flight displayed. (Holloway, *Straight and Level*, p. 13).

108 Holloway, *Straight and Level*, p. 14.

109 Ibid., p. 11.

110 An ASM is 'one airline seat, flown one mile, regardless of whether it is carrying a revenue passenger … Costs per ASM … [is] the cost of flying one aircraft seat for one mile' (Vasigh, Fleming and Tacker, *Introduction to Air Transport Economics*, p. 92).

111 *See* R. Doganis, *The Airline Business*, pp. 118–146 for extensive research on the importance of and challenges associate with labour costs in the airline business.

112 DOCs may be broken down further into 'variable or flying costs', 'fixed or standing costs', and 'indirect operating costs'. Ground crew salaries and costs associated with ticketing and sales constitute indirect operating costs. Because most airline sales and ticketing is now done online, the recent trend has been the decline of associated costs. (Source: Doganis, *Flying Off Course*, pp. 83–85; *See also* Doganis, *The Airline Business*, pp. 196–222 on the impact of e-commerce on the airline industry; and J.F. O'Connell, 'IT Innovations In Passenger Services', in O'Connell and Williams (eds), *Air Transport in the 21st Century*, pp. 353–374.

113 Vasigh, Fleming and Tacker, *Introduction to Air Transport Economics*, p. 79.

114 In 1994, DOCs represented 49 per cent of total operating costs but this figure rose to 61.9 per cent in 2007 and even further in 2008. (Doganis, *Flying Off Course*, p. 74)

115 Ibid., p. 8. The figures are available from ICAO.

116 Ibid.

have been phenomenal compared with other sectors, so it could be said that the innovation factor has generally had a positive effect on airline profitability. At the same time, however, the cost of purchasing aircraft has increased, which when taken together with the cyclical nature of the industry, has put increased strain on airline finances.[117] Because an aircraft typically takes between two and four years or more from order to fulfilment, the industry may have entered by that time into a different, downwards phase of the cycle, whereby causing airlines to struggle with cash flow and leading to further debt.

The basic LCC revenue model follows a simple price structure based on one-way sectors. With fewer manned check-in desks and customer service staff, no passenger lounges and minimum numbers of cabin crew, LCCs are able to minimize staffing costs.[118] The work of Vasigh, Fleming and Tacker shows, however, that while it may be the general assumption that LCCs pay the lowest salaries, this is not entirely correct. They show that in 2006, three US LCCs were lowest but a fourth LCC, Southwest Airlines, was near the middle in terms of flight crew costs. They also compare three US LCCs, Air Tran, Frontier and JetBlue, which all pay lower rates to younger crews who appear to accept this, to legacy carriers such as American Airlines and Continental Airlines, which 'have been around so long that many crew members are quite senior and command a higher pay rate than junior members'.[119]

LCCs keep their operational costs low through high aircraft seating density, offering refreshments for purchase only, and since LCCs do not usually offer interline routes, they are unlikely to hold responsibility for missed connections or the potentially associated costs. In the LCC cost model, relying on direct sales rather than through a computer reservation system(CRS) or a global distribution system (GDS) means lower distribution costs. LCCs will typically use secondary airports, which have lower charges for landing and take-off slots as well as lower passenger handling fees. Using so-called 'fast turnarounds' for high utilization of single-type fleet aircraft and by outsourcing external services such as passenger and aircraft handling, LCCs maximize value and flexibility of fixed costs.[120] LCCs can also perform general processes less expensively, for example, through the 'free seating' concept.

It should be noted that some LCCs have begun to differentiate themselves somewhat by offering a basket of services to customers willing to pay a premium. Most LCCs, for example, offer passengers seats with extra legroom or in the exit row at an extra cost. EasyJet offers premium check-in and boarding with its 'Speedy Boarding'

117 Ibid., pp. 12–13
118 Holloway, in *Straight and Level*, cites this as one way that legacy carriers differentiate themselves.
119 Vasigh, Fleming and Tacker, *Introduction to Air Transport Economics*, pp. 96–97; *See also* A. Knorr, and A. Arndt, 'Most Low-Cost Airlines Fail(ed): Why Did Southwest Airlines Prosper?', in P. Forsyth, D. Gillen, O.G. Mayer and H. Niemeier (eds), *Competition versus Predation in Aviation Markets: A Survey of Experience in North America, Europe and Australia* (Aldershot: Ashgate, 2005), pp. 145–170; *and* Doganis on the Southwest Airlines model and how it was followed in Europe (Doganis, *The Airline Business*, pp. 150–156, 164–170). *See also* B.M. Gilroy, E. Lukas and T. Volpert, 'The European 'No-Frills'-Aviation Market: Current and Future Developments', in Forsyth, Gillen, Mayer and Niemeier (eds), *Competition versus Predation*, pp. 203–233.
120 Holloway, *Straight and Level*, pp. 32–33.

product[121], while Ryanair charges for hold luggage[122]. The success of LCCs, particularly when encroaching on legacy carrier short-haul markets, has required legacy carriers to adjust their cost models, e.g. simplifying service delivery processes, 'depeaking' hubs, increasing aircraft utilization, and renegotiating input costs.[123]

At the same time, a handful of legacy carriers have also moved towards the low-cost model. 'When legacy carriers reduce their service product to equal that of LCCs, they are largely competing just on cost. And ... competing solely on cost is risky, since LCCs have much lower cost structures than legacy carriers.'[124] Other legacy carriers have launched subsidiary LCCs to compete in certain markets, e.g. KLM-Air France and Transavia; Lufthansa and Germanwings.[125]

Network economics

The global alliance strategy is rooted in the fundamentals of network economics within the global economy.[126] 'The economic pressures pushing the airlines into alliances are real since the benefits from joining alliances can be very substantial.'[127] Designing and developing an airline's network is crucial, both in terms of brand identity and to cost considerations.[128] In developing an alliance strategy, an airline must first 'identify and clarify its own objectives and aims'[129] before locating the appropriate partner or group to join. 'The final step in developing an alliance strategy is to assess and quantify the benefits and costs of different potential partners.'[130]

> Post deregulation, the legacy carrier business model on both sides of the Atlantic predicated on a 'from anywhere to everywhere' consumer proposition. However, no airline is able to efficiently serve every destination its customers require with its own aircraft.[131]

Since there is no single airline that fully matches every route for which there is demand, or 'demand linkages',[132] presently the only realistic matching of demand is characterized

---

121 *See* 'Speedy Boarding' on easyJet website. Available HTTP:<http://www.easyjet.com/en/book/speedy_boarding.html> (accessed 1 September 2011); 'Priority Boarding' on Ryanair website. Available HTTP: <http://www.ryanair.com/en/questions/how-do-i-book-priority-boarding> (accessed 1 September 2011).

122 *See* 'Baggage Allowances' on easyJet website. Available HTTP: <http://www.easyjet.com/en/planning/baggage.html> (accessed 1 September 2011); 'Checked Baggage Allowance' on Ryanair website. Available HTTP: <http://www.ryanair.com/en/questions/checked-baggage-allowance> (accessed 1 September 2011).

123 Holloway, *Straight and Level.*

124 Vasigh, Fleming and Tacker, *Introduction to Air Transport Economics*, p. 327.

125 Holloway, *Straight and Level*, p. 31.

126 ECDOT, 'Transatlantic Airline Alliances', p. 3.

127 Doganis, *The Airline Business*, p. 278.

128 Holloway, *Straight and Level*, p. 366.

129 Doganis, *The Airline Business*, p. 278.

130 Ibid., p. 279.

131 ECDOT, 'Transatlantic Airline Alliances', p. 3.

132 Holloway, *Straight and Level*, p. 366

by multi-stop and connecting flights, sometimes with different carriers.[133] This places airlines in the position of choosing which segment of the particular market to operate in based on their own identity as legacy carrier or LCC, economics of aircraft operation, economies of scope[134] and density.[135]

> Additionally, few city-pairs can generate sufficient demand on a daily basis to sustain non-stop service. To meet the demands of customers, carriers must seek commercial partners that can help them provide greater network coverage and increased service options.[136]

Applying the economies of scale[137] principle in microeconomics, as a firm's size increases through expansion of manufacturing, purchasing, diversification of financing or marketing through short-term investment, the firm's long-term average costs of production will reduce. Although an airline operating low frequency with larger aircraft has economies of scale since high frequency with small aircraft is generally more expensive, the trend over the past two decades has been to increase frequency with smaller planes, incidentally leading to more congestion.[138] Airlines are reluctant to reduce frequency of services, however, as they feel it will reduce their competitive advantage and damage their market position.

Inter-firm cooperation with a view to acquiring knowledge leads to the formation of strategic alliances that offer to expand a firm's capacity for innovation through the recombination of knowledge towards efficiency.[139] As this process is repeated

---

133 Ibid.

134 An airline has economies of scope where it is less costly per product to offer each additional unit, typically achieved through sharing of resources for multiple products (e.g. for airlines, a flight with passengers connecting to different flights and 'by operating various ancillary programmes/services, such as frequent flyer plans, maintenance activities, catering, and ground handling') (Vasigh, Fleming and Tacker, *Introduction to Air Transport Economics*, p. 100); *See also* O'Connell, 'Ancillary Revenues: The New Trend in Strategic Airline Marketing', in O'Connell and Williams, *Air Transport in the 21stCentury*, pp. 145–169.

135 An airline has economies of density, 'when unit cost declines as a result of increased volume of traffic being carried between points already served' and is highly dependent on aircraft size and length of flight (e.g. long-haul and non-stop flights usually have lower unit costs). (Holloway, *Straight and Level*, p. 369). Vasigh, Fleming and Tacker refer to airline hub-and-spoke systems as a form of consolidation of operations and thus achievement of economies of density and also contribute to their economies of scale (*Introduction to Air Transport Economics*, p. 90).

136 ECDOT, 'Transatlantic Airline Alliances', p. 3.

137 The airline and aircraft-manufacturing sector, the latter of which is effectively a duopoly comprised of Airbus and Boeing, are examples of high capital industries commonly with economies of scale. *See* Vasigh, Fleming and Tacker, *Introduction to Air Transport Economics*, pp. 89–91.

138 Holloway, *Straight and Level*, p. 371. On the risk of diseconomies of scale through consolidation, *see* Holloway, *Straight and Level*, p. 42; and A.M. Pilarski, *Why Can't We Make Money in Aviation?* (Aldershot: Ashgate, 2007), pp. 116–117.

139 R. Cowan, N. Jonard and J.B. Zimmermann, 'Bilateral Collaboration and the Emergence of Innovation Networks', *Management Science*, 57(7), 2007, 1051–1067; D. Lavie and L. Rosenkopf, 'Balancing Exploration and Exploitation in Alliance Formation', *Academy of Management Journal*, 49(4), 2006, pp. 797–818.

through the addition of new partners or altogether new alliances, innovation networks emerge. Whilst it is recognized that networks may emerge from individual behaviour[140], the focus here is on the effects of cooperation between firms. With firms increasing their 'non-market relations'[141] through the formation of strategic alliances, a new concept of 'network organization' develops. In coalitions where firms' boundaries are defined, the structure of the organization is stable according to Nash's game theory,[142] but tend to be inefficient. The network as non-traditional structure is more flexible – and thus potentially less stable – but enjoys a higher payoff.[143]

If the intention of the firm is to expand their innovative capacity, the degrees of interlinking and dependencies of firms through their relationships raise questions as to the nature of the strategic alliance: exploratory or exploitative. External forces on the firms from the industry or market may create turbulence, which may give rise to either exploration, exploitation, or both.[144] To summarize, exploration involves 'a pursuit of new knowledge' whereas exploitation involves 'the use and development of things already known'.[145] The risk is that firms will exploit their partners and the knowledge acquired *vis-à-vis* strategic alliances rather than work together towards innovation. As with organizational behaviour theory, there are both normative and behavioural perspectives to the balancing of exploration and exploitation within (innovative) networks[146]; however, for the purposes of this book, only the normative perspective is conferred. In the case of the air transport industry, the formation of innovation networks is sound evidence of industrial organization.

140 *See generally* B. Uzzi, and J. Sprio, 'Collaboration and Creativity: The Small World Problem', *American Journal of Sociology*, 111, 2005, 447–504.

141 This is a phrase used by Cowan, Jonard, and Zimmermann in their empirical work to describe the move from the traditionally dominant market or hierarchical form of economic organizations to more recent tactical and strategic alliances, which they suggest breaks down firms' once rigid boundaries to more porous, flexible boundaries in network structures (Cowan, Jonard and Zimmermann, 'Bilateral Collaboration', pp. 1051–1067).

142 *See generally* S. Hargreaves Heap and Y. Varoufakis, *Game Theory*, 2nd ed. (London: Routledge, 2004).

143 Ibid.

144 Lavie, and Rosenkopf, 'Balancing Exploration', pp. 797–818; For independent studies on exploration in alliance formation, *see* C.M. Beckman, P.R. Haunschild and D.J. Phillips, 'Friends or Strangers? Firm-Specific Uncertainty, Market Uncertainty, and Network Partner Selection', *Organization Science*, 15, 2004, 259–275; on exploitation *see* T. Rowley, D. Behrens and D. Krackhardt, 'Redundant Governance Structures: An Analysis of Structural and Relational Embeddedness in the Steel and Semi-Conductor Industries', *Strategic Management Journal*, 21, 2000, 369–386; and finally on situations where both are present, *see* M.P. Koza, and A.Y. Lewin, 'The Co-Evolution of Strategic Alliances', *Organization Science*, 9, 1998, 99–117.

145 D.A. Levinthal, and J.G. March, 'The Myopia of Learning', *Strategic Management Journal*, 14, 1993, 105, as cited in Lavie and Rosenkopf, 'Balancing Exploration, p. 798.

146 *See* Lavie and Rosenkopf, 'Balancing Exploration, pp. 800–801.

4 American and European competition law and policy

Introduction

Although they might appear *prima facie* to match up as transatlantic counterparts, European competition law and US antitrust law differ in far more than name. This topic is relevant to any discussion on the two forms of competition policy and law, especially in the present framework on the varied approaches of EU and US policy-makers to defining forms of cooperation and anti-competitive behaviour in the air transport sectors within their respective jurisdictions.

According to Jones and Sufrin, 'competition law or, in the US, antitrust law, exists to protect the process of competition in a free market economy'.[1] The 'free market economy' is considered as a theoretical concept and for the purposes of this study and the nature of air transport as a 'public utility', government intervention to some degree is expected, thereby limiting the concept to the latter two words 'market economy'. Semi-recent pronouncements on the issuance of grants and other loan guarantees by US authorities to American air carriers and the approval of state aid to European airlines despite the EU's transport policy objective of creating conditions for fair and equitable competition might suggest an unreasonable level of (continued) intervention.

In addition, the 'American terminology is more aggressive, and has a "disagreeably negative ring" to it'.[2] In this chapter, the idea that the distinction is simply one of terminology is defeated. The dissimilarities between EU competition law and US antitrust law are many. Amato and Peritz suggest that the inventors of US antitrust law were in fact politicians, and of European competition law, scholars, who viewed it as the solution to what they call a then crucial problem for democracy at the time:

> [T]he emergence from the company or firm as an expression of the fundamental freedom of individuals, of the opposite phenomenon of private power, a power devoid of legitimation and dangerously capable of infringing not just the

---

1 A. Jones and B. Sufrin, *EC Competition Law: Texts, Cases and Materials*, 4th ed. (Oxford: Oxford University Press, 2010), p. 3.

2 Jones and Sufrin, *EC Competition Law*, p. 3; *See also* F.M. Scherer, *Competition Policies for an Integrated World Economy* (Washington, DC: Brookings Institution, 1994); W. Pape, 'Socio-Cultural Differences and International Competition Law', *European Legal Journal*, 5, 1999, 444–445.

economic freedom of other private individuals, but also the balance of public decisions exposed to its domineering strength.[3]

This perhaps risks opening the 'floodgates' to a much deeper than intended discussion on the socio-legal construction of antitrust and competition laws, but indeed it is relevant to mention in the light of the two varied approaches. All in all, it is necessary to recognize at this point the idea that it is the citizens in a liberal democracy who give the relevant policymakers and the 'law' their legitimacy, and in turn expect these officials to make decisions in the interest of sustaining, if not improving, public welfare. With this in mind, a clearer picture of antitrust and competition law may be drawn, looking to their respective objectives, rather than as simply a source of decisions made by a body of 'domineering strength'.

American and European legislative perspectives

An objective observation of the statutory language of the two pieces of legislation relevant to the regulation of competition in the EU and US aids the explanation of the divergent regulatory approaches *vis-à-vis* the legal tests applied by the two respective competition authorities to their assessment of joint ventures and why their respective competition cultures might deserve the nicknames 'gentlemanly competition' and 'cowboy capitalism'.[4] The current state of the law leading to these categorizations, i.e. regulations as applied to the air transport industry in the EU, as well as the relevant sections of the competition law and US antitrust law will be examined in detail in this chapter.

The economies of scale principle[5] suggests that the fragmented air transport industry would benefit from expansion, particularly towards multinational corporate entities as mentioned earlier, but for the most part, airlines are prevented by domestic or regional cross-border merger and acquisition policies.[6] An international airline operating on a transatlantic route will be affected by at least one of these two systems of competition law and will also likely feel the effects of the others' extraterritorial reach. This study looks into the unprecedented level of cooperation and, to an extent, progress towards coordinated antitrust enforcement activity between competition authorities in the EU and US.

---

3 R.J.R. Peritz, *Competition Policy in America: History, Rhetoric, Law*, Rev. Ed. (Oxford: Oxford University Press, 1996).

4 O. Gersemann, 'Cowboy Capitalism: European Myths, American Reality', CATO Institute, 2004, as cited in J.B. McDonald, 'Section 2 and Article 82: Cowboys and Gentlemen', paper presented to the College of Europe, Brussels (16 June 2005). Online. Available HTTP: <http://www.justice.gov/atr/public/speeches/210873.htm> (accessed 13 September 2011).

5 The fundamental idea of the economies of scale principle in microeconomics is that with the increase of a firm's size (through expansion of manufacturing, purchasing, diversification of financing or marketing through short-term investment), long-term average costs of production are reduced.

6 IATA suggests that these economies of scale will be achieved if the industry is supported by proper competition supervision (C. Findlay and D. Round, 'The "Three Pillars of Stagnation": Challenges for Air Transport Reform', *World Trade Review*, 5(2), 2006, 251–270).

Deregulation and liberalization of the two air transport sectors are accepted as 'achieved' in the classical sense,[7] supported by the relevant legal framework for 'pro-competitive behaviour',[8] namely European competition law and American antitrust. Deregulation is, of course, not without regulation. In fact, to be efficient it is clear that deregulation and liberalization of markets require some effective forms of regulation through law and policy.[9] However, the degree to which this 'regulation' is required varies from a deregulated US to a liberalized European sector. Particularly in an industry in which regulators apply 'public interest' rhetoric, there is a risk that policymakers are conflicted and confused, choosing either to self-protect or to protect firms, as demonstrated by the use or misuse of competition and antitrust policies, instead of concerning themselves foremost with 'workable competition' in the market.

Statutory language

The immediate, quite apparent difference is in the language of the EU competition rules and US antitrust legislation. By way of comparison: Article 102 TFEU reads: 'Any abuse by one or more undertakings of a dominant position within the common market . . . shall be prohibited as incompatible with the common market.' Section 2 of the Sherman Act 1890 states: 'Every person who shall monopolize, or attempt to monopolize . . . shall be deemed guilty of a felony, and . . . shall be punished by fine . . . or by imprisonment'. The US courts have interpreted 'monopolize' as the wilful acquisition or maintenance of monopoly power and the use of exclusionary conduct. *Prima facie* then, the remit of EU competition rules is the policing of the conduct of dominant firms and a breach requires 'abuse', whereas US antitrust law prevents the creation or maintenance of monopolies and a breach requires 'exclusionary conduct'.

Upon closer examination, the US approach to anti-competitive behaviour is founded on 'protecting the public from the failure of the market', antitrust being 'concerned for public interest'. In 1986, US Judge Easterbrook famously said:

> Competition is a ruthless process. A firm that reduces cost and expands sales injures rivals – sometimes fatally . . . These injuries to rivals are by-products of vigorous competition, and the antitrust laws are not balm for rivals' wounds. The antitrust laws are for the benefit of competition, not competitors.[10]

---

7 Indicators such as administrative changes, less (direct) governmental intervention and to some degree more efficiency (through transparency and fair pricing) suggest that the key objectives of deregulation and liberalization have been achieved. The 'achievement' (as set apart from 'implementation' or 'successfulness') of these economic principles will be revisited below.

8 It is difficult to distinguish anti-competitive behaviour from healthy competitive practices, which might benefit competition but harm competitors. It is increasingly difficult, or impossible, 'for regulators to draw a clear line to divide appropriate competitive acts from inappropriate competitive acts.' (B. Vasigh, K. Fleming and T. Tacker, *Introduction to Air Transport Economics* (Farnham: Ashgate, 2008), p. 222).

9 As stated by Giovanni Bisignani, former IATA Director and CEO (Findlay and Round, 'Three Pillars of Stagnation', p. 263).

10 *Ball Memorial Hospital Inc v Mutual Hosp Ins Inc* 784 F.2d 1325, 1338 (7th Cir. 1986) (F.H. Easterbrook, J.).

Arguably more so than those in Europe, American firms are permitted, if not encouraged, to compete aggressively. The rationale is that the result of intense competition in a market promotes consumer interests. The successful firm's goal is to strive towards monopoly. This is viewed as 'successful (workable) competition', and as such, has become a sort of accepted business practice in the US. Another, US Judge Hand, argues that subjecting a firm's every action to judicial scrutiny would threaten to discourage the competitive enthusiasm that antitrust laws seek to promote.[11]

Thus the application of antitrust is restricted. Since breaches of US antitrust are difficult to prove, there appears to be more faith by antitrust legislation and regulators in the long-term benefits to competitive behaviour. This is combined with a strong belief in the market's ability to correct the anti-competitive behaviour. To that end, the American business environment has been called 'cowboy capitalism'.[12] When considering air transport, however, and its regulatory exception, it can be said that the US DoT takes a broader view of the public interest in its legal test applied to its assessment of joint ventures. The public interest test gives US DoT greater discretion in its decision making process under applications for antitrust immunity, not to forget its also being the transport policymaker in the US.

On the other hand, European firms are now neither required nor allowed to notify or apply to Commission for approval of a proposed joint venture,[13] so airlines 'must instead themselves conduct an assessment of whether their cooperation is in breach of the EU competition rules'.[14] Thus, the EU competition law expects firms to 'compete like gentlemen'[15] or quasi-self-regulate until and if the Commission or a competition authority in a Member State initiates an investigation. A so-called duty to deal with rivals is imposed by EU competition law. Conversely, American firms have the freedom to refuse to deal with rivals as this may have a better result for the market, so there is an expectation on the European firm, therefore, to 'maintain' competition.

In *British Airways plc v Commission*, the European Community (EC)[16] Court of First Instance (CFI)[17] stated:

> [W]hilst the finding that a dominant position does not in itself imply any reproach to the undertaking concerned, [the dominant undertaking] has a special responsibility, irrespective of the causes of that position, not to allow its conduct to impair genuine undistorted competition on the common market.[18]

---

11 *United States v Aluminium Co of Am* 148 F.2d 416, 430 (2d Cir. 1945) (L. Hand, J.).
12 Gersemann, 'Cowboy Capitalism', as cited in McDonald, 'Section 2 and Article 82: Cowboys and Gentlemen'.
13 Regulation 1/2003 abolished the previous notification system.
14 European Commission and US Department of Transportation (ECDOT), 'Transatlantic Airline Alliances: Competitive Issues and Regulatory Approaches' (2010), p. 17. Online. Available HTTP: <ec.europa.eu/competition/sectors/transport/reports/joint_alliance_report.pdf> (accessed 23 July 2011).
15 Remarks by Claes Bengtsson, 'Loyalty Discounts, the approach in EU,' Developments in the Law and Economics of Exclusionary Pricing Practices (18.3.2004), Washington, DC.
16 Now European Union.
17 Now called the General Court of the European Union.
18 Case T-219/99, *British Airways plc v Commission* [2003] ECR 242.

From an historical perspective, it should be remembered that EU competition policy was made in line with the primary objective of integration of national firms into the Union's single market, bringing an end to state-owned and sanctioned monopolies, and opening markets to competition. It could be said that EU policymakers are more confident that this system is able to predict outcomes, thus making *ex ante* intervention more likely. The general legal test of the European Commission is to apply and enforce the competition rules, while ensuring that any joint ventures do not ultimately harm consumers.

The EU and US governments take two different regulatory approaches to the extent that European firms, in particular those approaching a naturally dominant market position, must employ an element of self-regulation through carefully monitoring the competition by rivals, whereas American counterparts are 'free' to pursue their own success[19] albeit at their own risk. According to the findings of a 2010 report by the two competition regulators:

> The competitive assessments of both the Commission and DoT provide for the weighing of efficiencies and consumer benefits. However, the two authorities follow conceptually different approaches . . . Notwithstanding these important differences, decisions by the Commission and DoT are based on generally compatible analytical frameworks and are both subject to judicial review[20] by the respective courts in the EU and United States.'[21]

There is certainly evidence of general compatibility of the two frameworks. For instance, both systems 'condemn restraints by dominant firms that harm market competition. Both are committed to applying sound economics'.[22] Neither wants to protect inefficiencies and as economics suggests, 'each should steer away from protecting inefficient competitors at the expense of consumers'.[23]

Case study: Virgin Atlantic and British Airways

Before engaging with the details of European competition rules and American antitrust law, it is useful to first consider the divergent approaches to their application in practice. The following example helps to explain the divergent rationales.

In two cases between Virgin Atlantic (VS) and British Airways (BA),[24] VS challenged BA's granting of loyalty payments to travel agents both in EU and US courts.

---

19 McDonald, 'Section 2 and Article 82: Cowboys and Gentlemen'.

20 The US DoT procedures are publically available whereas the Commission procedures are not. This means that in practice, judicial review of Commission decisions occurs more frequently. (ECDOT, 'Transatlantic Airline Alliances', p. 17).

21 Ibid.

22 E.F. Fox, 'Monopolization, Abuse of Dominance, and the Indeterminacy of Economics: The U.S./ E.U. Divide', *Utah Law Review*, 2006, 739.

23 Ibid.

24 *See United States v Microsoft Corp* 253 F.3d 34, 84 (D.C. Cir. 2001) and Case COMP/C-3/37.792 *Microsoft* (24 March 2004) for an example of a situation where the US Court of Appeals required an

BA, the dominant UK carrier, offered rebates to travel agents who met sales targets under an incentives scheme. It would follow that the travel agents would promote BA over other carriers to receive the incentive payment. Despite the BA scheme, VS continued to be successful. It could be argued, however, that in the absence of BA's scheme, Virgin might have been more successful.

VS complained to the European Commission, which investigated and condemned BA's practice in 1999 under ex. Article 82 TEC (now Article 102 TFEU).[25] BA appealed to the former CFI, which ruled in 2003. VS, supported by the Commission, argued that a dominant firm should not be permitted to give discounts or incentives that encourage customer loyalty. BA argued that its rebates could not be held to constitute 'abuse' unless there was evidence showing an adverse effect on competitors, customers, or consumers.[26] The CFI agreed with the Commission that proof of an actual anti-competitive effect was unnecessary. It said: 'It is sufficient . . . to demonstrate that the position tends to restrict competition, or, in other words, that the conduct is capable of having, or likely to have, such an effect'.[27] The Commission's decision against BA was upheld.

In the US, VS brought a private action[28] against BA claiming breaches of Sections 1 and 2 of the Sherman Act. A Federal Court of Appeals upheld a summary judgment for BA in 2001. Section 1 prohibits agreements that unreasonably restrain trade, weighing up an agreement's pro and anti-competitive effects. The Court held that VS failed to evidence any actual anti-competitive effect, such as higher prices or lower output. VS argued under Section 2 that BA had, with its loyalty scheme, diverted passengers from purchasing tickets for VS and other airlines. The Court rejected these arguments on the basis that VS remained in business and there was no evidence that BA was charging monopoly prices.

The EU approach, which 'focused on the competitiveness of rival firms, which could indirectly benefit customers, but relied on presumed harm to rivals in the market and presumed indirect harm to consumers',[29] was proactive *vis-à-vis ex ante* regulation. By contrast, the American approach looked for actual anti-competitive effects, seeking *ex post* proof of harm to competition and consumers, was reactive.

---

investigation into the actual anti-competitive effects in the browser market, demanding proof of this, even though Microsoft held a 90 per cent share and undisputed monopoly in operating systems tied to its media player. The Commission Decision in 2004 was more generous as it held there was an unlawful tie between Microsoft's operating system and its media player without requiring any proof of the anti-competitive effect on consumers.

25 The European Commission found in its decision 2000/74 of 14 April 1999 in *Virgin/British Airways*, OJ L30/1, 4 February 2004, that British Airways abused its dominance on the UK market for the purchase of travel agent services by rewarding loyalty. In its judgement in Case T-219/99 *British Airways v Commission*, of 17 December 2003, the CFI dismissed an appeal against this decision.

26 Case T-219/99, *British Airways Plc v Commission* 2003 ECR 250 (2003). The original decision was based on the breach of ex. Article 82 TEU (now Article 102 TFEU) as evidenced by BA's commission payments. This was the appeal to the CFI (now the General Court of the European Union).

27 Ibid., p. 293.

28 257 F.3d 256 (2nd Cir. 2001).

29 McDonald, 'Section 2 and Article 82: Cowboys and Gentlemen', p. 11.

As Veljanovski sums it up:

> The choice between *ex ante* and *ex post* legal responses has been a perennial topic in both economic and social regulation . . . antitrust laws (and *ex post* response) or *ex ante* sector regulation . . . The European solution has been to develop a new system of *ex ante* sectoral regulation based on *ex post* competition law principles.[30]

It is interesting to note that nearly a decade later, the dialogue between European and American competition authorities has expanded to include discussions on analytical issues in competition cases and more:

> In their parallel but independent reviews of the proposed JV agreement among British Airways, American Airlines and Iberia, the Commission and DoT discussed their respective competitive assessments with a view aimed at avoiding conflicting applications of remedies.[31] In parallel to cooperation with DOT, the Commission has long-standing and productive cooperation with the US Department of Justice.[32]

EU competition rules

The EU air transport market was characterized prior to its liberalization by 'legacy' or 'national flag carriers' operating under the mandate of respective national governments, many of which were also state-owned. Under those conditions, national flag carriers benefited from a favourable position both in the domestic market and in international markets where travel originates and terminates in the home state. For flag carriers it is understandable that 'national prestige hangs upon [their] success . . . and they often enjoy considerable state support and privileged status.'[33]

Over the past decade and a half, the EU air transport market was liberalized incrementally under three 'liberalization packages', thereby influencing more *ouvert* national markets, the creation of a single European air transport market 'Single European Sky'.[34] It was not until between 1993–97 that this liberalization was fully realized,[35] and the EU competition rules could finally be efficiently applied to the air transport sector. Until 1993, there was much debate surrounding appropriate application of the

---

30 C. Veljanovski, 'Economic Approaches to Regulation', in R. Baldwin, M. Cave and M. Lodge (eds), *The Oxford Handbook of Regulation* (Oxford: Oxford University Press, 2010), p. 29.

31 *See* Oneworld Case, Docket DOT-OST-2008-0252, Order 2010–2–8 at 27 (Feb. 13, 2010); Order 2010–7–8 at 16–20 (20 July 2010).

32 ECDOT, 'Transatlantic Airline Alliances', p. 12.

33 B. Adkins, *Air Transport and E.C. Competition Law* (London: Sweet and Maxwell (European Competition Law Monographs), 2001), p. 1.

34 *See* Council Decision concerning the conclusion by the European Union of the Protocol on the accession of EUROCONTROL, Council Document 5565/1/04.

35 It is argued below that the liberalization of the internal EU market for air transport was not completed until the 'turning point' in 2002 or indeed fully liberalized, also externally, much later in 2008 following the EU–US Air Transport Agreement.

rules to the industry, but the best argument for the delay is that the sector was not yet sufficiently liberalized, and as such the EU competition rules would have had little or no real effect. Under Article 119(1) TFEU, activities of the Member States and the EU are conducted in accordance with the principle of an open market economy and free competition, which are essential for the development of the internal market.[36]

Whish summarizes the four main benefits[37] effective competition aims to achieve:

- competition promotes allocative and productive efficiency;
- competition leads to lower prices for consumers;
- competition means that firms will be innovative in order to win business: innovation and dynamic efficiency mean that there will be better products available on the market;
- where there is effective competition, consumers have a choice as to the products that they buy.[38]

It should also be noted that:

> Under the EU competition rules, the Commission conducts an analysis of possible negative competitive effects of a transaction, whereas the burden to demonstrate efficiencies [as is the case in the US] to the requisite legal standard lies entirely on the parties.[39]

The 'agreements' under the first point above include both horizontal and vertical cooperation. It is necessary first to distinguish between the two for the purposes of this study. In accordance with Article 101 TFEU, 'cooperation is of a "horizontal nature" if an agreement or concerted practice is entered into between companies at the same level(s) in the market. In most instances, horizontal cooperation amounts to cooperation between competitors'.[40] Instances of horizontal cooperation agreements include research and development, production, purchasing and commercialization.

As applied to Article 101(3) TFEU, vertical cooperation includes

> agreements for the purchase or sale of goods or services where these agreements are concluded between non-competing undertakings, between certain

---

36 *See* Regulation (EC) No 1008/2008 of the European Parliament and of the Council of 24 September 2008, on common rules for the operation of air services in the Community (Recast), [2008] OJ L293/3, 31 October 2008.

37 EU competition law as used here refers initially only to Articles 101–103 TFEU. The body of EC competition law also includes the separate aims of the EC Merger Regulation (on the control of concentrations between undertakings), which is considered below at point 4.4.2.5 'Concentrations and the ECMR', *see* Council Regulation (EC) No 193/2004 of 20 January 2004 on the control of concentrations between undertakings (the EC Merger Regulation), [2004] OJ L 24/1, 29.1.2004.

38 Whish, *Competition Law*, (Oxford: Oxford University Press, 2009), p. 18.

39 ECDOT, 'Transatlantic Airline Alliances', p. 20.

40 Commission Notice 2001/C 3/02, 'Guidelines on the applicability of Article 81 of the Treaty to horizontal cooperation agreements' (6 January 2001).

competitors or by certain associations of retailers of goods; [and] vertical agreements containing ancillary provisions on the assignment or use of intellectual
property rights; [and] the corresponding concerted practices.[41]

Non-pricing, pricing policies and predatory behaviour are abusive. In *Hoffman-La
Roche v Commission*, the Court of Justice of the European Union (CJEU) found:

> The concept of abuse is an objective concept relating to the behaviour of an
> undertaking which is such as to influence the structure of a market where, as a
> direct result of the presence of the undertaking in question, competition has been
> weakened and which, through recourse different from those governing normal
> competition in products or services based on trader's performance, have the
> effect of hindering the maintenance or development of competition still existing
> on the market.[42]

Exclusionary practices having the effect of deterring entry or forcing the exit of rivals
include both pricing and non-pricing strategies. Predatory pricing,[43] selective discounts and fidelity rebates[44] are examples of abusive pricing practices, whereas the
refusal to deal[45] and tying[46] are typical non-pricing strategies.

The actions of an oligopoly are likely to affect the market. 'Firms might, for
instance, sometimes practice "tacit collusion", where they keep prices relatively high
and "go along to get along" by avoiding any aggressive competitive act that would
lead to price wars'.[47] The phrase 'workable competition' suggests that tacit collusion, oligopoly and parallel behaviour may be balanced by careful application and

---

41 Commission Regulation (EC) No 2790/1999 of 22 December 1999 on the application of ex. Article
   81(3) TEC (now Article 101(3) TFEU) to categories of vertical agreements and concerted practices.
42 Case 85/76, *Hoffman-La Roche v Commission* [1979] ECR 461. In this case, it was held that different
   prices of different vitamins from Member State to Member State indirectly prejudiced consumers and
   thus was capable of affecting competition and trade between Member States, a breach of ex. Article
   82 TEC (now Article 102 TFEU).
43 Press Release IP/03/1025, 'High-speed Internet: Commission imposes a fine on Wanadoo for abuse
   of a dominant position' *Europa* (16 July 2003).
44 Case 322/81, *NV Nederlandsche Banden Industrie Michelin v Commission* [1983] ECR 3461, where automobile dealers in the Netherlands were bound to Michelin tyres by means of a discount which was evidence of abuse of a dominant position, a breach of ex. Article 82 TEC (now Article 102 TFEU). The
   rebates were not based on economic principles; Case T-203/01, *Manufacture française des pneumatiques
   Michelin v Commission* [2003] ECJ CELEX LEXIS 489, held as a serious infringement of ex. Article 82
   TEC (now Article 102 TFEU) where rebates paid were loyalty-inducing and thus had a foreclosure
   effect on the market.
45 Case COMP/C-3/37.792, *Microsoft*, 24 March 2004.
46 Case T-83/91, *Tetra Pak International SA v Commission* [1994] ECJ CELEX LEXIS 6909, where Tetra
   Pak held 90 per cent of the market in aseptic packaging for UHT milk and juices and thus was the
   favoured supplier. The products were not sufficiently interchangeable. Second, the filling machines
   and cartons were tied. Finally, the UK experience before showed the chance to recoup losses; Case C-
   333/94 *Tetra Pak v Commission* ('Tetra Pak II') [1996] ECR I-5951, where *AKZO* was restated. If price
   is less than the economic justification, this is evidence of abusive behaviour.
47 Vasigh, Fleming and Tacker, *Introduction to Air Transport Economics*, p. 209.

exemption of competition policies to and from some industries and markets. The OECD says that the 'notion of workable competition arises from the observation that since perfect competition does not exist; theories based on it do not provide reliable guidelines for competition policy'.[48] In 1940, economist J.M. Clark[49] argued that the goal of policy should be to make competition 'workable' rather than perfect, as this is unrealistic. Nevertheless, policymakers determine the definition of 'workable' according to which strategies and goals they may deem as 'appropriate'.

Competition law plays a vital role 'in the overriding goal of achieving single market integration'[50] in the EU. Whish continues,

> The very idea of the single market is that internal barriers to trade within the Community should be dismantled and that goods, services, workers and capital should have complete freedom of movement. Firms should outgrow their national markets and operate on a more efficient, trans-national, scale throughout the economy.[51]

The single European market's competition law seriously punishes national cartels, export bans and 'market sharing'. In the case of *Volkswagen*,[52] the automobile manufacturer sought to prevent exports of its cars from Italy to Germany and Austria and was imposed with a fine of EUR 102 million.[53] Likewise, a fine of EUR 167.8 million was imposed on *Nintendo*[54] for preventing exports of game consoles and related products from the UK to the Netherlands and Germany.[55] In 2010, eleven airlines were fined approximately EUR 799 million for their involvement in a price-fixing cartel.[56]

There is a difference between the penalty for cases resulting in the finding of cartels, market sharing or other behaviour deemed anti-competitive in the EU and US.

48 Glossary of Industrial Organisation Economics and Competition Law, compiled by R.S. Khemani and D.M. Shapiro, commissioned by the Directorate for Financial, Fiscal and Enterprise Affairs, OECD, 1993. Online. Available HTTP: <http://www.oecd.org/dataoecd/8/61/2376087.pdf> (accessed 25 June 2011).

49 J.M. Clark, 'Toward a Concept of Workable Competition', *American Economic Review*, 30(2), 1940, 241–256.

50 Whish, *Competition Law*, p. 22.; *See also* E.D. Ehlermann, 'The Contribution of EC Competition Policy to the Single Market', *CML Rev*, 29, 1992, 257; The Commission's XXIXth *Report on Competition Policy*, (1993) at point 3. Online. Available HTTP: < http://ec.europa.eu/competition/publications/annual_report/1998/en.pdf> (accessed 13 September 2011).

51 Whish, *Competition Law*, p. 22.

52 *Volkswagen*, [1998] OJ L 124/60, [1998] 5 CMLR 33, where in an agreement with Italian Audi (part of the Volkswagen Group) dealer (Autogermania) not to sell to non-Italian residents demonstrated concerted practice thereby constituting infringement of ex. Article 81 TEC (now Article 101 TFEU) on implementation of market-partitioning policy.

53 Ibid, 21; [1998] OJ L 124/60, [1998] 5 CMLR 33. On appeal the fine was reduced to EUR 90 million.

54 *See* Commission Press Release IP/02/1584, 'Commission fines Nintendo and seven of its European distributors for colluding to prevent trade in low-priced products ', 30 October 2002.

55 Ibid; *See* Commission Press Release IP/02/1584, 30.10.2002.

56 Case COMP/39258, *Airfreight*, Commission Decision of 9 November 2010 (unpublished); *see also* IP/10/1487 – 'Antitrust: Commission fines 11 air cargo carriers €799 million in price fixing cartel' – 9 November 2010, Brussels.

As examined in this chapter, it is commonplace in the EU to be given only a fine, albeit of quite high value, for such practices. In the next section on US antitrust law and breaches thereof, it will be shown that the penalties for these practices include indictment, charges of 'felony' and imprisonment for the parties responsible.

The Union's external aviation policy (European Transport Policy)

The previous Lisbon Agenda[57] encouraged industries' competitiveness through innovation, incorporating aspects of economic, social and environmental policies, including European transport policy, and culminating with the Treaty of Lisbon amending the Treaty of the European Union and the Treaty Establishing the European Union.[58] The European Council has developed a specific agenda for the Union's *external* aviation policy.[59]

In 2003, the European Council established a new legal framework for air transport between EU and third countries that is in line with Article 49 TFEU.[60] This is discussed in further detail below. At this point, the Council also urged the Commission to 'bring the current negotiations with the United States to a successful and mutually satisfactory conclusion as early as possible',[61] namely the first stage EU–US Air Transport Agreement, which was provisionally implemented in March 2008. On the environmental aspects of air transport, there has been progress since 2008[62] on the EU Emissions Trading Scheme (ETS).[63]

Articles 101 and 102 TFEU (European competition rules)

Articles 101 and 102 TFEU contain key provisions for forming the principles on which European competition policy is based. Article 101(1) prohibits

> all agreements between undertakings, decisions by associations of undertaking and concerted practices which may affect trade between Member States and which have as their objective or effect the prevention, restriction or distortion of competition within the common market, and in particular those which:

---

57 *See also* European Commission, 'White Paper: Road map to a Single European Transport Area – Towards a competitive and resource efficient transport system', COM (2011) 144 Final, Brussels, 28 March 2011.

58 Signed at Lisbon, Portugal, 13 December 2007, OJ C306/1.

59 Ibid.

60 Regulation (EC) No 847/2004; Council Decision of 05 June 2003 on authorizing the Commission to open negotiations with third countries on the replacement of certain provisions in existing bilateral agreements with a Community agreement; Council Decision of 05 June 2003 on authorizing the Commission to open negotiations with the United States in the field of air transport.

61 Ibid.

62 *See* 'Opinion of the European Economic and Social Committee on Climate Change and the Lisbon Strategy', [2008] OJ C 044, 16 February 2008, pp. 69–73.

63 Founded upon Directive 2003/87/EC of the European Parliament and of the Council of 13 October 2003 establishing a scheme for greenhouse gas emission allowance trading within the Community and amending Council Directive 96/61/EC [2003] OJ L275/32.

a)   directly or indirectly fix purchase or selling prices or any other trading conditions;
b)   limit or control production, markets, technical development, or investment;
c)   share markets or sources of supply;
d)   apply dissimilar conditions to equivalent transactions with other trading parties, thereby placing them at a competitive disadvantage;
e)   make the conclusion of contracts subject to acceptance by the other parties of supplementary obligations, which, by their nature or according to commercial usage, have no connection with the subject of such contracts.[64]

Article 101(2) simply states that these agreements are void. However, Article 101(3) provides that the provisions of 101(1) may be declared 'inapplicable' if the agreement, decision or concerted practice

> contributes to improving the production or distribution of goods or to promoting technical or economic progress, while allowing consumers a fair share of the resulting benefit, and which does not:
>
> a)   impose on the undertakings concerted restrictions which are not indispensable to the attainment of these objectives;
> b)   afford such undertakings the possibility of eliminating competition in respect of a substantial part of the products in question.[65]

In addition, the Council conferred exclusive power on the Commission to grant exemptions from the prohibitions under Article 101(1).[66]

Article 102 TFEU, which includes no provision for exemptions, provides:

> Any abuse by one or more undertakings in a dominant position within the common market or in a substantial part of it shall be prohibited as incompatible with the common market insofar as it may affect trade between Member States.[67]

Article 101(1) TFEU prohibits unjustifiable price-fixing as incompatible with the Common Market in all industries.[68] In *Ahmed Saeed*,[69] the CJEU confirmed that

---

64 Treaty on the Functioning of the European Union (the Treaty), Title VII (ex. Title VI), s1, Article 101(1)(a-e) TFEU (ex. Article 81(1)(a-e) TEC).
65 Ibid., Art. 101(3)(a-b) TFEU.
66 Reg. 17 [1959–1962] OJ Spec. Ed. 87, Art. 9.
67 Treaty on the Functioning of the European Union (the Treaty), Title VII (ex. Title VI), s1, Article 102 (ex. Article 82).
68 Ibid., Art. 101(1)(a) TFEU.
69 Case 66/86, *Ahmed Saeed Flugreisen and Silver Line Reisebüro GmbHv Zentrale zur Bekampfung unlauteren Wettbewerbs E.V.* [1989] ECR 803, [1990] 4 CMLR 102, involving price-fixing. Travel agents obtained and sold tickets from outside their Member State at a discounted rate constituting abuse as there was no distinction between international flights. The problem with this case was that there was at the time no implementing legislation to achieve applicability of Article 101(3) to the air transport sector within a Member State. This led to Regulation 411/2004 on the intra and extraterritorial powers of the Commission with respect to air transport, [2004] OJ L68/1.

agreements to fix prices were automatically void unless they had been granted an exemption from ex. Article 81(3) TEC (now Article 101(3) TFEU) under Regulations 3975/87 and 3976/87,[70] the former of which details the application of ex. Articles 81 and 82 TEC (now Articles 101 and 102 TFEU) to intra-Union flights whereas the latter gave permission to the Commission to grant block exemptions.[71] The *Ahmed Saeed* case is quite an important one in this area insofar as the Court recognized the need to distinguish between price-fixing and a 'consultation' on tariffs to determine application of now Article 101(3) TFEU to the actual circumstances in the industry.

Consultations on tariffs or fares are common worldwide practice in the airline industry. These consultations are held on a bilateral or multilateral 'conference' basis. The major international conference for scheduling and fares is held biannually in June and November under the framework and oversight of IATA. 'As many as 300 airline companies are members of the association and these represent more than 98 per cent of all international scheduled air traffic.'[72]

The 'undertaking' concept

Although the term 'undertaking' is not defined in TFEU, it is widely used in Articles 101 and 102. It has been held that the term 'undertaking' as applied in Articles 101 and 102 has the same meaning.[73] A clear meaning of the term 'undertaking' as applied here was given in *Polypropylene*, where the Commission stated:

> The subjects of [EU] competition rules are undertakings, a concept which is not identical to the question of legal personality for the purposes of company law and fiscal law . . . It may, however, refer to any entity engaged in commercial activities.[74]

This 'quasi-severed' position was confirmed in *Höfner and Elser v Macrotron*, where the CJEU stated that 'the concept of undertaking encompasses every entity engaged in an economic activity regardless of the legal status of the entity and the way in which it is financed'.[75]

---

70 Regulations 3975/87, which was repealed by Council Regulation (EC) No 411/2004, and Regulation 3976/87 were replaced by Regulation 487/09 of 25.05.2009 on the application of Article 81(3) TEU to certain categories of agreements and concerted practices in the air transport sector, [2009] OJ L148/1, 11 June 2009.

71 Whereby renewing the now expired 'IATA exemption'.

72 Figures taken from the IATA website. Available HTTP: <http://www.iata.org/whatwedo/scheduling/schedules_conference.htm> (accessed 10 August 2011).

73 *See* the consecutive Decisions in Cases T-68, 77 and 78/89, *Società Italiana Vetro v Commission* [1992] ECR 11–1403, [1992] 5 CMLR 302, where three automobile/non-automobile glassmakers were investigated for cartelistic behaviour. It was decided that no cartel existed. This case is significant to EU competition law as it is an example of where the undertaking concept was applied to more than one firm.

74 [1986] OJ L 230/1, [1988] 4 CMLR 347, para. 99.

75 [1991] ECR I-1979, [1993] 4 CMLR 306, para. 21; *See* also *The Distribution of Package Tours During the 1990 World Cup* [1992] L326/31, [1994] 5 CMLR 253 for another illustration of multiple travel agents (associations) carrying out 'economic activities' considered 'undertakings' by the Commission.

In the absence of language in the Treaty to the contrary, the term 'undertaking' must be taken to include those products and services offered by a Member State.[76] It should be noted that whether the entity is profit seeking or was set up for an economic purpose is irrelevant in this context, as has been confirmed by the Commission in *IAZ International Belgium NV v Commission*[77] and *Saachi*,[78] respectively.

One institution that does not fit the criteria and is therefore not considered 'undertakings' for the purposes of Article 101 or Article 102 is Eurocontrol,[79] the European air traffic control organization. It was held in *SAT Fluggesellschaft v Eurocontrol*:

> Eurocontrol's activities, by their nature, their aim and the rules to which they are subject, are connected with the exercise of powers relating to the control and supervision of air space which are typically those of a public authority. They are not of an economic nature justifying the application of the Treaty rules of competition.[80]

Thus airlines, whether passenger or cargo, and most likely airports, in which states have a vested interest, are to be considered as undertakings, and relevant competition rules do apply, whereas an institution which serves the public interest, namely those of air traffic and transportation safety, are exempt. There is a fine line between whether, for the purposes of the application of Articles 101 or 102 TFEU, an organization or institution is 'public'. It is evident that claims based on these articles will be taken on a case-by-case basis.

Defining 'agreements'

Agreements appear to be caught no matter what form they take.[81]

Although Article 101(1) prohibits all forms of explicit collusion in the form of agreements, decision and concerted practices, the irrefutably broad construction of the word 'agreement' makes distinguishing between 'agreements' and 'concerted practices' difficult.

In *ICI and CSC v Commission*, the term 'concerted practice' was defined as

> co-ordination between undertakings which, without having reached the stage where an agreement, properly so called, has been concluded, knowingly substitutes practical co-operation between them for the risks of competition which

---

76 *See* Jones and Sufrin, *EC Competition Law*, pp. 128–129.
77 [1983] ECR 3369, [1984] 3 CMLR 276, where the producer of washing machines were to display health and safety labels under national (Belgian) law. This led to a quality-protection barrier to trade as it indirectly appointed a sole provider of washing machines in Belgium.
78 Case 155/73, [1974] ECR 409, [1974] 2 CMLR 177.
79 *See* Regulation (EC) No 1108/09 laying down the framework for the creation of the single European sky [2009] *OJ L309/51*.
80 Case C-364/92, [1994] ECR I-43, [1994] 5 CMLR 208, para. 30. A claim brought on refusal to pay fees to Eurocontrol under allegations that it abuse of a dominant position was dismissed.
81 *See* Jones and Sufrin, *EC Competition Law*, pp. 148–149.

do not correspond to the normal conditions of the market, having regard to the nature of the products, the importance and number of the undertakings, as well as the size and importance of the said market.[82]

It should be noted that 'a concerted practice may be operated horizontally between colluding competitors but also vertically between a manufacturer and its distributors'.[83] It is also needful to clarify that Article 101(1) prohibits agreements that have as either their 'object or effect the prevention, restriction, or distortion of competition'.[84]

Regarded as a pivotal case in the field of EU competition law, *ICI v Commission* removed the previous requirement that an actual agreement come into existence between the parties before their relationship and any future business intentions of those parties be assessed under the competition rules. This judgment leads to a policy dilemma, especially in markets where a few large firms exist. Under such oligopoly-type market conditions as those found in the global airline industry for instance, it may be difficult for the law to distinguish between the strategic pursuit of a firm's best interests, say for instance a 'coordinated, joint policy' and outright tacit collusion.[85]

This case highlights the concept of 'concerted practices' as a form of collusion pre-agreement, and will most likely have severe implications for the future tone of cooperative behaviour between firms. For instance, two firms or individuals may not coordinate business if that coordination is anti-competitive in nature. This calls upon, in most cases, a kind of principle of moral obligation to self-regulate, to pre-empt any potential breaches of the competition rules. It is not this self-prescription that calls for greatest concern, however, it is the threat to cooperation between firms, a practice highly regarded in most cases as good for firms, industry and consumers.

Although the air transport sector certainly represents an atypical industry in the wider scheme of business practices and competition rules, the measures taken by airlines in response to the current regulatory, political and economic environment to compete tend to be on the basis of cooperation, which includes a very distinct element of coordination between firms. Thus the notion of 'coordinative' behaviour, which is not yet governed by a contractual 'agreement' in the language of the competition rules, is just as exposed as the agreement itself – and this might pose a significant threat to the future of cooperative dealings between airlines. However, the *ICI v Commission* case did not involve the air transport sector, so until a decision is handed

82 Cases 48, 49, 51–7/69, *ICI v Commission* [1972] ECR 619, [1972] CMLR 557, paras. 64–65. In this case although the undertaking consisted of an EU and non-EU supplier, one of the two firms (ICI) bought surplus and resold within the Community. It was held that undertakings which hold a dominant position within the market whose behaviour is characterized by 'united action' must be regarded as an 'economic unit'. Therefore ICI and CSC were jointly and severally liable.

83 Jones and Sufrin, *EC Competition Law*, p.179.

84 *See* Case 56/65, *Société Technique Minière v Maschinenbau Ulm GmbH* [1966] ECR 234, 249, [1966] 1 CMLR 357. In this case, a clause 'granting an exclusive right of sale' was not considered automatically void. It is required to assess whether the effect partitions markets within the Member State.

85 Utton, M. 'Going European: Britain's New Competition Law', Working Paper – University of Reading. Online. Available HTTP: <http://www.rdg.ac.uk/Econ/Econ/workingpapers/emdp403.pdf> (accessed 12 August 2011).

down which finds itself within the realm of air transport, and thereby governed by its often atypical sub-rules, it is difficult to make a clear pre-assessment of the effect of this particular subject.

Market power

In competition assessments, perhaps the most important issue is whether a firm or group of firms has market power. Article 102 TFEU prohibits the abuse of a dominant position by an undertaking, which includes imposing unfair prices, restricting production or markets, and preferential or discriminatory practices that put firms at a competitive disadvantage or force the conclusion of unrelated contracts.[86]

In order to assess whether there has been abuse of a dominant position by an undertaking, it is first necessary to determine if that undertaking enjoys a dominant position in the relevant market. To achieve this, it is essential to define the relevant market and consider the product or service market in relation to its geographic market, which is not always as simple as it would appear.

From a general, economic perspective, Korah suggests:

> [M]arkets do not always have clear limits, and the insistence on definition rather than analysis may be misleading. There may be no substitutes perfect, in which case selecting a narrow definition will overstate the market power of a firm supplying a large proportion of the defined product . . . A wide definition will usually indicate a smaller market share that understates a firm's market power.[87]

From the legal perspective, however, and in the light of rationale applied by the Commission and CJEU, the 'test' of the definition of the relevant market is a bit clearer. In *Ahmed Saeed*, the CJEU stated:

> The test to be employed is whether the scheduled flight on a particular route can be distinguished from the possible alternatives by virtue of specific characteristics as a result of which it is not interchangeable with those alternatives and is affected only to an insignificant degree by competition from them. The application of the test does not necessarily yield identical results in the various cases that may arise; indeed, some airline routes are in a situation where no effective competition is likely to arise. In principle, however, and in particular as far as intra-community routes are concerned, the economic strength of an airline on a route served by scheduled flights may depend on the competitive position of other carriers operating on the same route or on a route capable of serving as a substitute.[88]

---

86 Article 102(a-d) TFEU.
87 V. Korah, *An Introductory Guide to EC Competition Law and Practice*, 9thed., (Oxford: Hart Publishing, 2007), p. 95.
88 Case 66/86, *Ahmed Saeed Flugreisen and Silver Line Reisebüro GmbH v Zentrale zur Bekämpfung unlauteren Wettbewerbs E.V.* [1989] ECR 803, [1990] 4 CMLR 102, paras 40–41.

To conduct the 'market power' analysis, the relevant market first must be defined. Defining the relevant market in the air transport sector is particularly complex. It is not a simple task of defining the market and then deeming a percentage of market share as equal to a firm's or group of firms' market power. Each assessment must be taken on a case-by-case basis, as the facts and potential for substitutability of products or services may differ from industry to industry, and market to market.

To determine whether a firm or group of firms has market power, competition authorities look at the concept of 'concentrations', that is whether there exists a concentration of a particular market, which indicates that the market is quite likely uncompetitive. The Commission uses concentration ratios and the *Herfindahl-Hirschman Index*, in addition to considering barriers to entry and exit from the market and the degree of buying power as producers over suppliers, to determine whether a market is concentrated.[89]

Identifying 'appreciability'

Article 101(1) requires that an agreement should affect trade and that the resulting 'restriction' should be 'appreciable'. An analysis of the market will be required.[90]

The criteria of Article 101(1) and (3) TFEU should also be applied to 'joint ventures performing on a lasting basis, all the functions of autonomous economic entities, to the extent that their creation has as its consequence an appreciable restriction of competition between undertakings that remain independent'.[91]

In *Société Technique Minière v Maschinenbau Ulm GmbH,*[92] the effect of the agreement was discussed:

> Where . . . an analysis of the said clauses does not reveal the effect on competition to be sufficiently deleterious, the consequence of agreement should then be considered and for it to be caught by the prohibition it is then necessary to find that those factors are present that show the competition has in fact been prevented or restricted or distorted to an appreciable extent. The competition in question must be understood within the actual context in which it would occur in the absence of the agreement in dispute.[93]

If the total production is less than 0.15 per cent, there will be no attachment of the powers of the Treaty, and the restriction will be deemed *de minimis*. This was also the

---

89 The same index is also used to measure the level of consolidation in the US market, *see* Vasigh, Fleming and Tacker, *Introduction to Air Transport Economics*, pp. 14–15 and Ch.9; The CJEU has decided a number of cases involving airlines where the issue of relevant market was pivotal.

90 *See* Jones and Sufrin, *EC Competition Law*, pp. 191–198.

91 Council Regulation (EC) No 193/2004 of 20 January 2004 on the control of concentrations between undertakings (the EC Merger Regulation), [2004] OJ L 24/4, 29 January 2004.

92 Case 56/65, *Société Technique Minière v Maschinenbau Ulm GmbH* [1966] ECR 234, 249, [1966] 1 CMLR 357.

93 Ibid.

case in *Völk v Vervaecke*,[94] where the Commission stated that the total production, in this case of washing machines, amounted to 0.8 per cent of the total production of the common market.

'Concentrations' under the ECMR

Despite the applicability of Articles 101 and 102 TFEU to certain (market) concentrations as evidenced by the plethora of case law of the CJEU, the European Council responded in 2004 to the lack of sufficient control of all operations that might 'prove incompatible with the system of undistorted competition envisaged by the Treaty'.[95] The Council adopted Regulation 139/2004[96] on the control of concentrations between undertakings (the EC Merger Regulation), based on ex. Articles 83 and 308 TEU (now Articles 103 and 352 TFEU).[97] The provisions of the EC Merger Regulation (ECMR) apply to 'significant structural changes, the impact of which goes beyond the national borders of any one Member State'.[98] Any other concentrations not covered by the ECMR as they do not have a 'Union dimension'[99] should be covered within the jurisdiction of the Member States. The Commission implements (quantitative) thresholds[100] that determine whether the concentration has a 'Union dimension'. The Commission reviews the thresholds and reports to the Council on the implementation of the applicable thresholds and criteria[101]:

> A concentration that would not significantly impede effective competition in the common market or in a substantial part of it, in particular as a result of the creation or strengthening of a dominant position, shall be declared compatible with the common market.[102]

---

94 Case 5/69 *Franz Völk v Vervaecke*, [1969] ECR 295, 302.

95 Council Regulation (EC) No 139/2004 of 20.1.2004 on the control of concentrations between undertakings (the EC Merger Regulation), [2004] OJ L 24/1, 29.1. 2004.

96 Ibid., as implemented by Commission Regulation (EC) No 802/2004 of 07.04.2004, OJ L133/1, 30 April 2004, and amended by Commission Regulation (EC) No 1033/2008 of 20.10.2008, OJ L279/3, 22 October 2008.

97 Under Article 352 TFEU, the Union may give itself additional powers of action necessary for the attainment of its objectives, including powers of action regarding concentrations on the markets for agricultural products listed in Annex 1 TFEU.

98 Council Regulation (EC) No 193/2004 of 20.1.2004 on the control of concentrations between undertakings (the EC Merger Regulation), [2004] OJ L 24/2, 29 January 2004.

99 Concentrations are deemed to have a Union dimension where their worldwide turnover is more than EUR 5 billion and the Union aggregate turnover of each of at least two of the undertakings concerned is more than EUR 250 million ('the thresholds'). If the concentration does not meet these thresholds, it has a Union dimension if the combined worldwide is EUR 2,5 billion, in each Member State the aggregate is more than EUR 100 million, in at least three Member States the aggregate turnover of each of at least two is more than EUR 25 million and the aggregate Union-wide turnover of at least two is greater than EUR 100 million (Source: Council Regulation (EC) No 193/2004 of 20 January 2004 on the control of concentrations between undertakings (the EC Merger Regulation), [2004] OJ L 24/6, 291.2004).

100 These thresholds are set out above.

101 The Council reviews the thresholds and criteria in line with Article 202 TFEU.

102 Council Regulation (EC) No 193/2004 of 20.1.2004 on the control of concentrations between undertakings (the EC Merger Regulation), [2004] OJ L 24/7, 29.1. 2004.

A concentration that would significantly impede effective competition, in the common market or in a substantial part of it, in particular as a result of the creation or strengthening of a dominant position, shall be declared incompatible with the common market.[103]

Where concentrations exist in oligopolistic market structures, such as is the case in the air transport sector, the Council and Commission view the maintenance of effective competition very necessary in these markets. At the time, although the Community courts had not

expressly interpreted Regulation (EEC) 4054/89 as requiring concentrations giving rise to such non-coordinated effects to be declared incompatible with the common market . . . [the ECMR] permits effective control of all such concentrations by providing that any concentration which would significantly impede competition, in the common market or in a substantial part of it, should be declared incompatible with the common market . . . extending beyond the concept of dominance, only to the anti-competitive effects of a concentration resulting from the non-coordinated behaviour of undertakings which would not have a dominant position on the market concerned.[104]

The EU regulatory framework for air transport

Policymakers at the national and international level have been called upon to provide a regulatory framework that promotes a competitive 'Union' air transport industry. The four main objectives[105] for this regulatory framework are: (i) facilitating the airlines' financing ability; (ii) ensuring the respect of the internal market rules; (iii) creating conditions for fair and equitable competition[106]; and (iv) extending the liberalization policy to third-country routes.

During the liberalization of the EU air transport sector, a number of legal measures were devised by the Commission to apply EU competition law to the sector in a gradual and effective manner until 2004. The liberalization process involved a slow relinquishing of Member State controls in the sector and vesting future oversight centrally to the EU. This process may be best seen in the area of market access and traffic rights, which is detailed below.

As part of the third and final phase of the 'liberalization packages' applied to the sector,[107] a number of regulations have been made to ensure equal market access and traffic rights for all Union carriers; provide an appropriate procedure and relevant

---

103 Ibid.

104 Ibid., p. 4.

105 Trier Academy of European Union Law, 'Deregulation and Regulation of the European "Airscape"', Vol. 23, Cologne (Germany): *Bundesanzeiger Verlags*, 1997.

106 This point includes the problematic on-going experience of state aid offered to flag carriers by the respective (Member) States discussed in greater detail below.

107 It could be argued that full sector liberalization did not happen until between 2002–08.

criteria for the licensing of Union carriers; see to the deregulation of air fares and cargo rates; develop a code of conduct for computer reservations systems (CRSs) and establish procedural rules for the application of the competition rules on state aid in the air transport sector.

Single market for air transport

Council Decision 87/602 under the first phase of the liberalization process and Council Regulation 2343/90[108] were 'measures designed to introduce greater freedom of access to air transport markets to bring about a single market for air transport, albeit gradually'.[109] These regulations assign substantive rights and obligations to individual Member States and the EC as regards Community air transport, in particular the free market access to all intra-Union air routes.

Established under the auspices of the so-called third phase of air transport liberalization, Council Regulation 2408/92 provided that Union air carriers may exercise traffic rights between civilian airports in the Union without distinction between passenger and cargo sectors, or scheduled and charter air services.[110]

Member States retain the right to regulate through intervention through allocation of traffic to airports, without discrimination and with concern for Union, national, regional or local rules relating to safety, the protection of the environment and slot allocation. This Regulation was quite significant, nonetheless, 'to the extent that the conferment of a general freedom of access has removed a substantial margin of discretion from the national authorities of Member States in the licensing of [Union] carriers and routes'.[111]

In late 2004, the Italian Republic asked the Commission to publish a notice in the *Official Journal of the European Union* imposing public service obligations[112] (PSOs) on 18 routes between three Sardinian airports and the main national airports, thereby restricting market access for non-Italian Union carriers. Dissatisfied with the evidence presented with the request, the Commission gave its decision in 2005 to carry out an investigation to examine the conformity of the PSO referred to in Article 4 of the regulation.[113] These practices were deemed acceptable when required to sustain services to remote locations.

---

108 Council Regulation (EEC) No 2343/90 of 24 July 1990 on access for air carriers to scheduled intra-Community air service routes and on the sharing of passenger capacity between air carriers on scheduled air services between Member States, [1990] OJ L217/8–14, 11 August 1990.

109 Council Regulation (EEC) No 2408/92 of 23 July 1992 on access for Community air carriers to intra-Community air routes, subsequently amended these provisions under the third wave of the Community's market liberalization process, [1992] OJ L240/8–14, 24 August 1992, as amended.

110 This cabotage-type provision was laid down by Council Regulation (EEC) No 2408/92 of 23 July 1992 on access for Community air carriers to intra-community air routes; [1992] OJ L 240 of 24 August 1992, as amended.

111 J. Goh, *European Air Transport Law and Competition* (Chichester: John Wiley & Sons, 1997), p. 127.

112 According to Article 8, Council Regulation (EEC) 2408/92, as amended: A 'Member State . . . may impose a public service obligation in respect of scheduled air services to an airport serving a peripheral or development region in its territory' subject to a number of conditions being satisfied.

113 Commission Decision of 3 March 2005, [2005] OJ L 075, 22 March 2005, pp. 53–57.

Council Regulations 411/2004 and 487/2009 lay down the procedure for application of the rules on competition to undertakings in the air transport sector.[114] Since May 2004, enforcement of EU competition rules is now the joint responsibility of the Commission and the national competition authorities in Member States, together with the European Competition Network (ECN). Council Regulation 411/2004 addresses the appropriate procedure for the future negotiation and implementation of multilateral air service agreements between Member States and third countries.[115] Regulation 847/2004 established a new legal framework for the EU's relations on aviation with third countries and provides for the compatible standardization of the pre-existing bilateral air service agreements between Member States and the US and other third countries.[116]

Council Regulation 2410/92 amended Council Regulation 3975/87 by removing the word 'international' in Article 1. The former Council Regulation 3975/87 was applied to the following cases on code share agreements between European carriers: *Lufthansa–SAS*,[117] *Finnair–Maersk*,[118] *Austrian–Lufthansa*,[119] and *SAS–Maersk Air*,[120] which will be discussed in detail later in the context of multilateral cooperative agreements between airlines.[121]

In July 2001, in *SAS–Maersk Air*,[122] the Commission

---

114 The original procedure was laid down by Council Regulation No 3975/87. This was since amended by Regulation 2410/92 No 2410/92 of 23 July 1992, [1992] OJ L240/18, 24 August 1992, and repealed by Council Regulation (EC) No 411/2004 of 26 February 2004, which also amended Regulations (EEC) No 3976/87 and (EC) No1/2003, in connection with air transport between the Community and third countries, [2004] OJ L68/1, 06 March 2004. These were replaced by Council Regulation (EC) No 487/2009 of 25.05.2009 on the application of Article 81(3) TEC to certain categories of agreements and concerted practices in the air transport sector, [1990] OJ L148/1, 11 June 2009.

115 Ibid.; this will be discussed in further detail below. It is of interest to note that in the same year, Regulation (EC) No 868/2004 of 30 April 2004 concerning protection against subsidisation and unfair pricing practices causing injury to Community air carriers in the supply of air services from countries not members of the European Community came into force.

116 Regulation (EC) No 847/2004 of the European Parliament and of the Council of 29 April 2004 on the negotiation and implementation of air service agreements between Member States and third countries, [2004] OJ L157/7, 30 April 2004.

117 *Lufthansa/SAS* [1996] OJ L 54/28, [1996] 4 CMLR 845, *See* also (1998) 19 ECLR 116. In the decision, the two airlines were required to drop alliances, freeze frequencies on key routes and divest in slots.

118 *See* The Commission's XXVIIIth Report on Competition Policy, 1998, p. 146–147. Online. Available HTML: <http://ec.europa.eu/competition/publications/annual_report/1998/en.pdf> (accessed 25 September 2011).

119 *Austrian/Lufthansa* [2002] OJ L 242/25, [2003] 4 CMLR 252. The exemption was granted on the condition that slots would be released within 45 minutes of proposed cooperative flights, the decrease in fares would be proportional and not only on the Frankfurt–Vienna route, access to frequent flyer programmes would be available to new entrants as well as access to established intermodal services.

120 *SAS/Maersk Air* [2001] OJ L 265/15, [2001] 5 CMLR 1119, *See* also the appeal: *SAS v Community* T-241/01 [2001] OJ L 265/15.

121 It should be noted that the EU position on certain agreements was further clarified *vis-à-vis* Commission Regulation (EEC) No 1617/93 of 25.06.1993 on the application of Article 85(3) TEC to certain categories of agreements and concerted practices concerning joint planning and coordination of schedules, joint operations, consultations on passenger and cargo tariffs on scheduled air services and slot allocation at airports, [1993] OJ L155/18, 26 June 1993.

122 Ibid.

decided to impose fines of EUR 39.375 million and EUR 13.125 million respectively on SAS and Maersk Air for implementing an agreement to share out routes to and from Denmark. The Commission discovered the agreement's existence in June 2000, following inspections at the companies' headquarters. The agreement contained an overall non-compete clause under which Maersk Air undertook not to launch a new international route from Copenhagen without SAS's consent. Conversely, SAS undertook not to operate on Maersk Air's routes out of Billund, Denmark's second airport. Both airlines had also undertaken to abide by the existing share-out of domestic routes.[123]

More recently in November 2010, in the *Airfreight*[124] case, the European Commission fined 11 airline companies a total of approximately EUR 799 million. The alleged infringements involved for air freight services on routes between airports within the European Economic Area (EEA); with the EU and outside the EEA; routes between EEA but not EU countries and third countries; and EU–Switzerland. The alleged infringements included coordination related to fuel and security surcharges, and the payment of commission on freight surcharges. *British Airways*,[125] *Air France–KLM*,[126] *Lufthansa*,[127] *Martinair*[128] and *Cathay Pacific*[129] brought actions in protest to these allegations in January 2011. Arguments that have been put against the Commission include, *inter alia*, that it acted without sufficient evidence, lacked the jurisdiction for many of the flight routes concerned (which involved destinations such as Hong Kong and Brazil), and infringed the principle of proportionality.[130] Two things are of interest to note in this price-fixing case. The Commission increased the fine (recidivism uplift of 50 per cent) for SAS as a repeat offender, albeit it this offence was on different grounds than the 2001 case discussed above. All airlines' fines were reduced by 15 per cent owing to 'the general regulatory environment in the sector which can be seen as encouraging price coordination'.[131] These cases clearly exemplify the sheer penalty power of the Commission in instances of clear breaches of the competition rules.

Between the years 1995–2002, individual Member States negotiated 'open skies' air service agreements on a bilateral basis with the US. In 2002, however, following the CJEU 'open skies judgments',[132] the way was finally paved for the liberalization

---

123 Bulletin EU 7/8–2001, Competition (1/54); *see also* Commission Press Release IP/01/1999, 'Commission Fines SAS and Maersk Air for market-sharing agreement', Brussels (18 July 2001).

124 *CASE COMP/39258 – AIR FREIGHT)* (C(2010)7694 TO /19; SEC(2010)1382).

125 *British Airways v Commission* (Case T-48/11) (2011/C 80/57).

126 *Air France – KLM v Commission* (Case T-62/11)(2011/C 95/13).

127 *Deutsche Lufthansa and Others v Commission* (Case T-46/11) (2011/C 80/56).

128 *Martinair Holland v Commission* (Case T-67/11) (2011/C 95/15).

129 Cathay Pacific Airways *v Commission* (Case T 38/11) (2011/C 72/50)

130 At the time of publication, these cases were still on-going.

131 Case COMP/39258, *Airfreight*, Commission Decision of 9/11/2010 (unpublished); *see also* IP/10/1487 – 'Antitrust: Commission fines 11 air cargo carriers €799 million in price fixing cartel' – 9 November 2010, Brussels.

132 *See* Case C-466/98 *Commission v United Kingdom*, [2002] ECR I-9427; Case C-467/98 *Commission v Kingdom of Denmark* [2002] ECR 9519; Case C-468/98 *Commission v Kingdom of Sweden* [2002] ECR

of international air services at the EU level.[133] The judgments clarified the EU's powers with respect to external aviation policy and ruled that Member States could not reserve benefits for national carriers under the fundamental freedom of establishment laid down in Article 49 TFEU.

Before the European Council adopted Regulation 411/2004[134] in connection with the air transport between the Union and third countries, the Commission did not have full procedural powers in relation to such agreements. Regulation 411/2004[135] provides for the procedural application of the EU competition rules and under it, the Commission obtains jurisdiction to investigate practices between EU airlines and third country airlines. Prior to this regulation, the Commission

> did not enjoy powers of investigation and enforcement with regard to infringements of Articles 81 and 82 [TEU] in respect of air transport between the Community and third countries equivalent to those enjoyed as regards air transport within the Community.[136]

For instance, the Commission initiated proceedings into cooperation between United Airlines (UA), Lufthansa (LH) and SAS under ex. Article 81(1) TEU in 1996,[137] but the Commission 'lacked effective enforcement powers to enable it to issue a decision relating to the international air transport . . . [and] the case was closed on the basis of commitments proposed by the parties in 2002'.[138]

Taking the view of Doganis:

> The European Court's decision in opening up the nationality issue is the first crack in the door. It will take time before third countries are willing to renegotiate their air service agreements so as to change the nationality article. But the effects are already being felt.[139]

9575; Case C-469/98 *Commission v Republic of Finland* [2002] ECR 9627; Case C-471/98 *Commission v Kingdom of Belgium* [2002] ECR 9681; Case C-472/98 *Commission v Grand Duchy of Luxembourg* [2002] ECR 9741; Case C-475/98 *Commission v Republic of Austria* [2002] ECR 9797; Case C-476/98 *Commission v Federal Republic of Germany* [2002] ECR 9855. In these decisions, so-called 'nationality clauses' were deemed to infringe Article 43 TEU as they were inconsistent with the single European market for air transport.

133 *See* R. Doganis, *The Airline Business in the 21st Century*, 2nd ed. (London: Routledge, 2006), pp. 54–66.

134 Council Regulation (EC) No 411/2004 of 26.02.2004, in connection with air transport between the Community and third countries, [2004] OJ L 68/1. This repealed Regulation (EEC) No 3975/87 and amended Regulations (EEC) No 3976/87 and (EC) No 1/2003 (with respect to air transport). It is of interest to note that similarly, Council Regulation (EC) No 1419/2006 of 25.09.2006, repealed Regulation (EEC) No 4056/86 laying down detailed rules for the application of Articles 85 and 86 TEC to maritime transport, and amended Regulation (EC) No 1/2003 as regards the extension of its scope to include cabotage and international tramp services, [2006] OJ L269/1, 28.09.2006.

135 [2004] OJ L 68/1.

136 Ibid.

137 The resulting decision: *Lufthansa/SAS* [1996] OJ L 54/28, [1996] 4 CMLR 845.

138 ECDOT, 'Transatlantic Airline Alliances', p. 15.

139 Doganis, *The Airline Business*, p. 20.

It seems only proper that air services agreements concluded between Member States or the EU and third countries should be duly considered, most importantly for the purposes of assessing the degree of competition, in respect of Articles 101 and 102 TFEU, in the relevant air transport markets.[140] Previously, the Commission lacked in particular 'requisite fact-finding tools and the powers to impose remedies which are necessary to bring infringements to an end or to impose penalties in respect of proven infringements'.[141] Now the EU has competency to enter into, for instance, a single horizontal agreement with a third country; this laid the foundation for the initiation and negotiation of reciprocal 'freedoms' in the EU–US Air Transport Agreement.[142]

This widens the extraterritorial scope of EU competition law to include practices (including cooperation) between Union airlines and third country airlines. Though controversial, it would seem appropriate in this context that EU competition law include in its purview not only intra-Union practices, but extra-Union practices as well. This brings the EU competition rules as they apply to the air transport sector, in particular the extraterritorial concept, roughly in line with US antitrust law as regards the applicable scope of the rules.

In an effort to encourage the 'single market' concept the Council adopted Common Position 7/2004 on the negotiation and implementation of air service agreements between Member States and third countries in the wake of the CJEU 'open skies judgments' introduced above.

> These judgements confirmed that the agreements in question included provisions falling within the exclusive competence of the [Union] . . . [and] in effect the Court confirmed that Member States are not exclusively competent to negotiate and conclude a classical bilateral air service agreement.[143]

Prior to the EU–US Air Transport Agreement in 2008, air service agreements by Sweden, Finland, Belgium, Luxembourg, Austria, the Netherlands, Denmark and the United Kingdom had been concluded with the US. Citing the provisions of Regulation 847/2004,[144] the CJEU's reasoning for renegotiation was that since the US had the authority to withdraw, suspend or limit air traffic rights of air carriers

---

140 Ibid.
141 Ibid.
142 The turning point in the legal framework came following Regulation (EC) No 847/2004 of the European Parliament and of the Council of 29 April 2004, on the negotiation and implementation of air service agreements between Member States and third countries, OJ L157/7, 30 April 2004; Council Decision of 05 June 2003, on authorizing the Commission to open negotiations with third countries on the replacement of certain provisions in existing bilateral agreements with a Community agreement; and Council Decision of 05 June 2003, on authorizing the Commission to open negotiations with the United States in the field of air transport.
143 Common Position (EC) No 7/2004/C 54 E at 37; *See also Commission v Netherlands* (C-523/04) [2007] ECR I-3267.
144 Regulation (EC) No 847/2004 of the European Parliament and of the Council of 29 April 2004, on the negotiation and implementation of air service agreements between Member States and third countries, [2004] OJ L157/7, 20 April 2004; Corrigendum: [2004] OJ L195/3, 02 June 2004.

designated by these signatories, these agreements infringed EU law with the inclusion of discriminatory nationality clauses restricting equal market access for all Union carriers and contravene the authority of the EU legislation.

> This regulation establishes a procedure for notifying and authorising the bilateral negotiations conducted by Member States with a view to ensuring the introduction of standard clauses to make existing agreements compliant with EU law [and] . . . imposes certain obligations on Member States to ensure that non-discriminatory procedures are established for the consultation of stakeholders and for the distribution of traffic rights during negotiations.[145]

Licensing

Under Article 17 of the Convention on International Civil Aviation (Chicago Convention) in 1944,[146] aircraft hold the nationality of the state where they have been registered. The state hosting the registry or granting the operating licence is therefore responsible for overseeing the respective aircraft. In the case of the EU, aircraft may be registered in its state's national register or in the Community register.[147] Member States have opted for the national register, as will be discussed below.

Previously, Regulation 2407/92[148] laid down the economic and technical competency requirements in place for air carriers to obtain or maintain an operating licence. An air carrier licence could only be issued by a Member State when air transport is the main activity of the undertaking concerned and its registered office and principal place of business are located in the issuing Member State. Article 4(2) of the Regulation provided that Community air carriers must be majority owned and effectively controlled by Member States or nationals of Member States.

The first ever case[149] to be considered under Regulation 2407/92 was in May 1995. In this case, the Belgian State and the *Société Anonyme Suissepour la Navigation Aérienne* (then Swissair, now Swiss International Airlines) entered into an

---

145 Regulation (EC) No 847/2004. Online. Available HTML: <http://eur-lex.europa.eu/LexUriServ/LexUriServ.do?uri=OJ:L:2004:195:0003:0006:EN:PDF> (accessed 8 October 2011).

146 'Convention on International Civil Aviation, 9th ed., Doc. 7300/9, 2006' (Chicago Convention 1944). Online. Available HTML <html://www.icao.int/icaonet/arch/doc/7300/7300_9ed.pdf> (accessed 12 May 2011).

147 *See* Article 8(2)(a), Regulation (EEC) No 2407/92 of 23.7.1992 on licensing of air carriers [1992] OJ L 240 of 24 August 1992.

148 Ibid. It should be noted that the position was clarified and consolidated into one single regulation during the third liberalization package, whereby substantial changes were made to Council Regulations (EEC) No 2407/92 of 23 July 1992 on licensing of air carriers, (EEC) No 2408/92 of 23 July 1992 on access of Community air carriers to intra-Community air routes, and (EEC) No 2409/92 of 23 July 1992 on fares and rates for air services when in 2003, the Commission announced a revision of the third package so as to adapt the current rules to these changes. *See* Regulation (EC) No 1008/2008 of the European Parliament and of the Council of 24 September 2008, on common rules for the operation of air services in the Community (Recast), [2008] OJ L293/3, 31 October 2008.

149 Commission Decision 95/404/EC of 19 July 2005; [1995] OJ L 239/19–28, 7 October 1995.

agreement under which the latter was to acquire 49.5 per cent of the share capital of the Belgian air carrier Sabena SA. The agreement detailed the terms and conditions of that acquisition, as well as the rights and obligations of the parties in the thereafter governance of Sabena. The question before the Commission was whether Sabena complied with the requirements of Article 4 of the Regulation as regards the licensing and subsequent ownership and control of the business 'in Swiss hands'. Because Switzerland was neither a member of the EEA nor a Community Member State, it was not therefore entitled to obtain an operating licence by virtue of this Regulation. The Commission held that the existing ownership restrictions between the Community and Switzerland were only transitional measures pending reciprocity agreements on the matter, and additionally that Sabena remained effectively controlled by Belgian shareholders.

Although the rules have changed for Europeans under the 'Single European Sky', the European licensing rules certainly demonstrate, as seen in the *Swissair* case above, an element of 'safeguarding' against foreign ownership. The US approach to foreign ownership discussed below is presently capped at 25 per cent of controlling stock and 49 per cent of overall stock held. The American rules governing foreign ownership are not contained in licensing arrangements, but simply outright 'take it or leave it' protectionist. It could be argued that the European approach is more liberal than that of its American counterpart with its 'majority' national ownership provisions to gain an operating licence.

Deregulation of airfares and air cargo rates

Under the third phase of air transport liberalization, Regulation 1008/2008[150] lays down the criteria and procedures governing the establishment of airfares and air cargo rates charged by air carriers on air services within the Union. Although Union air carriers may freely set air fares and cargo rates for services operated within the internal market under these rules, individual Member States may require air fares to be filed with them as they so prescribe, withdraw basis fares that are excessively high, or stop decreases in airfares in markets where market forces have led to sustained downward development of airfares, resulting in widespread losses amongst air carriers.

Computer reservations and global distribution systems

Computer reservations systems (CRSs) and global distribution systems (GDSs) became integral to the global air transport sector in the mid-1970s in the US. Primarily a medium for searching airfares and making bookings, CRSs are integral to the

---

150 Council Regulation (EC) No 1008/2008 of the European Parliament and of the Council of 24 September 2008, on common rules for the operation of air services in the Community (Recast), [2008] OJ L293/3, 31 October 2008.

operation of a structured and efficient industry. Individual and groups of airlines have been actively enrolled in the development of CRSs to promote their services.

Regulation 2299/89[151] sets out the criteria for the use of CRSs to query fares and make bookings from within the Union. The 'code of conduct' includes certain rules for fair, neutral displays and booking procedures, to provide for a competitive, yet equal medium for the booking of seats and cargo space.

Since the 1990s, the impact of the growth of Internet services has meant that online travel search engines such as 'Travelocity', 'Expedia', 'Opodo' and 'ebookers' are the preferred sales platforms for consumers. Making travel arrangements, from flights and hotels to hire cars, is now a simple matter of logging on, entering one's criteria on one of these search engine webpages, and searching. The search engines will access one or more GDSs attached to any number of CRSs to find the best-priced deals available according to one's search criteria. A typical consumer will not approach a travel agent or the airline direct, in most cases, to book tickets, as this will be more time-consuming and often more expensive. By conducting a search online, a list of possible itineraries is produced in a matter of seconds. For reasons relating to subcontracts with providers and booking fee arrangements, one rarely tends to find the exact same list of search results on two different platforms.

Slot allocation

An issue of mounting concern particularly in the EU but also worldwide is airport capacity.[152] The challenges relating to slot allocation is seldom raised at airports with sufficient excess capacity for new carriers and routes, yet at congested airports. There is very little, if any, excess capacity for new entry. Where new regulations have come into force, some airlines retain grandfather rights to continue use of its previously granted or purchased slots. Perhaps the most prevalent example of grandfather rights in slots is BA at London-Heathrow Airport (LHR).

The most popular airports, owing either to a location proximate to nearby cities or with excellent interline connections, tend to be the largest and most overcrowded. Runway and gate capacities at a number of EU airports are at or approaching maximum limits, presenting a significant barrier to the growth of and new entry into the air transport sector. The high demand for these airports cannot be adequately accommodated and thus impedes effective competition in the Union's air transport sector.

In response to the problems faced in the sector owing to lack of airport capacity, IATA and the EU have adopted various procedures for slot allocation. In light of the severity of the 'capacity problem' to the industry, agreements on capacity, coordination and consultation of fares and slot allocation has therefore been granted an exemption by the Commission.

---

151 Council Regulation (EEC) 2299/89 on a code of conduct for computer reservations systems (CRSs) [1989] OJ L220/1, as modified [2009] OJ L35/47.
152 *See* P. Forsyth, D. Gillen, O.G. Mayer and H. Niemeier (eds), *Competition versus Predation in Aviation Markets: A Survey of Experience in North America, Europe and Australia* (Aldershot: Ashgate, 2005).

The implementation of Regulation 793/2004[153] on slot allocation within the Union and Regulation 1105/2002[154] regarding consultations on passenger tariffs and slot allocations are intended to assist, beginning with the Lisbon Agenda,[155] with the implementation of a Community-wide slot allocation procedure towards realizing the need for 'adequate' transport links.

Regulators utilize the slot allocation system as a remedy in response to the question of regulatory approval of alliances of airlines, often requiring that certain airlines divest certain slots to make way for new entrants and increased competition. In the markets for US–London services, *British Airways–American Airlines* and *Lufthansa–SAS–United Air Lines*as discussed below, were required to give up slots until competitors provided at least 55 per cent of the total number of services on hub–hub routes.[156] The potential problem with this is that the definition of 'competitor', since the advent of alliances and cooperative agreements, is constantly changing. Individual airlines may be competitors, or groups of airlines in the form of alliances may be competitors. This raises the question of substitutability of services.

In the *Lufthansa–SAS*[157] case mentioned above, the European Commission approved alliance formation with the caveat that airlines

> must freeze the number of daily frequencies they operate on a route when a new entrant decides to serve that route. This condition is designed to prevent the airlines already present from increasing substantially their number of frequencies with a view of squeezing the new entrant from the market. Lufthansa and SAS must nevertheless be allowed to exercise the necessary degree of flexibility in operating their services, in the event of a new competitor starting up on a route, they should be able to increase the number of daily frequencies by one frequency on the relevant route.[158]

Concerns raised by the likes of the OECD are that the requiring of divestment of slots as a remedy to approving mergers and alliances are that 'this alone may not be enough

---

153 Of 21 April 2004, amending Council Regulation (EEC) No 95/93 on common rules for the allocation of slots at Community airports, as modified [2009] OJ L167/24.

154 Of 22 June 2002, amending Regulation (EEC) No 1617/93 as regards consultations on passenger tariffs and slot allocations at airports. *See also* Commission Press Releases IP/02/924, 'Commission renews block exemption for the IATA passenger tariff conferences', Brussels, 25 June 2002; IP/06/1294, 'Competition: Commission revises Block Exemption for IATA passenger tariff conferences', Brussels, 02 October 2006.

155 In March 2000, the European Council met in Lisbon, Portugal, to set out the development plan for the European Union, known as the 'Lisbon Agenda'. The 10-year plan stresses innovation, incorporating aspects of economic, social and environmental policies, including European transport policy. *See* B. Daley, and C. Thomas, 'Challenges to Growth: Environmental Issues and the Development of the Air Transport Industry', in O'Connell and Williams (eds), *Air Transport in the 21st Century*, pp. 269–294.

156 OECD Annual Report (2003). Online. Available HTTP: <http://www.oecd.org/dataoecd/45/28/2506789.pdf> (accessed 11 March 2011).

157 *Lufthansa/SAS* [1996] OJ L 54/28, [1996] 4 CMLR 845, *See also* (1998) 19 ECLR 116.

158 OECD Annual Report.

to eliminate competition concern (new point-to-point entry on the hub–hub route of an existing network is extremely difficult, especially for a network, which does not itself operate a hub at one or both ends)'.[159]

EU and IATA

Current worldwide systems of slot allocation have been greatly influenced by the relevant procedures developed by IATA. In its *Scheduling Procedures Guide*,[160] IATA sets out the procedures for slot allocation. 'Slots are typically allocated by a scheduling committee of an airport consisting of representatives from the airlines, the airport and the regulatory authority'.[161]

Whilst these scheduling practices have been challenged on the basis of anti-competitive concerns, it has been argued by IATA that much of its work is essential to maintaining an efficient international air transport system. To that end, IATA tariff conferences previously had a block exemption from EU competition rules under Commission Regulation 1617/93.[162]

Regulation 1617/93, which renewed Regulation 2671/88 on revenue pooling, exempted from Article 81(3) TEC certain categories of agreements and concerted practices concerning joint planning and coordination of schedules (capacity), joint operations, consultations on passenger and cargo tariffs on scheduled air services and slot allocation at airports with the aim of facilitating 'interlining', subject to certain *a priori* conditions.[163]

It should be noted that following Regulation 3976/87 (repealed by Regulation 487/2009),[164] specific block exemptions had been granted to capacity, coordination and consultation on fares and slot allocation within the Union. The original block exemption[165] provided for the exemption of joint planning and coordination, tariff consultations and slot allocation, but was revised in 2003[166] to exempt only IATA tariff conferences.[167] The Commission elected not to renew the block exemptions,

---

159　Ibid.
160　Available at the IATA website. HTTP: <http://www.iata.org/whatwedo/standards/scheduling. htm> (accessed 10 August 2011).
161　Goh, *European Air Transport Law*, p. 166.
162　Commission Regulation 1617/93, [1993] OJ L 155/18, 26 June 1993, as amended by Commission Regulations (EC) No 1523/96, [1996] OJ L190/11, 31.07.1996 and (EC) No 1083/1999, OJ L131/27, 27 May 1999.
163　[1988] OJ L 239/9. The position has since been amended such that practices are subject to increased scrutiny and less outright immunity from the competition rules. *See* Commission Regulations (EC) No 1523/96, [1996] OJ L190/11, 31.07.1996 and (EC) No 1083/1999, OJ L131/27, 27 May 1999.
164　Council Regulation (EC) No 487/2009 on the application of Article 81(3) TEC to certain categories of agreements and concerted practices in the air transport sector, [2009] OJ L 148/1, 11 June 2009.
165　Regulation 2671/88.
166　Regulation 1617/93.
167　The IATA block exemption continued until 30 June 2007 for routes between the EU and the US or Australia, and 31 October 2007 for routes between the EU and third countries. *See* Commission Press Releases IP/02/924, 'Commission renews block exemption for the IATA passenger tariff conferences', Brussels, 25 June 2002; IP/06/1294, 'Competition: Commission revises Block Exemption

however, which expired on 30 June 2007 for routes between the EU and the US Australia, and 31 October 2007 for routes between the EU and third countrie͏ As a result, IATA and individual carriers must now ensure that their agreements a͏͏ compatible with the EU competition rules.

State aid

It is generally speaking prohibited for a Member State of the EU to give financial aid to an ailing company, as this is unfair to its competitors and is thus detrimental to competition and ultimately the consumer. Firms that are not financially viable are, through this mechanism, kept alive through artificial means. There are exceptions to this rule, however, where it would be detrimental to the market if a particular firm went out of business and exit. There are several conditions necessary for the commission to approve state aid measures, one of which is that a company is 'in difficulty'.[169] This requirement is problematic as an ambiguous concept with many possible interpretations. Nevertheless, there are cases where this conceptual uncertainty has been overcome and aid has been approved, and yet others where state aid measures were deemed anti-competitive.

The EU air transport sector has long been characterized by 'flag carriers' representing each of the Member States, high levels of state intervention and 'traditional' bilateralism, e.g. reciprocity arrangements. The Council completed its liberalization programme in 1993 and removed all remaining restrictions from the industry by 1997.

The most notable cases involving state aid granted to European airlines after the final liberalization package was implemented in 1993 include *Sabena*,[170] *Iberia*,[171] *Aer Lingus*,[172] *TAP Air Portugal*,[173] *Air France*,[174] *Olympic Airlines*,[175] *Alitalia*,[176]

---

for IATA passenger tariff conferences', Brussels, 02 October 2006; IP/07/973 'Competition: Commission ends block exemption for IATA passenger tariff conferences for routes between the EU and non-EU countries', Brussels, 29 June 2007.

168 On the one hand, although air transport services were once subject to exceptional treatment in the EU vis-à-vis block exemptions, there are now no sector-specific competition rules in aviation. Unlike the existing regulatory exception in the US, however, where US DoJ handles all antitrust issues except for aviation, which is delegated to US DoT, the EU has one department charged with the application of EU competition and merger rules, the DG for Competition. On the other hand, the US DoT has dual powers of enforcement and transport policymaker, whereas in the EU, these are separated between the DG for Competition on enforcement and the DG for Transport and Mobility on general transport policy setting.

169 N. Farantouris, 'Firms in Difficulty and State Aids: A Compatibility Analysis'. *ECLR* 30(10), 2009, 496.

170 [1991] OJ L 300/48, 31.10.2001.

171 The Commission's XXIInd Report on Competition Policy (1992), p. 269.

172 Commission Decision 94/118/EC, 21 December 1993.

173 Commission Decision 94/698/EC, 6 July 1994.

174 Commission Decision 94/653/EC, 27 July 1994.

175 Commission Decision 94/696/EC, 7 October 1994.

176 See the relevant decisions listed below under 'Alitalia'.

and more recently *Austrian Airlines*,[177] *Ryanair*,[178] *Cyprus Airways*[179] and *Malév*,[180] as detailed below.

In the Commission's first major investigation[181] into state aid to airlines in 1991, it approved the Belgian government to give 'restructuring' aid to its then-flag carrier, Sabena (SB). The conditions of this authorization included that the Belgian government not become involved in the management of the airline and that it would be the last injection of public funds into the airline. Then, in 1992 and 1995, there were two large injections into Iberia, the Spanish flag carrier. In short, the Spanish government sought to recapitalize Iberia by selling shares to international investors, which resulted in the actual price paid for these shares at an average discount of 20 per cent.[182] The discount was funded by the public purse, raising a state aid issue.

TAP Air Portugal (TP)[183] was granted approval by the Commission in 1994[184] to increase capital and the amount of credit guarantees, and to take a tax exemption ('the state aid') on the condition that the Portuguese Republic honour its undertaking[185] to apply the state aid to the autonomous regions of Madeira and the Azores in establishing public service obligations for routes to these destinations. Later, in 2000, TAT European Airlines (IJ) brought an action[186] for annulment of the third *tranche* of state aid previously approved by the Commission,[187] against which two actions were brought in 1994 by several airline companies, including BD and BA. The validity of the original decision remained unchanged in the Commission's 2000 judgment. In 2002, the French government notified the Commission of a compensation scheme for losses they had implemented in the French aviation sector from 15 September 2001. As a result of the terrorist attacks in the United States on 11 September 2001, certain areas of air space were closed for several days. The United States air space was closed from 11 to 14 September 2001 and gradually opened thereafter. Airlines were forced to cancel flights and special compensation schemes were developed in the

---

177 Case No COMP/M.5440 –*LUFTHANSA/AUSTRIAN AIRLINES*

178 *Ryanair Ltd v Commission of the European Communities (Association of European Airlines (AEA), intervening)* (T-196/04) [2009] 2 CMLR 7.

179 Commission press release IP/07/297, 'European Commission Raises Doubts About Cyprus'. Online. Available HTML: http://europa.eu/rapid/pressReleasesAction.do?reference=IP/06/352&format=HTML&aged=1&language=EN (accessed 1 October 2011).

180 Case C38/2010 (ex NN 69/2010 CP 63/2010), Malév Hungarian Airlines, Negative decision and recovery, 09 January 2012. The non-confidential version of the decision is due to be published once any confidentiality issues have been resolved. It will be published in the Official Journal of the European Union and will be made available under the case number SA. 30584(NN 69/2010) in the State Aid Register on the DG Competition website.

181 [1991] OJ L 300/48, 31.10.2001.

182 The Commission's XXIInd Report on Competition Policy, p. 269.

183 Commission Decision 94/698/EC of 6 July 1994 concerning increase in capital, credit guarantees and tax exemption in favour of TAP, Article 1(e).

184 Ibid.

185 Under Article 4, Regulation 2408/92, [1992] OJ L/240/8, as amended.

186 Commission Decision 94/653/EC, 27 July 1994.

187 Decision 94/653/EEC of 2 concerning the notified capital increase of Air France [1994] OJ L 254/73.

Union and received Commission approval.[188] The budget authorized for France for this initial period was EUR 54.9 million.[189]

The compensation scheme continued in France from 15 to 19 September 2001. It is this subsequent period, for which the Commission decided to initiate the procedure laid down in Article 108(2) TFEU (ex. Article 88(2) TEC) on state aid. The Commission stated:

> The French authorities thus recognise that, after 14 September 2001, the situation was no longer marked by traffic disruption but by tighter operating arrangements for airlines in terms of security measures. Though unusual, such additional costs cannot be considered to be exceptional occurrences within the meaning of [ex.] Article 87(2)(b) [TEC].[190]

The state aid, which France proposed to implement in favour of French airlines beyond 14 September 2001 for losses sustained on account of the partial closure of air space, was held incompatible with the common market and therefore could not be implemented.

In September 2003, the Commission brought an action[191] against the Hellenic Republic (Greece) under Article 108(2) TFEU (ex. Article 88(2) TEC) for failure to fulfil obligations in accordance with the Commission Decision 2003/372/EC[192] and the Treaty. Article 1 of the Decision outlines the types of 'restructuring aid' granted by Greece to Olympic Airlines (OA), the national carrier. Article 2 addresses state aid 'given' in the form of 'a persistent non-payment of social security obligations, of value-added tax (VAT) on fuel and spare parts payable by Olympic Aviation, of rentals for different airports, of airport charges payable to Athens International Airport and other airports [and] of *Spatosimo* tax' and the incompatibility with the common market. Article 3 of the Decision states that Greece must take appropriate measures to recover from the beneficiary, Olympic Airlines (OA) (the new company to which the personnel and assets were transferred from OA under Greek law[193]), the aid of GRD 14 billion (EUR 41 million), as referred to in Articles 1 and 2 of the Decision.

The European Court held that Greece had granted illegal state aid, has not fulfilled its obligations to recover that state aid and must therefore pay the costs.[194] In addition, OA were ordered to repay EUR 160 million in illegal aid. The rationale behind

---

188 COM (2001) 574 final, 'The repercussions of the terrorist attacks in the United States on the air transport industry', Communication from the Commission to the European Parliament and the Council, 10 October 2001.

189 [2002] OJ C 59/25, Decision N 806/2001 of 30 January 2002 on 'state aid', 6 March 2002.

190 [2003] OJ L 77/61, 24 March 2003, Commission Decision of 11 December 2002 concerning State aid scheme C 42/2002 (ex N 286/2002) which France proposed to implement to assist French airlines, at point 37.

191 Commission Decision 94/696/EC, 7 October 1994.

192 [2003] OJ L 132/1, Decision 2003/372/EC of 11 December 2002.

193 Law No 3185/2003, FEKA 229/26 September 2003.

194 Case C-415/03, *Commission v Hellenic Republic*, Judgement of the European Court (Second Chamber), 12 May 2005.

the Court's Decision is that 'by granting this aid, Greece has given Olympic Airlines an advantage not available to their competitors'.[195] The new aid payments were held a violation of the 'one time, last time' principle discussed above, as OA had already benefited from regarding restructuring aid in the past.[196]

In 1996, Alitalia (AZ) developed a restructuring plan for the period 1996–2000 including an injection of capital totalling ITL 2.75 billion (approximately EUR 1.42 million) to be paid in three instalments by the airline's majority shareholder, the *Istituto per la Ricostruzione Industriale* (the Italian State). The Commission reviewed this plan and declared the state aid compatible with the common market in 1997, subject to some conditions.[197] AZ brought an action in 1997, on which the CFI annulled the Commission's first decision.[198] The Commission adopted a new decision on the subsequent adjustments to AZ's restructuring plan in 2001, declaring the state aid compatible with the common market.[199] AZ brought another action, which was dismissed by the CFI who confirmed the Commission's 2001 decision as valid.[200]

In November 2001, the EU Energy and Transport Directorate at General (DG) gave a negative decision with recovery of EUR 300 million restructuring aid given to AZ funded through a public enterprises scheme.[201] The DG also undertook an investigation into a guarantee scheme to restructure Cyprus Airways and reached a positive decision in February 2008.[202] Most recently, an application was made to the DG for restructuring aid (by direct grant) to Austrian Airlines in December 2008. In February 2009, a decision was taken to initiate a formal investigation.[203]

The *Lufthansa–Austrian Airlines* case[204] involved a proposed takeover by Lufthansa of the Austrian State's 41.56 per cent stake in the company. The additional shareholders would also be bought out. The price to be paid by Lufthansa contained three elements: a purchase price of approximately EUR 366,000; a debtor warrant issued to the Austrian state (which may lead to further payment); and a recapitalization of Austrian Airline's historical debt, which totalled roughly EUR 500 million.[205]

---

195 Press Release, IP/05/1139, 'Commission finds that Greece has granted illegal State aid to Olympic Airways and Olympic Airlines, Brussels' (14 September 2005).

196 *See* Decision 1999/332/EC of 14.8.1998, [1999] OJ L 128/1.

197 Decision 97/789/EC of 15 July 1997 concerning the recapitalisation of the company Alitalia, [1997] OJ L 322/44.

198 Case T-296/97, *Alitalia v Commission*, 12 December 2000.

199 Decision 2001/1723/EC of 18 July 2001 concerning the recapitalization of the company Alitalia, [2001] OJ L 271/28.

200 Decision of 9 June 2002, [2002] OJ C 239/2.

201 Case C26/2008 (ex. NN31/2008) *Prêt de 300 millions d'euros à ALITALIA* (Recovery of EUR 300 million from Alitalia), 12 November 2008.

202 [2008] OJ L 49/51, Commission Decision of 7 March 2007 regarding state aid case C 10/06 (ex N555/05) – Cyprus Airways Public Ltd's restructuring plan, 22 February 2008.

203 Case number C6/2009 (ex. N663/2008) Restructuring of Austrian Airlines AG.

204 Case No COMP/M.5440- *LUFTHANSA/AUSTRIAN AIRLINES*.

205 Press Release IP/09/1256, 'State aid: Commission approves the restructuring of Austrian Airlines', *Europa* (28 August 2009). Online. Available HTML: <http://europa.eu/rapid/pressReleasesAction. do?reference=IP/09/1256&format=HTML&aged=0&language=EN&guiLanguage=en> (accessed 25 July 2011).

The last condition meant there would be an aggregate negative purchase price, which was tantamount to state aid. Thus bankruptcy of the airline would have been a less costly option for the Austrian state. The Commission declared this concentration, however, to be compatible with the internal market.[206] Although the price to be paid by Lufthansa included state aid, this was justified by the Community Framework of rescuing and restructuring firms in difficulty. Furthermore, aid was kept to a minimum, and a reduction in capacity (15 per cent) and a cap on growth[207] were sufficient to satisfy the rules regarding competition and state aid.

In 1998, Ryanair[208] lodged an application for annulment of the Commission's decision[209] authorizing the Irish government to inject (a second) round of state aid into EI as approved in 1993,[210] which was rejected. In a more recent case involving Ryanair,[211] the Commission initially found that there had been illegal aid in the form of financial benefits given to Ryanair by two airports in Brussels, and ordered this to be repaid. Ryanair had set up a base at Charleroi Airport and entered into two separate agreements, one with the Walloon region (the contested agreement) and owner of Charleroi airport, and the other with Brussels-South Charleroi Airport (CRL), a public sector company. Under the contested decision with the Walloon region, Ryanair was given a discount on landing charges and was insured against any loss of profit resulting from a change in regulation of airport opening hours or charges. Under the second agreement, Ryanair and CRL undertook several reciprocal agreements, which were not notified to the Commission. The Commission found these agreements to constitute advantages within the meaning of Article 87(1) TEC (now Article 107 TFEU) and satisfied the other criteria for state aid. Thus the agreements were held to be incompatible with the common market. Ryanair appealed, arguing the two airports ought to be viewed as a single economic entity and the private investor principle[212] ought to apply. Upon appeal, the Commission was found to have made an error in law; the fact that the Walloon region was a public body did not mean it could not engage in commercial activity, and Ryanair's terms were held to be obtained through commercial negotiation rather than illegal state aid.

In the *Cyprus Airways* case, a restructuring of the airline by the state was deemed to be compatible with the internal market. In March 2006, the Commission decided to

206 Commission Decision of 28 August 2009 declaring a concentration to be compatible with the common market and the EEA Agreement. Online. Available HTML: <http://ec.europa.eu/competition/mergers/cases/decisions/m5440_20090828_20600_en.pdf> (accessed 27 July 2011).

207 Press Release IP/09/1256, 'State Aid: Commission approves the restructuring of Austrian Airlines', *Europa* (28 August 2009). Growth is defined as average of the growth rate observed for member airlines of the Association of European Airlines until the end of 2015 or whenever Austrian Airlines hit an operational break even.

208 Commission Decision 94/118/EC, 21 December 1993.

209 [1994] OJ C 399/1 of 31 December 1994.

210 Commission Decision 94/118/EC of 21.12.1993 concerning aid to be provided by the Irish government to the Aer Lingus group [1994] OJ L 54/30, 25 February 1994.

211 *Ryanair Ltd v Commission of the European Communities (Association of European Airlines (AEA), intervening)* (T-196/04) [2009] 2 CMLR 7.

212 Ibid. This principle asks whether similar conditions could have been obtained from a rational private actor on the market.

open an investigation into whether this restructuring constituted illegal state aid.[213] On concluding the investigation one year later, the Commission declared that it was satisfied that the restructuring plan would lead to the long-term viability of the airline, and met the other requisite conditions for the rescue of a firm in difficulty.[214] In the case regarding the Hungarian Airline *Malév*,[215] the Commission found that the Hungarian Authorities granted to its national airline capital injections and shareholder loans.[216] In particular, the Commission doubted that Malév would have been able to obtain the same favourable conditions from a private investor in normal market conditions, or for that matter been able to borrow money at all given its precarious financial position. Suspicious capital injections occurred in February and September 2010, while shareholder loans were granted between April and July, and again in September 2010.[217] The Commission found that the necessary criteria for rescuing and restructuring firms in difficulty had not been satisfied.[218]

More than a decade later, increased competition on intra- and extra-Union markets has ushered structural changes and new comprehensive agreements with other airlines and industries. Although the Union has enforced a stricter application of rules on state aid, a number of European airlines remain heavily state-owned.[219] According to the Commission:

> In the more competitive environment state aids might be of substantially increased interest of their own airlines. This could lead to a subsidy race, which would jeopardise both the common interest and the basic objectives of the liberalisation process.[220]

The conflict that arises for individual Member States is the obligation to provide an adequate, sustainable means of air transportation for its public, and at the same time abide by the Union regulations on state aid. This struggle between national and Union policy and objectives often leads to a conflict of interest and in some cases leaves the Member State feeling that there are no alternatives available.

---

213 Press Release IP/06/352, 'European Commission raises doubts about Cyprus Airways restructuring', *Europa* (22 March 2006).

214 Press Release IP/07/297, 'Cyprus Airways: Commission authorises restructuring plan', *Europa* (7 March 2007).

215 Notice 2011/C 156/09, 28 May 2011.

216 Press Release IP/12/7, 'State aid: Commission orders Hungary to recover incompatible state aid from national air carrier Malév', *Europa* (9 January 2012).

217 Press Release IP/10/1753, 'State aid: Commission opens in-depth investigation into Hungarian support measures for national airline Malév', *Europa* (21 December 2010).

218 See MEMO/04/172. The non-confidential version of the decision is due to be published once any confidentiality issues have been resolved. It will be published in the Official Journal of the European Union and will be made available under the case number SA. 30584 (NN 69/2010) in the State Aid Register on the DG Competition website.

219 *See Table 4.1.*

220 [2005] OJ 94/C 350/07, Application of Articles 92 and 93 TEC and Article 61of the EEA agreement to state aid in the aviation sector.

Under Articles 107 to 109 TFEU, the Commission has the power to deal with state aid that could distort competition in the common market. Article 107(1) TFEU provides that:

> Save as otherwise provided in this Treaty, any aid granted by a Member State or through State resources in any form whatsoever which distorts or threatens to distort competition by favouring certain undertakings or the production of certain goods shall, in so far as it affects trade between Member States, be incompatible with the internal market.[221]

Article 107(2) TFEU provides that certain categories of state aid shall be compatible with the common market. These include aid having a social character, in such instances as national disasters or markets under PSOs, as provided for under Regulation 2408/92,[222] such as travel between the Azores islands and mainland Portugal and the Greek islands and mainland Greece. Subsidies to operating costs are only permissible in this PSO category.

In the case *Presidente del Consiglio dei MinistrivRegione Sardegna*,[223] which was a reference from the Italian *Corte Costituzionale* for a preliminary ruling under Article 234 TEC (now Article 267 TFEU), the region of Sardinia imposed a tax on tourist and recreational flight stopovers that were domiciled for tax purposes outside of Sardinia. The question was whether this constituted state aid for the purposes of Article 87 TEC (now Article 107 TFEU). It was held that in order to qualify as a 'service' under Article 50 TEC (now Article 32 TFEU), it was not required that the provider come to the beneficiary; it could just as equally be the reverse, meaning that this tax contravened the EU fundamental principle of freedom of movement of goods and services. The four criteria for an action to be considered state aid under Article 107 TFEU are that there must be an intervention by the State or through State resources; the intervention has to be liable to affect trade between Member States; it must confer an advantage on the recipient; and it must distort or threaten to distort competition.[224] The region of Sardinia argued that its policy was justified by public interest as they sought to offset the environmental damage caused by tourism, but this was rejected on the basis that pollution had nothing to do with the origin of the aircraft. Furthermore, there was no evidence that the legislation was enacted on public health grounds.

Latest developments: 'Temporary Framework'

In response to the current financial crisis, the Commission adopted the Communication 'A European Economic Recovery Plan' in November 2008[225] based on

221 Art. 107(1) TFEU, OJ C115/91, 9 May 2008.
222 [1992] OJ L240/8, as amended.
223 Case C-169/09, [2010] OJ C24/6, 30 January 2010.
224 Ibid.
225 Communication from the Commission to the European Council, COM(2008) 800.

short-term measures to 'boost demand, save jobs and help restore confidence' and through 'smart investment' yield 'higher growth and sustainable prosperity in the longer term' in line with the Lisbon Agenda reforms. The Commission communicated a Temporary Framework for State Aid in 2009, outlining the need for temporary state aid measures, including the unblocking of bank lending to small and medium sized enterprises (SMEs).[226] The Temporary Framework Communication (TFC) reinforces that state aid is still possible under existing instruments,[227] including *de minimis* aid[228] and aid to improve environmental performance beyond Union standards.[229] On the applicability of Article 107(3)(b) TFEU,[230] under which the Commission may declare common market aid 'to remedy a serious disturbance in the economy of a Member State' as compatible with the common market, the Commission considers in the TFC that 'certain categories of state aid are justified, for a limited period, to remedy those difficulties and that they may be declared compatible with the common market on the basis of this power.[231]

The compatible amount of aid (financial and in the form of guarantees) is limited by the following conditions. The aid:

- must not exceed a cash grant of EUR 500,000 per undertaking;
- must be granted in the form of a scheme;
- may be granted to firms who were not in difficulty on 1 July 2008 but entered in difficulty thereafter as a result of the global financial and economic crisis; and
- must be granted no later than 31 December 2010.[232]

Under the new measure of the TFC, aid in the form of guarantees will be considered compatible with the common market where:

---

226 Communication from the Commission – Temporary Community framework for State aid measures to support access to finance in the current financial and economic crisis, [2009] OJ C/16/1, 22 January 2009. This is following on from the earlier Communication from the Commission to the Council, the European Economic and Social Committee, and the Committee of the Regions 'Think Small First' – A 'Small Business Act' for Europe of 25 June 2008, COM(2008) 394 final.

227 As simplified and streamlined by Commission Regulation (EC) No 800/2008 of 6 August 2008 declaring certain categories of aid compatible with the common market in application of Articles 87 and 88 TEC ('the General Block Exemption Regulation'), [2008] OJ L 214/3, 8 February 2008.

228 The *'de minimis'* Regulation specifies that support measures up to EUR 200,000 per company over a three-year period or guarantees of up to EUR 1,5 million do not exceed the *de minimis* threshold and therefore do not constitute state aid. (Source: Commission Regulation (EC) No 1998/2006 of 15 December 2006 on the application of Articles 87 and 88 TEC [now Articles 107 and 108 TFEU] to *de minimis* aid, [2006] OJ L379/5, 28 December 2006.)

229 *See* Community Guidelines on State aid for environmental protection, [2008] OJ C/82/1, 1 April 2008.

230 On strict interpretation of Article 107(3)(b) (ex. Article 87(3)(b) TEC), *see* Joined Cases T-132/96 and T-143/96, *Freistaat Sachsen and Volkswagen AG v Commission* [1999] ECR II-3663, para. 167.

231 Communication from the Commission – Temporary Community framework for State aid measures to support access to finance in the current financial and economic crisis, [2009] OJ C/16/4, 22 January 2009.

232 Ibid.

- in the case of SMEs, Member States grant a reduction of up to 25 per cent of the annual premium to be paid for new guarantees granted;
- for large companies, Member States grant a reduction of up to 15 per cent of the annual premium for new guarantees;
- may be granted to firms who were not in difficulty on 1 July 2008 but entered in difficulty thereafter as a result of the global financial and economic crisis;
- the guarantee does not exceed 90 per cent of the loan; and
- the reduction of the guarantee premium is applied during a maximum period of two years following the granting of the guarantee.[233]

The Commission amended the TFC in 2009:

> Member States have to show that the state aid measures notified to the Commission under this framework are necessary, appropriate and proportionate to remedy a serious disturbance in the economy of a Member Sate and that all the conditions are fully respected.[234]

The Volcanic Ash Crisis of April 2010 presented a different situation where advantages given to airlines by member states may not constitute illegal state aid. A package of short-term and medium-term measures was given support by a wide range of ministers in a meeting in May 2010.[235] The consensus was that more flexibility was required to ease the pressure on airlines, more coordination was needed between member states to deal with the crisis, a new regulator framework ought to be set up, and certain loans and guarantees granted under normal market conditions would not amount to state aid.[236] Ministers did concede, however, that competition ought to be preserved as much as possible.

Adopted in January 2009, the TFC continues to support access to finance in the current financial and economic crisis. The rationale of the TFC is to facilitate firms' access to cash and to encourage innovation even in a difficult economic climate. Indicated by the title, this framework was meant to be temporary, and has been under constant evaluation every since its inception. The first evaluation came in October 2009; initially, the framework was due to expire in December 2010, and the Commission sought to evaluate whether the deadline ought to be extended.

The Commission considered whether there had been any significant developments in the economic climate and the capacity of markets to supply adequate funds, whether this framework was an appropriate vehicle for recovery, and whether there had been any detrimental effects on competition between firms. Despite some improvement in the banking industry, the financial markets were still highly

---

233 Ibid., pp. 5–6.
234 Communication from the Commission – Amendment of the Temporary framework for State aid measures to support access to finance in the current financial and economic crisis – adopted on 25 February 2009.
235 Commission MEMO/10/162.
236 'Responses to "Ash Crisis" for Air Transport Outlined', *EU Focus*, 272, 2010, 34–35.

ttile, which the Commission deemed sufficient justification of a prolongation of framework until December 2011.[237] Bearing in mind that the framework is due be phased out at some point, the Commission tightened the restrictions in July 2010.[238] This is meant to ease the transition back to normal state aid conditions and limit the anti-competitive impact of the framework. It would seem the TFC has certainly had an impact on the market. For instance, 23 Member States have made use of the TFC during its lifespan, although only about 7 per cent of financial help approved by the Commission was actually paid out. The majority was spent by Germany (78 per cent) with other states contributing significantly less (Britain 1.1 per cent and Italy 8 per cent). Thus, there are apparently still some disparities in the internal market.[239]

State ownership

If an airline is partially or wholly state-owned, state subsidies into the airline are more prevalent.[240] Table 4.1 illustrates the proportion of flag carriers, which to 2010 remain wholly or partially state-owned. Between 2002 and 2010, there was a reduction in the percentage of state ownership of flag carriers, notwithstanding the appending of new airlines to the list following the accession of new Member States since 2004 and 2007.[241]

Low-cost carriers and 'start-up aid'[242]

Ryanair, an Irish low-cost passenger airline, typically flies to smaller, regional airports where congestion and costs are at a minimum. Rather than fly to the main airport in Brussels, for instance, it strategically[243] flies to Brussels South Charleroi Airport (CRL), a public undertaking controlled by the Walloon Region of Belgium. Although not as conveniently accessible to the city of Brussels as the main airport, which lies only eight miles away, Ryanair has managed to develop new competition in the intra-Union markets to and from the Brussels catchment area, despite the airport being the 'second best' choice for travellers. By choosing the CRL option over BRU, Ryanair received certain benefits including a 50 per cent reduction in landing fees, substantial

237 Communication of the Commission – Temporary Union framework for State aid measures to support access to finance in the current financial and economic crisis. Official Journal C6, 11 January 2011, p. 5. Online. Available HTTP: <http://eur-lex.europa.eu/LexUriServ/LexUriServ.do?uri=CELEX: 52011XC0111(01):EN:NOT> (accessed 26 July 2011).
238 See Directorate General Competition Commission Staff Working Document of 30 April 2010: The application of State aid rules to Government Guarantee schemes covering bank debt to be issued after 30 June 2010. For specific details on how conditions were restricted, see footnote 16.
239 Communication of the Commission – Temporary Union framework for State aid measures to support access to finance in the current financial and economic crisis. Official Journal C6, 11 January 2011.
240 *See* Doganis, *The Airline Business*, pp. 223–257 on state-owned airlines.
241 *See Table 4.1.*
242 *See* S.D. Barrett, *Deregulation and the Airline Business in Europe: Selected Readings* (London: Routledge, 2009), pp. 104–119.
243 This is only one case-in-point. Ryanair operates to/from many European 'second-best' airports. In another case, Ryanair flies to an airport 90 minutes by coach from Oslo, Norway. The airline offers discounted coach tickets on board to passengers travelling to the city.

Table 4.1 Change in state ownership of flag carriers 2002–2010[a]

Flag carrier	Country	State ownership 2002	State ownership 2010
Adria	Slovenia	n/a*	87 %
Aer Lingus	Ireland	95 %	25.35 %
Air Baltic	Latvia	n/a*	52.6 %
Air France	France	56 %	18.6 %[b]
Air Malta	Malta	96.4 %	98 %
Alitalia[c,d]	Italy	53 %	49.9 %
Croatia Airlines	Croatia	n/a*	94.08 %
CSA Czech Airlines	Czech Republic	n/a*	91.75 %
Cyprus Airways	Cyprus	69.62 %	69.57 %
Finnair	Finland	58.43 %	55.81 %
LOT	Poland	n/a*	67.97 % (unchanged)
Jat Airways	Serbia	n/a*	100 %
Lufthansa	Germany	10.05 %	Nil
Luxair	Luxembourg	23.1 %	Unchanged/ 26.85 %
Malév	Hungary	n/a*	95 %
Montenegro Airlines	Montenegro	n/a*	99.88 %
Olympic Air[e]	Greece	100 %	unchanged
SAS Scandinavian Airlines	Sweden	21.4 %	
	Denmark	14.3 %	
	Norway	14.3%	unchanged
Swiss International Air Lines	Switzerland	23 %	Nil
TAP Air Portugal	Portugal	100 %	unchanged
Tarom	Romania	n/a*	95 % / 96.95 %

* In 2002, these countries were not yet Member States of the EU.

a Data in this table reproduced (with permission) from *Association of European Airlines Yearbook 2002*, AEA Website. Available HTTP: <http://www.aea.be/sms/datafiles/yearbook02.pdf> (accessed 1 October 2011); *Association of European Airlines Yearbook 2007*, AEA Website. Available HTTP: <http://www.aea.be/sms/datafiles/yearbook07.pdf> (accessed 1 October 2011). *AEA Profile AEA 2010, AEA* website. Available HTTP: <http://files.aea.be/Downloads/PROFILES10.pdf> (accessed 1 October 2011).

b Post-merger with KLM in 2004.

c AZ was fully privatized in late-2008, the Air France-KLM Group taking a 25 per cent stake under a strategic partnership.

d Alitalia – Compagnia Aerea Italiana started operations in January 2009. (*Association of European Airlines Profiles 2010*, AEA website, p. 9. Available HTTP: http://files.aea.be/Downloads/PROFILES10.pdf (accessed September 2009)).

e Olympic Air started trading in October 2009 after acquiring assets from Olympic Airlines. (*Association of European Airlines Profiles 2010*, AEA website, p. 29. Available HTTP: <http://files.aea.be/Downloads/PROFILES10.pdf> (accessed 7 September 2011)).

start-up aid such as accommodation costs, subsistence and the recruitment of pilots and cabin crew.[244]

The Commission received a complaint in January 2002 concerning these advantages and concluded a formal investigation including contributions from 12 airlines, including Ryanair, airport management bodies and other parties. In its decision, *Charleroi*,[245] the

244 'Ryanair Under Fire at Charleroi', *EIRO*. Online. Available HTTP: <www.eiro.eurofound.eu.int/2003/12/inbrief/be0312302n.html> (accessed 5 May 2011).

245 [2003] OJ C 18/03. The Walloon Region of Belgium granted by private law contract 'infrastructure and operational aid'. In a landmark decision, some of the aid was declared compatible. Aid for the

Commission set out to determine whether the measures taken in favour of Ryanair by the Walloon Region and CRL were consistent with the private 'market economy' investor principle, which looks at the likelihood of a hypothetical private investor acting in the same manner as happened in the actual situation. Since this was not the case, the Commission determined that the benefits granted to Ryanair constituted state aid. Accordingly, the Commission looked to whether the aid granted to Ryanair was compatible with the common market. They found that, in the context of air transport policy, 'insofar as they permit the development and improved use of secondary airport infrastructure which is currently under used and represents a cost to the community as a whole', certain forms of aid could be allowed. So-called 'one-shot' incentives for the launch of new air routes, including marketing and publicity, should be allowed, but aid that takes the form of discounted airport service charges[246] (i.e. ground handling) could not be authorized.[247]

In February 2005, the Commission published its draft *Community guidelines on the financing of airports and start-up aid to airlines departing from regional airports*[248] for consultation. It has been argued by Völcker that the Draft Guidelines' statements on start-up aid 'seek to integrate the Commission's statements in [the 2004] *Charleroi* decision into a consistent state aid policy framework . . . [and] that such an attempt is highly problematic, given the absence of a coherent and objective justification for start-up aid in its proposed form'.[249]

Following a wide-ranging public consultation,[250] the Commission in September 2005 set out new limits for state aid to regional airports. In short, the new guidelines provide that no single airline should receive start-up aid[251] for using regional European airports that handle fewer than five million passengers annually. This is intended to encourage new routes to regional airports, while ensuring fair competition between airport operators and air carriers.[252] In a statement, then-Transport Commissioner and Vice-President of the Commission Jacques Barrot,[253] said: 'The European

Dublin-Charleroi route, reduced fees at Charleroi for Ryanair and others and one-shot incentives for new routes were declared incompatible with the competition rules.

246 The reduction was EUR 2 per passenger. *See* S. Smith, 'The Strategies and Effects of Low-Cost Carriers', *Steer Davies Gleave,* 2005 (available at www.icea.co.uk/archive.htm) as cited in Vasigh, Fleming and Tacker, *Introduction to Air Transport Economics,* p. 315.

247 Press Release, IP/04/157, 'The Commission's Decision on Charleroi airport promotes the activities of low-cost airlines and regional development', *Europa* (3 February 2004).

248 Press Release IP/05/149, 'Fair conditions of competition for regional airports: Commission launches consultation', *Europa* (8 February 2005).

249 S. Völcker, 'Start-Up Aid for Low Cost Carriers – A Policy Perspective', *Competition Law Insight* (Informa Professional) 4.6(3), 2005.

250 Press Release IP/05/149, 'Fair conditions of competition for regional airports: Commission launches consultation', *Europa* 8 February 2005.

251 The start-up aid may be granted for a maximum of three years (five years for those airports in lesser developed regions) to cover up between 30 and 50 per cent of costs associated with the opening of new routes or increasing frequencies of existing routes.

252 'Commission Sets Out Limits for State Aid to Regional Airports', *EU News and Policy Positions* (6 September 2005). Online. Available HTTP: <http://www.euractiv.com/en/transport/commission-sets-limits-state-aid-regional-airports/article-143875> (accessed 10 August 2011).

253 At the time of publication, the current Transport Commissioner is Mr Siim Kallas.

Commission wishes to encourage the development of regional and personal mobility. These new rules give regional airports the legal certainty they need for their future development and for their relations with airlines and the authorities'.[254]

Medium-sized airports handling between five and ten million passengers annually may receive subsidies on an exceptional basis. For larger airports, the Commission has deemed that state aid is outright unjustified. The Commission's approach appears to be reasonable given present conditions and their objective: to support more growth at smaller regional airports, promoting regional commerce and relieving, at least in the short-term, capacity restrictions at the larger Union airports.

US antitrust

The American approach

The US air transport market has undergone considerable changes since its deregulation in 1978. Suddenly for the first time exposed to 'free' market forces, carriers faced a new challenge: an economic version of Darwin's 'survival of the fittest'. As a result, the past two and a half decades have seen many new US carriers come and go, merge with or be acquired by competitors, and generally work quite diligently to improve efficiencies and cut costs independently and collectively. Competition in the sector has been robust for the most part, while instances of conduct in breach of antitrust policies have been numerous. These include class action suits on airline mergers, monopolization cases, so-called 'freeze-out' mergers and the issues surrounding airline stocks and airline cargo carrier cartel investigations.

Whilst the US air transport sector may seem to be a truly open market, its character as a public utility for transportation remains a significant influencing factor for American policymakers. In the context of 'public' transportation, American antitrust law has its foundations in trust and cartel investigations on the railway sector.[255] Originally, antitrust issues surrounded interstate commerce[256] and the transport of goods as the primary source of fast, reliable transportation.

The primary objectives of US antitrust laws are embodied in three broadly worded statutes: the Sherman Act of 1890,[257] which 'forbids both concerted conduct that unreasonably restrains trade and unlawful monopolisation'; the Clayton Act of 1914,[258] which 'forbids anti-competitive mergers and acquisitions'; and the Federal Trade

---

254 Press Release IP/05/1097, 'European Commission encourages the development of regional airports and mobility in Europe', *Europa* (6 September 2005).

255 *See* landmark cases involving railroads as the common carrier and the jurisprudential debate over 'public interest' and the 'liberty to contract' (doctrinal common-law) and state police power through eminent domain (constitutional): *Munn v Illinois* 94 U.S. 113 (1877) and *Chicago, Milwaukee and Saint Paul Railway v Minnesota* 134 U.S. 418 (1890). These cases illustrate federal powers to investigate trusts and cartels in the context of interstate railroads under 14th Amendment of the US Constitution on state police powers. This is, as Peritz argues in *Competition Policy in America*, the foundation of US antitrust ideology.

256 *See* the Interstate Commerce Act 1877.

257 15 U.S.C. §1.

258 15 U.S.C. §12.

Commission Act of 1914,[259] which gives the Federal Trade Commission 'authority to prevent firms and individuals from engaging in unfair methods of competition'.

According to the US Supreme Court, the fundamental purpose of antitrust law

> is not to protect businesses from the working of the market; it is to protect the public from the failure of the market. The law directs itself not against conduct which is competitive, even severely so, but against conduct which unfairly tends to destroy competition itself. It does so not out of solicitude for private concerns but out of concern for the public interest.[260]

This viewpoint would appear to go hand-in-hand with deregulation theory, which suggests that deregulation leads to an increase in efficiency of an industry at lower costs, the savings from which are then passed on to consumers. Good, or even robust, competition is integral to any deregulated sector and the antitrust law seems to step in to oversee that competition remains fair and the market is allowed to work for itself.

Sherman Antitrust and Clayton Acts

The Sherman Antitrust Act[261] provides that 'every contract, combination in the form of trust or otherwise, or conspiracy, in restraint of trade or commerce among the several States, or with foreign nations, is declared to be illegal'[262] and that 'every person who shall monopolize, or attempt to monopolize, or combine or conspire with any other person or persons, or with foreign nationals, shall be deemed guilty of a *felony*'.[263] This approach, much unlike that in Europe, makes anti-competitive behaviour both at home and with foreign counterparts a criminal offence. This serves as a deterring reminder that 'trusts' are not to be tolerated under American law, and that those entering into agreements or other coordinated or cooperative behaviour should rather 'think twice'.

The Foreign Trade Antitrust Improvements Act of 1982[264] was enacted as an amendment to the Sherman Antitrust Act. It provides certain conditions that must be fulfilled in order for the Sherman Antitrust Act to apply to conduct involving trade or commerce with foreign nations. Nonetheless, it should be noted that US Federal courts have often disagreed over the extraterritorial scope of the Sherman Antitrust Act. The US Supreme Court has applied the Act to foreign defendants, when some of the 'conduct' under investigation occurred on US territory.[265] This is particularly relevant in the

---

259 15 U.S.C. §41.

260 *Spectrum Sports Inc v McQuillan* 506 U.S. 447, 458 (1993).

261 15 U.S.C. §§1–7, 2.7.1890.

262 15 U.S.C. §1.

263 15 U.S.C. §2 (emphasis added).

264 §7, Sherman Act, 15 U.S.C. §6a.

265 *See United States v Sisal Sales Corp*, 274 U.S. 268, 275–76, 71 L. Ed. 1042, 47 S. Ct. 592 (1927). In this case it was alleged that US companies conspired with Mexican counterparts to monopolize the importation of sisal. The alleged infringement was in the US and therefore US antitrust rules were applicable. However, this case demonstrates that antitrust has extraterritorial limits.

scope of international airlines and the cross-border agreements they form. Although the Sherman Act has suffered immeasurable scrutiny from the moment it was proposed, it has remained in force and should therefore be regarded as potentially applicable to international cooperative 'conduct' and any subsequent agreements.

The Clayton Act[266] of 1914 prohibits discrimination in price,[267] services or facilities; discrimination in rebates,[268] discounts, or advertising service charges, or underselling in particular localities, or penalties; cooperative association[269]; and sales on agreement not to use goods of competitor.[270] The language used in the Clayton Act is noticeably less aggressive than that found in the Sherman Act, and it certainly more resembles that used in the competition rules found under EU law.

US antitrust immunity

Antitrust exemption procedures also remain regulated. Prior to the enactment of the ADA, the CAB had the sole authority to approve and immunize agreements affecting international air transportation. Under the amended Act, however, the authority to grant antitrust immunity to agreements between US and foreign carriers was transferred to the US DoT in 1984; however, the US DoJ reviews domestic airline mergers, acquisitions and interlocking directorates under the antitrust laws, much the same as it does in other industries.

The US DoT also gained the responsibility for overseeing and maintaining essential air service, for instance on regional routes to small communities. Under the auspices of their US DoT's Essential Air Service programme, the US DoT may grant certain subsidies to airlines to operate services to smaller airports, which might be otherwise unprofitable, in a similar fashion to the EU PSOs discussed above.

Safety programmes and criteria are centrally managed by the FAA, which has been the case since 1958. It should also be noted that the US Congress began taking steps towards parallel deregulation of the air cargo sector from as early as 1977. Deregulation and liberalization of the air transport industry, supported by the World Trade Organization (WTO) agreements and other regional accords with the EU, North American Free Trade Agreement (NAFTA) and the Association of South East Asian Nations (ASEAN), for instance, have contributed to an immense growth in the air cargo industry.[271]

The situation post-deregulation

One year following deregulation of the US air transport sector, the International Air Transportation Competition Act of 1979 amended the Federal Aviation Act of 1958. In a speech, then-President Jimmy Carter discussed the new legislation's objectives:

266 15 U.S.C. §§12–27, U.S.C. §§52–53, 15.10.1914.
267 15 U.S.C. §13.
268 15 U.S.C. §13(a).
269 15 U.S.C. §13(b).
270 15 U.S.C. §14.
271 'The TIACA Manifesto', The International Air Cargo Association. Online. Available HTTP: <http://www.tiaca.org/content/chapter1.asp> (accessed 10 September 2011). In addition to the EU, there

This legislation affirms and strengthens our commitment to deregulation. The bill reduces statutory barriers against the entry of individual carriers into new international markets and authorizes carriers to change their fares within a zone of reasonableness without interference from the Civil Aeronautics Board. The bill also authorizes the Board and the President to take quick and effective countermeasures against a foreign government that engages in discriminatory or anti-competitive practices against American carriers or tries to impair their operating rights.[272]

According to Kahn, the two main consequences of deregulation of the US air transport sector have been positive: lower fares and higher productivity. The hub-and-spoke model,[273] a direct result of deregulation, created an industry operating structure from which main carriers operated from one or more 'hubs' to smaller non-hubs, on what are known as 'spoke' routes. The prices on more frequently served routes (for instance hub-to-hub, hub-to-mini hub or hub-to-competitors' hub) are generally lower than those on thinner routes (hub-to-spoke). This follows economic theory in that the cost to the airline of operating the thinner routes, both in terms of smaller planes and fewer passengers, are much higher with the demand much lower than those where there is steady demand and availability of aircraft.

Furthermore, in terms of increased productivity, Kahn noted that

> deregulation has compelled improvements in efficiency through the intense pressures of the price competition it unleashed. Carriers have put more seats on their planes – the average went up from 136.9 in 1977 to 153.1 in 1988 – and succeeded in filling a greater percentage of those seats – from an average of 52.6 per cent in the ten years before 1978 to 61.0 per cent in the twelve years after.[274]

The less positive consequences of deregulation, according to Kahn, are seen in the tendencies towards increased concentrations between firms and price discrimination.

exist a number of other labour and regional trade agreements, which might also deserve further investigation in the airline context. They are the Dominican Republic–Central America Free Trade Agreement (DR-CAFTA), US–Jordan Free Trade Agreement (JFTA), US–Australia Free Trade Agreement (FTA), Union of South American Nations (UNASUL), AFTA (ASEAN Free Trade Area), African Union (AU), Greater Arab Free Trade Area (GAFTA), South Asian Free Trade Area (SAFTA), Trans-Pacific Strategic Economic Partnership (TP SEP), Pacific Regional Trade Agreement (PARTA), Caribbean Community (CARICOM) and Central American Common Market (CACM). (Vasigh, Fleming and Tacker, *Introduction to Air Transport Economics*, pp. 143–151).

272 Speech by President Jimmy Carter, 'International Air Transportation Competition Act Statement on Signing S. 1300 Into Law', 15 February 1980, University of California at Santa Barbara Presidency Project. Online. Available HTTP: <http://www.presidency.ucsb.edu/ws/index.php?pid=32939#> (accessed 10 March 2011).

273 Also known as the spoke-hub distribution paradigm pioneered by FedEx founder Fred Smith in the mid-1970s.

274 A.E. Kahn, 'Airline Deregulation', *The Concise Encyclopaedia of Economics,* Library of Economics and Liberty. Online. Available HTTP: website at <http://www.econlib.org/library/Enc/Airline Deregulation.html> (accessed 11 September 2011).

'By wiping out all these restrictions [i.e. deregulating] and freeing carriers to enter any market, deregulation produced an estimated 25 per cent increase in the average number of airlines per route despite the recent mergers'.[275] Because most hubs can only adequately accommodate as a hub one airline, the history of the US air transport sector post-deregulation has seen many airlines come and go, some merging, but most being acquired by bigger prior competitors. As a potential remedy, Kahn argues that if the government agencies assigned the tasks of ensuring fair competition in the sector would not neglect their responsibilities, by for instance enforcing antitrust laws on mergers and other 'concentration' behaviour, the frequency of concentrations would be diminished and the subsequent anti-competitive effects reduced or reversed.

Indeed, two decades after the ADA, the US air transport sector had 'matured' in its deregulated market state to the extent that efficiency could be measured and evidence of the abuse of market power existed. The US government stepped up re-regulation at a time when some discipline seemed appropriate and necessary. The US DoT responded with new rules to prevent price predation at 'hub' airports,[276] the US DoJ scrutinized proposed mergers and international cooperation (e.g. alliances[277]) and began to exercise its power to deny those 'arrangements' that threatened competition.

To that end, and to contend with Kahn, there have been a number of antitrust policy adjustments made in the form of refusing mergers and other 'concentrations' and at the very least requiring certain amendments to the terms of such arrangements to ensure they are pro-competitive. A middle road for good public policy may be an unobtainable goal, as critics and supporters of policy measures will debate endlessly over the correct course. There will always be problems with deregulation, which its advocates sometimes fail to realize and accept, whereas advocates of regulation sometimes refuse to acknowledge the positive efficiency improvements under deregulation.[278]

US and IATA

The CAB approved the organization of IATA in 1946 under the IATA Traffic Conference Resolution.[279] It was founded by the then-major international airlines, with the goals of promoting international air transportation and providing a means for industry collaboration.[280] In 1955, the CAB granted indefinite approval to the IATA after several one-year temporary approvals.[281] Before the passage of the ADA,

---

275 Ibid.

276 Department of Transportation, Docket No. OST 98–3713.

277 The first of which to be 'remedied' was that relationship between British Airways and AA in 1999.

278 M. Cooper, 'Freeing Public Policy from the Deregulation Debate: The Airline Industry Comes of Age (and Should Be Held Accountable for Its Anti-Competitive Behaviour)', Consumer Federation of America Paper, 1999, p.2. Online. Available HTTP: <http://www.consumerfed.org/pdfs/abaair1.pdf> (accessed 2 June 2011).

279 6 CAB §639 (1945).

280 *See* the IATA website, www.iata.org.

281 CAB Order E-9305, 15 June 1955.

agreements affecting foreign air transport were approved and immunized by the CAB under broad public interest standards. Following the passage of the ADA, IATA amended its previous agreement, known as the 'Provisions for the Conduct of the IATA Traffic Conferences'.[282] The US DoT has since been exercising its regulatory oversight over the provisions of operation of the tariff conferences.[283]

US major air carriers have delegated the licensing of travel agents to their trade association, IATA. As such, all US travel agencies must have an IATA licence to access reservation systems of US-based airlines. In 2002, a number of *Travel Agencies*[284] brought a class action suit against four major US airlines[285] and IATA, alleging that the defendants illegally conspired to lower their sales commissions. At the July 1999 IATA Passenger Tariff Coordinating Conference in Montreal, Canada, an alliance made up of several principal Central American airlines announced it would only pay Central American travel agents a 6 per cent commission, rather than previously enjoyed variable commissions of up to 11 per cent. The next day, a number of other airlines followed suit.

The District Court held that the Federal Trade Antitrust Improvements Act[286] deprived it of subject matter jurisdiction, thereby barring the plaintiff's claim. A Federal Court of Appeals affirmed, on statutory interpretation, that the Act bars the plaintiff's proposed Sherman Act class action. The Court of Appeal considered whether the conduct in fact involves 'trade or commerce (other than import trade or import commerce) with foreign nations[287] [and] . . . whether [the] defendants' conduct has a direct, substantial, and reasonably foreseeable' anti-competitive effect on United States commerce and whether that conduct gives rise to a Sherman Act claim.[288]

On the first question, it was held that the plaintiffs could not demonstrate that the defendants' conduct reduced the import of goods or services into the US. In addition, the defendants were not involved in 'import trade or import commerce',[289] but rather 'conduct involving trade or commerce (other than import trade or import commerce) with foreign nations'.[290]

US government bailouts

Following the terrorist acts of 11 September 2001, then-President Bush signed into law the Air Transportation Safety and System Stabilization Act[291] establishing among

---

282 *See* CAB Order 80–4–113 for a description of the amendment.

283 *See* DOT Order 88–3–67, 31 March 1988.

284 SA. Truicentro; Centro America Travel Agencie, Ltd; Negocios Globo, SA; Fronteras del Aire, SA (on behalf of themselves and those similarly situated).

285 AA, DL, CO and UA.

286 15 U.S.C. §6(a).

287 Ibid.

288 *Travel Agencies* 303 F.3d 293, 2002 US App LEXIS 18467; 2002–2 Trade Cas (CCH) P73, 795; 1 ALR Fed 2d 719.

289 15 U.S.C. §6(a).

290 Ibid.

291 Public Law 107–42, 22.9.2001.

other things the Air Transportation Stabilization Board. The Board has the authority to issue independently up to USD 10 billion in Federal credit instrument-based subsidies such as loan guarantees to airlines. Applications for loan guarantees were subject to the Air Carrier Guarantee Loan Program Regulations,[292] which list the minimum requirements and application procedures under the 'Aviation Disaster Relief–Air Carrier Guarantee Loan Program'. Applications by air carriers were accepted between 12 October 2001 and 28 June 2002. Air carrier borrowers, or 'obligors' as referred to in the Regulations, were required to submit evidence that they fulfilled all the relevant criteria under the Act, a statement to the effect that the carrier was not under bankruptcy protection,[293] copies of financial statements,[294] evaluations and forecasts,[295] and a business plan detailing how the loan will be used for the operational needs of the carrier.[296]

Section 101(a)(2) of the Act gave Presidential power through the Executive Order to compensate air carriers through direct grants of up to USD 5 billion[297] for direct losses incurred during the grounding of aircraft from 11 September 2001 and incremental losses which followed up to 31 December 2001.

The first application was received by America West Airlines on 13 November 2001, which was approved for a USD 429 million loan supported by the Federal loan guarantee.[298] Subsequent applications made by Evergreen International Airlines, AQ, Frontier Airlines (F9), America Trans Air (AT), US Airways and World Airways were all approved.[299] Applications were denied by the Board for UA, Gemini Air Cargo, Great Plains Airlines, MED jet International Airlines, Corporate Airlines, National Airlines, Spirit Airlines, Frontier Flying Service and Vanguard Airlines.[300]

In the case of America West Airlines, the Board was issued with a warrant to purchase 18.8 million shares at USD 3 per share under the provisions of the loan guarantee, representing a third of the company's common stock. When the Board approved the merger of America West with US Airways in 2005 and the loan was

---

292 Under §101(a)(1) of the Air Transportation Safety and System Stabilization Act, 14 CFR Chapter VI and Part 1300, Federal Register Vol. 66 No.198, 12.10.2001, pp. 52270–52275.

293 §1300.16(5).

294 §1300.16(6).

295 §1300.16(7).

296 §1300.16(8), paras (i) and (iv).

297 The amount of an affected air carrier's direct and incremental losses is to be determined according to the product of USD 4.5 million and the ratio of available seat miles to the actual total available seat miles in August 2001. (§103(a)(2)(A) of the Act).

298 US Treasury website. Available HTTP: <http://www.ustreas.gov/offices/domestic-finance/atsb/recent-activity.shtml> (accessed 12 September 2011).

299 Ibid.; most of these loans were conditionally approved. The conditions usually included a resubmission of business plans or other documentary evidence. However, the Board considered warrants of various percentages of the applicants' reorganized equity offered to the US government in the application, subject to the government's own (business and legal) due diligence. In the case of US Airways, this was agreed at 10 per cent (Letter from the Board to then President and CEO of US Airways, David Siegel. Online. Available HTTP: <fl1.findlaw.com/news.findlaw.com/hdocs/docs/usair/ats-busair21103ltr.pdf> (accessed 1 July 2011)).

300 Ibid.

repaid in full, the Board cashed out the shares at the accrued stock price of USD 9 per share. It has been argued that through similar conditions on loan guarantees to airlines granted under the Act, commonly referred to as the 'bailout bill' or 'Corzine-Fitzgerald Amendment',[301] the Board 'earned' the Treasury roughly USD 130 million in profits.[302] Whilst this is controversial and might be viewed as a 'bailout bounty', the magnitude of the loans guaranteed by the US government in this 'lucrative' case and others validates to some degree the Board's protectionist intention to mitigate the Treasury and taxpayer losses. For instance, when US Airways filed for protection under Chapter 11[303] in September 2004, the Board became more intensely involved in the airline's restructuring and with the bankruptcy court 'to ensure that the taxpayers' interests [were] protected'.[304] This does not seem unreasonable from the Board's perspective and helps to substantiate the purchase and subsequent sale of warrants.

Foreign ownership rules

US rules on foreign ownership of companies have befallen much criticism over the years, especially in the face of liberalization and globalization. The current restriction on foreign ownership of US airlines stands at 25 per cent of the controlling stock and 49 per cent of the total stock. This limitation proves difficult to the forging of international relationships within the industry, in particular international joint ventures and of course multinational mergers, as it demonstrates a high level of risk for any significant investment. Investment in US airlines is controlled by the Federal Aviation Act of 1958, which only permits aircraft registered[305] in the US the domestic air carriage of passengers and cargo.[306] Yet the only two industries located in which foreign ownership is so heavily restricted are the airline industry and broadcasting.[307] In 1998, automobile manufacturers Daimler–Benz (Germany) and Chrysler (US) merged to become a new company, Daimler Chrysler. This serves as an example of a successful international merger, in organized labour no less, for a key US industry and manufacturer. The arguments against increasing foreign ownership of US carriers typically include national security issues supported by the US Department of Defense, safety

---

301 This represents the names of the Congressmen who presented it.

302 The information in this paragraph is taken from J. Birger, 'The Bailout Bounty', *Fortune* 155(4), 2007 24–26.

303 Chapter 11 of the US Bankruptcy Code providing (generally) for reorganization. (11 U.S.C. §§301, 303).

304 US Treasury website, Press Room. Online. Available HTTP: <http://www.ustreas.gov/press/releases/js1902.htm> (accessed 3 October 2011).

305 Registration of an aircraft is limited to US citizens, partnerships in which all partners are US citizens or US registered corporations in which the CEO and two-thirds of the directors are US citizens and 75 per cent of the controlling stock is held by US citizens.

306 49 U.S.C. §§40101–49101, 41101; 14 C.F.R. §§211–298.

307 The Communications Act of 1934 (47 U.S.C. §310(b)) prohibits the Federal Communications Commission from granting radio or television broadcast licenses to foreign governments, individuals, corporations or other entities.

issues, labour group objections and restrictions in existing international bilateral avia-tion agreements.[308]

In the November 2005 round of 'open skies' negotiations with the EU, the US was presented with demands to change the restrictions on foreign ownership.[309] The US DoT has proposed new rules allowing foreign interests to control US airlines, but in June 2006, the US House of Representatives rejected the bill, 291 to 137. The US DoT was expected to announce new rules governing the ownership of US carriers in August 2006, but the Bush administration delayed its new rules as it is caught up in a struggle over executive power and Congressional legislative power to change existing restrictions.

Many US airlines, including United Airlines, support the proposed rule. The American Federation of Labor and Congress of Industrial Organizations (AFL-CIO) Transport Trades Department, Air Pilots Association and a number of Congress-men, however, starkly object to the proposal, saying it 'is not good for the US avia-tion industry and would threaten the jobs and rights of thousands of workers'.[310] There is fear that, if amended, the rules could lead to another 'Dubai situation'.[311] In Europe, airports operator BAA in the UK accepted a GBP 10.3 billion takeover bid by Spanish consortium *Ferrovial* in August 2006.[312] In March 2009, the UK Competi-tion Commission ordered BAA to sell LGW, STN and either Edinburgh (EDI) or Glasgow (GLA) airports[313] as the common ownership gives rise to adverse effects on competition. The UK Enterprise Act 2002 requires the UK Competition Commis-sion to carry out investigations into whether competition is prevented, restricted or distorted in connection with the supply or acquisition of any good or service in the UK or part of the UK.

308 M. Whitaker, 'Liberalized Airline Ownership and Control: Good for Consumers, Airlines and the United States', Seminar paper for AT Conf/5, 2003, ICAO Worldwide Air Transport Conference, 22–23 March 2003; *See also* R. Abeyratne, 'Competition and Predation: Legal Aspects', in Forsyth, Gillen, Mayer and Niemeier (eds), *Competition versus Predation*, pp. 57–77.

309 The existing update 'open skies' agreements do not require a change in the foreign ownership restric-tions to be successfully performed, however the EU is increasing pressure on Member States to relin-quish control of their bilateral agreements under the Union agenda. The 2005 round of negotiations was unsuccessful.

310 M. Hall, 'House Rejects Foreign Ownership of US Airlines – But the Fight Isn't Over', *AFL-CIO* (15 June 2006). Online. Available HTTP: <http://blog.aflcio.org/2006/06/15/house-rejects-foreign-ownership-of-us-airlines%E2%80%94but-the-fight-isn%E2%80%99t-over/>.

311 DP World, owned by the Dubai government, took over a British company that manages terminals at several US ports, to which the US Congress reacted to ban it for security reasons, even though it almost immediately announced that it would sell its US operations to a US entity. (A. Zwaniecki 'House Approves Moratorium on Airline Foreign Ownership Rule', 2006, American Information Web website, HTTP: <http://usinfo.org/wf-archive/2006/060317/epf507.htm> (accessed 12 August 2011)).

312 BAA Website, www.baa.com.

313 'BAA Airports Market Investigation: A Report on the Supply of Airport Services by the BAA in the UK', UK Competition Commission, 19 March 2009 (final). Online. Available HTTP: <http://www.competition-commission.org.uk/rep_pub/reports/2009/fulltext/545.pdf> (accessed 12 July 2011).

The Oberstar Bill

Congressman James L. Oberstar in February 2009 introduced a bill to study the effects of airline alliances and antitrust immunity on consumers, questioning whether the perceived benefits outweighed the loss of competition.[314] Oberstar saw such joint ventures as *de facto* mergers, and pointed towards evidence suggesting that the granting of antitrust immunity would lead to less competition and a loss of consumer welfare.[315]

In May 2009, Christine Varney, head of the Department of Justice, spoke before the Chamber of Commerce and announced that the Obama administration would be taking a tougher line than the previous administration towards antitrust. In particular, they would reverse the policy on single firm conduct under Section 2 of the Sherman Act that had been employed by the Bush administration. She rejected the economic arguments behind self-regulation and self-policing, condemning such passive approaches, and was adamant that consumer welfare ought to be protected, rather than simply focusing on efficiency of the dominant players on the market.[316]

For all this tough rhetoric, the actions by the US DoJ have not shown as much resolve. In July 2009, the already immunized Star Alliance was granted permission to expand and bring CO into its network.[317] Star Alliance claimed that adding CO would allow it to 'increase the range of competitive service options available to passengers . . . generate new online service and routing options for millions of passengers . . . [and] lower fares to more than 15 million annual passengers in . . . nearly 43,000 global airport-pairs'.[318] As a condition, however, the US DoT carved out four non-stop overlaps, namely the NYC–Stockholm, Lisbon, Geneva and Copenhagen routes.[319] On the grounds that the oneworld alliance in turn applied for antitrust immunity, the US DoJ thought this might have anti-competitive effects and rejected the application.[320] It might actually have created more competition in the market by allowing oneworld, one of three major global alliances, to compete more effectively with the other two. A study using data from between 2005–10 found that a reduction in one competitor in the market for non-stop transatlantic routes led to an increase in fares of 7 per cent,[321] but whether this can be applied to the global networks is yet unclear. In any

---

314 Statement of the Honourable James L. Oberstar, 'A Bill to Ensure Adequate Airline Competition Between the United States and Europe', H.R. 831, 111th Cong. (3 February 2009).

315 V. Bilotkach and K. Huschelrath, 'Antitrust Immunity for Airline Alliances', *Journal of Competition Law and Economics*, 7(2), 2011, 335–380.

316 R. Miller, and J. Chua (eds), *Airlines – 2009 World Wide Competition Law Review*. A Civil Aviation Authority (CAA) policy document. Online. Available HTTP: <http://www.caa.co.uk/default.aspx?catid=5&pagetype=90&pageid=6264> (accessed 18 July 2011). Contributions by: Joanne Young and David Kirstein.

317 B. Bradshaw and B. Patel, 'Final Descent? The Future of Antitrust Immunity in International Aviation', *GCP: ANTITRUST CHRON* 1, 2010, 1–8.

318 DOT-OST-2008-0234-0001, pp. 33, 35, 37.

319 W. Gillespie and O.M. Richard, *Antitrust Immunity and International Airline Alliances*, Economic Analysis Group Discussion Paper, Antitrust Division, U.S. Department of Justice, Washington D.C., EAG 11–1, February 2011.

320 Comments of the Dep't of Justice, DOT-OST-2008-0252 (21 December 2009).

321 Gillespie and Richard, *Antitrust Immunity and International Airline Alliances*, p. 2

case, while this evidence would suggest antitrust immunity is not a good policy to begin with, it certainly does not justify granting it only to selective alliances. Perhaps realizing this, oneworld were finally granted antitrust immunity by the US DoT in 2010, after they had divested four slots at LHR.[322]

Conclusion

After several rounds of failed negotiations and whilst the 2007 (stage one) agreement did not address the issue of reform of US rules on airline ownership and control, the EU and US signed a protocol to amend the first stage agreement that entered into provisional application in 2010, which 'includes a commitment to engage in progress towards such reform'.[323] Article 21 of the EU–US Air Transport Agreement reads:

> The Parties commit to the shared goal of continuing to remove market access barriers in order to maximise benefits for consumers, airline, labour, and communities on both sides of the Atlantic, including enhancing the access of their airlines to global capital markets, so as better to reflect the realities of a global aviation industry, the strengthening of the transatlantic air transportation system, and the establishment of a framework that will encourage other countries to open up their own air services markets . . . The Joint Committee shall develop a process of cooperation in this regard including appropriate recommendations to the Parties.[324]

In a press release on this topic, the European Commission said:

> When the United States changes its legislation to allow EU investors majority ownership of US airlines, the EU will reciprocally allow major ownership of EU airlines by US investors and US airlines will benefit from additional market access rights to and from the EU.[325]

This chapter has investigated the legal situation in the context of 'regulatory regimes' in Europe post-liberalization and in the United States post-deregulation.[326] This investigation provides a framework for understanding the intentions of regulators

---

322 DOT Order 2010-7-8.

323 Press release IP/10/371, 'Breakthrough in the EU–US second-stage Open Skies negotiations: Vice-President Kallas welcomes draft agreement', *Europa* (25 March 2010).

324 Article 21 of the EU–US Air Transport Agreement, as amended by the Second Stage Agreement (Protocol amending the First Stage Agreement) on 24 March 2010.

325 Press release IP/10/371, 'Breakthrough in the EU–US second-stage Open Skies negotiations: Vice-President Kallas welcomes draft agreement', *Europa* (25 March 2010).

326 Deregulation and liberalization of the two air transport sectors are accepted as 'achieved' in the classical sense. *See* Rhoades, D.L. 'State of US Aviation: Clinging to Old Ways in a New Century', in O'Connell and Williams (eds), *Air Transport in the 21st Century*, pp. 97–111.

ng rules to promote or protect pro-competitive practices in a free mar-
. On review of the varied approaches taken by European and American
ith reference to competition rules and antitrust legislation through con-
market re-regulation – representing the current 'state of the law' – the
s revealed. The European competition rules have a very proactive and pre-
r *ex ante* character, insofar as they hold the airlines accountable through
a qu... :lf-regulation for numerous aspects of the airline business in the form of
sector-specific legislation. In the US, the duty to 'play fair' on the part of airlines is
far more reactive, as breaches of antitrust law are dealt with upon petition. Thus it
could be said that while dissimilarities between EU competition rules and US antitrust
are many, these policy approaches have been shaped by the mixed deregulation and
liberalization policies, influenced by a myriad of economic principles considered by
regulators, their separate environments and historical developments.

The issuance of grants and other loan guarantees by US authorities to American
air carriers and the approval of state aid to European airlines despite the Union's
transport policy objective of creating conditions for fair and equitable competition
suggest an unreasonable level of intervention from the standpoint of competition. It
is accepted that keeping (sufficient) airlines in business is also important to consumers and therefore also to competition. It should be remembered that the European air
transport market has in particular been characterized by national flag carriers operated
under the mandate and with the financial backing of respective national governments.
This suggests some rationale behind some ethereal state 'obligation' to offer their
flag carriers different forms of state aid. Yet there is now a single market for Union
air transport and by law, these flag-loyalties should no longer be acted upon in such
a fashion. It could be asked whether 'national pride' is in fact a justifiable means of
supporting or indeed preserving an inefficient or failing flag carrier. In a deregulated
sector, 'the flag carrier is free to market itself to travelers on the basis of national pride
– if consumers feel it is important to support the flag carrier they can do so'.[327] If they
do not, it must follow that consumers in question do not value this 'national pride' in
line with the price they are prepared to pay for the premium.

The post-2008 era has seen the biggest downturn in the aviation market since the
serious downturn following the 11th September terrorist attacks. The number of
flights in 2010 was 14 per cent lower than it would have been had the pre 2008 trend
continued; Eurocontrol estimate in total about five years of growth has been lost.[328]
This will only be compounded by the increasing capacity constraints at many of the
busiest airports, with only Frankfurt/Main (FRA) expanding sufficiently to cope
with growing demand.[329] Thus it seems likely airlines will continue to pursue a policy
of cooperation in an effort to reap higher efficiencies, and the market will become

---

327 Vasigh, Fleming and Tacker, *Introduction to Air Transport Economics*, p. 137.
328 S.D. Gleave *Impact Assessment of Revisions to Regulation 95/93, Final Report (Section 1–12)*. European Commission, March 2011, p. 2. Online. Available HTTP: <http://ec.europa.eu/transport/air/studies/
doc/airports/2011-03-impact-assessment-revisions-regulation-95-93.pdf> (accessed 20 July 2011).
329 Ibid.

increasingly amalgamated. In the transatlantic market at present, 82 per cent of the market share is held by three groups of carriers with antitrust immunity – one from each of the major alliances, SkyTeam, oneworld, and Star.[330] This concentration is significant when one considers that in 1995, 13 independent carriers with a market share of at least 2 per cent were operating on the transatlantic market.[331] Whether these joint ventures are beneficial to the consumer has been a matter of intense debate, with much regulatory activity occurring on both sides of the Atlantic.

Looking towards the future with the economic and social forces of globalization in focus, the opening up of air transport through multilateral open skies agreements and other standardized air service agreements offers new competitive benefits. These include actual or constructive[332] market entry, increased capacities, and direct competition between firms on a global scale that raises industry standards and levels of innovation.

'Liberalization' and 'deregulation' are not to be taken as the simple act of 'privatizing' and removing governmental control from a sector. Indeed there are economic[333] and social dimensions that build on the post-deregulatory re-regulation, as has been shown in this chapter. Thus the incentive to cooperate, whether the rationale is strategic (voluntary) or defensive (involuntary in the face of demise), is far more complex than originally estimated. With respect to the regulatory environments in the EU and US as reviewed, the sheer multitude of regulatory instrumentalities creates a confusing state of the law. Being mindful that the air transport sector possesses unique characteristics with which no other industry may sufficiently compete, there is a persuasive impetus to conduct a study into the phenomenon of strategic, increasingly intimate alliance-forming within this 'regulatory space'.[334]

Furthermore, the US and European approaches to market regulation and 'workable competition' are divergent. American firms are permitted to compete aggressively, whereas European firms are expected to maintain competition on certain relevant markets and generally to deal with rivals. Although a firm in a position of dominance in a market seems unimportant for either system of market regulation, the firm's distorting of competition through any prohibited behaviours will constitute a breach under EU law but not necessarily under US law. Although this chapter has focused

---

330 DOT Order 2010-2-8 at 14, cited in Gillespie, William and Richard, Oliver M. *Antitrust Immunity and International Airline Alliances*. Economic Analysis Group Discussion Paper, Antitrust Division, U.S. Department of Justice, Washington D.C., EAG 11–1, February 2011.

331 Bilotkach and Huschelrath, 'Antitrust Immunity for Airline Alliances', p. 360.

332 Accesses to national markets through code share agreements support this point.

333 Instances of this introduced in this chapter include the deregulation of airfares and air cargo rates, slot allocation, computer reservations systems, the standardization of air service agreements and to some extent a relaxation of the rules on foreign ownership. *See* Regulation (EC) No 1008/2008 of the European Parliament and of the Council of 24 September 2008, on common rules for the operation of air services in the Community (Recast), [2008] OJ L293/3, 31 October 2008.

334 *See* C. Scott, 'Analysing Regulatory Space: Fragmented Resources and Institutional Design', *Public Law*, 2001, 329–353; R. Baldwin, M. Cave, and M. Lodge 'Introduction: Regulation – The field and the developing agenda', in Baldwin, Cave and Lodge, *Oxford Handbook of Regulation*, pp. 3–16.

on market regulation, it is thought that regulation of airports[335] at the US Federal or EU level would have a significant impact on the liberalization and deregulation of the air transport sectors. The positive experience of the opening up the ground handling market in the EU under the Ground Handling Directive[336] and the Commission's 'Airport Package'[337] communication under the Lisbon Agenda and the EU's 'Transport 2030' White Paper suggest that steps towards efficiency through airport regulation, innovation and environmental thinking is underway.[338]

335 For a study on 'Reforming Airport Regulation', using the UK as the case study, *see* Starkie, *Aviation Markets: Studies in Competition and Regulatory Reform*, pp. 51–67.

336 Directive 96/97/EC on access to the ground handling market at Community airports, [1996] OJ L 302, 26 November 1996. Ground handling was most recently dealt with in Regulation (EC) No 1008/2008 of the European Parliament and of the Council of 24 September 2008, on common rules for the operation of air services in the Community (Recast), [2008] OJ L293/3, 31 October 2008.

337 The package consists of three key initiatives: 'a proposal for a directive on airport charges, a communication on airport capacity, efficiency and safety in Europe and a report on the implementation of the ground handling directive'. (Commission Communication of 24 January 2007 to the Council, the European Parliament, the European Economic and Social Committee and the Committee of the Regions entitled 'An action plan for airport capacity, efficiency and safety in Europe', COM (2006) 819 final.) *See also* Press Release IP/07/78, 'Commission proposes a landmark regulatory package for airlines', *Europa* (24 January 2007).

338 European Commission, 'White Paper: Road map to a Single European Transport Area – Towards a competitive and resource efficient transport system', COM (2011) 144 Final, Brussels, 28 March 2011.

5 The development of tactical and strategic alliances

Progress and challenges

Introduction

In this chapter, the perceptions of how deregulation impacts on airlines and the industry *vis-à-vis* the current regulatory regimes in the EU and US identified in the preceding chapters will be rigorously questioned, challenged and tested against the measures devised and taken by airlines to 'cope' in the liberalized environment.

Airlines have devised and adopted several tactical and strategic commercial measures[1] over the past three decades, with the expressed objective of increased competitiveness and economic efficiency, e.g. mergers,[2] global alliances, codeshare and block-space agreements, franchising, links between frequent flyer programmes, management contracts, and joint ventures in catering, ground handling and aircraft maintenance.[3] These multilateral cooperative ventures and agreements come as responsive 'solutions' to the regulation and the perceived impediment to the industry's economic objectives. The two key benefits to tactical and strategic alliances are expanded and optimized route networks, cost reductions in maintenance and operational activities, or so-called 'one-roof initiatives'.[4]

Consider this hypothetical example: BA cannot merge with AA[5] owing to restrictions on US foreign ownership and antitrust laws, but they have entered into bilateral

---

1 The distinction between the words tactical and strategic as used here is adopted from a report on transatlantic airline alliances. Whereas strategic alliances are global multilateral alliances, 'tactical alliances often involve at least one independent carrier that is not a member of a larger strategic alliance' (European Commission and Department of US Transportation (ECDOT), *Transatlantic Airline Alliances: Competitive Issues and Regulatory Approaches*, A report by the European Commission and the United States Department of Transportation (16 November 2010), p. 4. Online. Available HTTP: <http://ec.europa.eu/competition/sectors/transport/reports/joint_alliance_report.pdf> (accessed 2 August 2011)).

2 *See* cases mentioned above including *Sabena and Swissair* (1995) *and Lufthansa and SAS* (1996) for examples of codeshare agreements/mergers between carriers.

3 These are categorized alternatively as: 'cost sharing ventures, asset pools, pro rate agreements, codeshare agreements, feeder, marketing alliances, joint ventures, integrated feeder and equity stakes' (B. Kleymann and H. Seristö *Managing Strategic Airline Alliances* (Aldershot: Ashgate, 2004) pp. 12–15).

4 B. Vasigh, K. Fleming and T. Tacker, *Introduction to Air Transport Economics* (Farnham: Ashgate, 2008), p. 171–172.

5 In fact, British Airways and AA attempted to merge in 2001, but competition authorities on both sides of the Atlantic denied the merger. This merger attempt shall be examined in greater detail below.

codeshare and block space agreements under the 'oneworld' alliance, and clearly enjoy many of the benefits of an actual merger, in spite of laws prohibiting mergers. Of interest here are the influences on these airlines to construct a 'virtual merger', the measure of success of this action using corporate and business strategy models and the legal question.

The research in this chapter examines the ways in which airlines are responding to competition in the current environment and to what extent these 'responses' have been influenced by the current regulatory climate.[6] The actions taken by EU and US airlines are scrutinized to determine to what extent they are lawful, 'extra-legal' or as yet unclear, and will lead a discussion on whether the said measures are taken to 'cope with' or 'survive' the deregulated environment, or 'circumvent' the law.

It is the aim of this chapter to investigate the phenomenal trend of two or more firms taking the decision to manage their business jointly, whether that includes routes, aircraft, uniforms or standards of quality, with a common goal – purely economic or a public relations campaign. As these new types of business organizations grow through the recruitment of ever more members, they gain their own 'virtual' brand awareness and reputation, thereby increasing the value of the group and its membership. The impact this has on the airline industry and the implications for it, through a wide-range of cooperation methods from franchising to mergers, might be taken objectively to change it, or simply arise as a by-product of that cooperation.

Competition law recognizes two different types of agreement–alliances: horizontal and vertical, according to their structure. A horizontal alliance is one between firms selling on the same product or service market, whereas a vertical alliance is one between a firm and its suppliers, distributors or buyers. So-called 'external alliances are drawn up with potential entrants or with the producers of substitutes or complements in other industries'[7] and for the purposes of this study correspond to unilateral contractual agreements outside the sphere of international airlines.

Against the backdrop of economic theories that support cooperation and relevant motivations for forming a tactical or strategic alliance, in this chapter attention shifts to various forms of vertical and horizontal alliances and mergers currently operating in the air transport sector.[8] Each type of alliance varies in its construction – from contractual to cross-investment – and level of commitment – from association to acquisition. The ten different categories of cooperative integration offered in this book as relevant to the airline industry are set out below in order of increasing level of intimacy:

6   The methodological aim of this examination is to conceptualize the responsiveness of airlines to the autonomy engendered by deregulation and liberalization principles in a 'free market' environment *vis-à-vis* contractual arrangements and network forming. The airline manoeuvring infers adaptation to the situational factors present in that environment, including in part the state of competition guided by relevant competition policies.

7   J.P. Hanlon, *Global Airlines: Competition in a Transnational Industry*, (Oxford: Butterworth-Heinemann, 1996), p. 204.

8   The tactical and strategic alliances discussed in this chapter are primarily horizontal in nature. However, it should be mentioned that in particular franchising and global alliances do have something of a vertical nature about them. Partners supply traffic and other services to one another. Although it may not be the impetus for the alliance, it should be noted that horizontal alliances are generally the weakest form of industry consolidation.

- interline agreement
- franchising
- block space arrangements (wet lease)
- codeshare agreements
- global alliances
- cargo alliances
- joint ventures
- networks
- stock investment
- mergers.

After examining the rudiments of each type of cooperation and identifying relevant case studies to give demonstration of each application, a brief discussion will be led on the links between two or more airline frequent flyer programmes. It is noted that although each of the following types of cooperative agreements may exist independently, they may also be used as 'building blocks', in the sense that firms may choose to extract features of several in combination to produce a suitable agreement for the venture's objectives.

'Interlining'

A key feature visible in the workings of the airline industry is the interline agreement.[9] Interlining is an agreement between two carriers, under which each carrier may accept the other's tickets in exchange for transport.[10] Passengers therefore have the opportunity to travel with a ticket issued by one carrier on flights operated by any number of other carriers worldwide. The arrangement is fundamental to the operation of the industry from both a corporate and competition perspective. From Abeyratne's perspective:

> Airlines have developed both a corporate strategy and a competition strategy to cope with competition. Both these strategies are becoming increasingly complementary rather than mutually exclusive, which they were at the inception of the airline industry.[11]

With few exceptions, interline agreements are now inherent in the airline industry. They support operation of the industry, connecting nearly all carriers by means of indirect cooperation. The external motivation for this is the benefit it brings not only to consumers, but also to the industry's growth and stability. If a flight is delayed or

9 The prevalence of interline arrangements in the shipping industry and public transport systems should also be noted.

10 To determine each airline's share of the revenue from an interlined journey, airlines depend on Multilateral Prorate Agreement–Passenger and Multilateral Prorate Agreement–Cargo. These are overseen by IATA's Prorate Agency. *See* IATA, 'Finance – Proration'. Online. Available HTTP: <http://www.iata.org/whatwedo/finance/pages.proration.aspx> (accessed 2 September 2011).

11 R. Abeyratne, *Aviation Trends in the New Millennium*, (Aldershot: Ashgate, 2001), pp. 4–5.

cancelled, it is generally fairly simple for an airline to rebook its passengers on other carriers to ensure they are expedited to their final destinations. Thus the interline agreement, when the required capacity aboard the other airline is available, prevents costly 'gridlock' in transport systems.

The exception to this seemingly competent 'back-up plan' of a system is in the arena of low-cost, or relatively new, carriers. For instance, if a new carrier comes on the market, it will not generally have such connections with larger incumbent competitors to rely upon as a failsafe for delayed or cancelled passengers. If this new airline only serves that particular market, say once a day, the absence of any interline agreement with other carriers will mean that a cancelled flight will delay the passenger until the next day. The other option would be for the new carrier to divert the passenger aboard one of its other aircraft. However, depending on whether there is in fact an existing network in place to enable this re-routing, this may leave the passenger or cargo stranded.

In the case of a low-cost carrier (LCC), whereas a flight route network may be in place, there is little to ensure that a passenger will be duly accommodated aboard another flight. To protect consumers, the EU has developed a number of rules[12] governing reasonable compensation for delayed or stranded passengers, which will amount in most cases to monetary or voucher remuneration, but in contrast to, say, a flight delayed or cancelled by a larger, better connected carrier in terms of its interline agreements airline, this means that a 'low-cost' passenger stands in a worse-off position than the 'traditional' passenger. Whilst there has been some advancement of cooperation between low-cost and new carriers in recent years,[13] the interline agreement is argued to be a benefit of the larger incumbent carriers in most markets.

An interline agreement may also be used with some creativity to open up access to markets otherwise prohibited between domestic and international carriers, as highlighted earlier as facilitating a firm's entry into alliances in the first instance. Prior to deregulation, an interline agreement between TWA (domestic) and PanAm (international) gave TWA passengers access to PanAm's Frankfurt/Main (FRA) hub and added domestic destinations to PanAm's profile. At the time, other US airlines concentrated rather on building strong domestic networks and once these were established in the post-deregulation years, TWA and PanAm could not cope with the changed market conditions.[14]

Hanlon points out that:

> One of the most important marketing objectives of alliances is to encourage interline 'hubbing' by facilitating co-operation between domestic and international services where restrictions on cabotage prevent the international carrier

---

12 EC Regulation No 261/2004 of the European Parliament and Council of 11.2.2004 establishing common rules on compensation and assistance to passengers in the event of denied boarding and of cancellation or long delay of flights (repealing EEC Regulation No 295/91).

13 For instance, the hugely successful Southwest Airlines has partnered up with ATA in the US. However, newer carriers do not always stand in a good bargaining position to secure interline agreements with larger, 'trunk' carriers.

14 ECDOT, *Transatlantic Airline Alliances*, p. 3.

from serving domestic routes and where, under existing bilateral air service agreements, the domestic carrier has no traffic rights on the relevant international routes.[15]

This is perhaps most prevalent in the US, where air traffic rights on the domestic market are strictly reserved for US-licensed carriers. Indeed, even if they US would give cabotage rights[16] to foreign-owned airlines, 'the immediate results, though beneficial, are unlikely to be spectacular. US airlines have been deregulated for a long time and are quite efficient by world standards – the market is not an easy one to make a profit in'.[17]

Franchising

The next form of agreement, the franchise, is one that is quite commonly found in various industries around the globe and may be vertical or horizontal in design. Blair and Lafontaine put forward this definition for a franchise:

> a contractual arrangement between two legally independent firms in which one firm, the *franchisee*, pays the other firm, the *franchiser*, for the right to sell the franchiser's product and/or the right to use its trademarks and business format in a given location for a specific period of time.[18]

In practice, a franchiser sells the rights to use the business name and sell a product or service to the franchisee. Parties enter into a franchise agreement, binding the parties together through contractual provisions, specifying their rights and obligations such as the territory the franchisee may use and the extent to which they will be supported by the franchiser.

Unique to the franchise contract are monetary terms, such as franchise fees, royalty rates, on-going fixed payments, and advertising fees. The terms, however, of a franchise contract are typically uniform.[19] A franchise fee is an initial lump-sum fee paid at the start of the contract. Royalty rates are an on-going payment made throughout the life of the franchise contract. The 'fee' is usually determined as a percentage rate with a fixed minimum value. As an alternative or in addition to royalty rates, some franchisers require on-going fixed payments to be made as a sort of 'rent'. Finally, 'many franchisers may stipulate in their contracts that the franchisee must make contributions to support national, regional, and/or local advertising'.[20] It should be noted that franchise agreements might also include non-monetary clauses such as exclusive territory, property ownership, restraint of trade and termination.

---

15 Hanlon, *Global Airlines*, p. 210.
16 Cabotage, which can be interpreted as a form of protectionism, is the regulation of transport services between two points in the same country, restricting it to carriers from the country. This is also referred to in Table 1.1, Chapter 1) where this point is illustrated as 'Eighth freedom rights'.
17 Vasigh, Fleming and Tacker, *Introduction to Air Transport Economics*, p. 136.
18 R.D. Blair and F. Lafontaine, *The Economics of Franchising* (Cambridge: Cambridge University Press, 2005), p. 3.
19 *See* Ibid., Ch.3.
20 Ibid., p. 69.

A franchise agreement may be another method by which to achieve higher profits and greater efficiencies without fully integrating vertically.[21] That is, a firm must not necessarily own and operate all of its outlets, or as applied to the airline industry, a 'trunk' carrier must not necessarily own and operate all of its 'feeder' services, to be economically efficient. A firm may enjoy cost-saving benefits through franchising, while maintaining an image of great (market) size and reputation. For this reason, the franchise agreement is the least 'intimate' of the contract-based manoeuvres by airlines.

The franchising trend began as early as the 1930s with sit-down restaurants and then exploded in the 1950s with fast-food restaurants, such as McDonald's. 'For example, at the end of 2001, McDonald's had 30,093 restaurants worldwide. [Only] 8,378, or almost 28 per cent of them, were company-owned and operated.'[22] In the airline industry, 'branding of third level services under the colours of major airlines has been one of the most significant and lasting by-products of deregulation'[23] in the US and Canada, while it remains in its infancy in Europe.

Franchising in North America has had tremendous success. Although most common in food and other service industries, franchising is thriving in many other enterprises, perhaps the most profitable of which are the energy (e.g. Esso, Texaco, Chevron and Amaco) and automobile sectors (e.g. General Motors, Ford and Chrysler). There are thousands upon thousands of franchising opportunities available daily, with large companies inviting an attractively smaller, less risky investment from entrepreneurs, and in most cases feature start-up assistance, and financing and consultant advice as part of the franchise fee. Franchising in the airline industry is a welcomed, successful business venture in the US, especially on so-called 'feeder', commuter or regional routes.

Examples of successful franchising ventures in other industries include exclusive agreements between automobile manufacturers and local dealerships, and between large trunk and commuter, or 'feeder' airlines. To provide for a better understanding of the economic benefits to franchising, it would be helpful to turn consideration at this point to the theory of competitive advantage. Airlines typically gain a competitive advantage in a market in one of two ways. An airline may possess certain values that set it apart from competitors, say for instance hard values such as type or age of aircraft and flight schedules, or soft values such as staff, in-flight meals and entertainment. Then again, an airline may derive its competitive advantage from a current or previous position as the national flag carrier.

Case study on feeder services: British Airways and GB Airways (now defunct)

Feeder services are perhaps the most prevalent example of franchising in the airline industry. BA announced its first franchise agreement with a company outside the UK in May 1996 named Sun-Air A/S, a Danish regional airline. Under the existing

---

21 However, a franchise agreement is among the most 'vertical' of the tactical alliances discussed in this study.

22 Blair and Lafontaine, *The Economics of Franchising*, p. 83.

23 Hanlon, *Global Airlines*, p. 95.

agreement, Sun-Air operates as 'BA Express' from the UK to locations in Scandinavia, with its base in Billund, Denmark.[24] In the same year, BA signed an additional three franchise agreements,[25] with South African-based Comair, Gibraltar-based GB Airways[26] and the UK-based Airline of Britain Group.[27] In 1997, BA reached a similar agreement with what was previously known as British Mediterranean Airlines (BMED). BA's fifth franchisee is Glasgow-based Loganair.

Before British European Airlines (BEA) became BA in 1973, it held a 49 per cent stake in GibAir, which became GB Airways Ltd in 1989. In 1995, BA relinquished its financial holding in GB Airways, when it became a full BA franchise operator. Under the former franchise agreement, GB Airways traded as BA, with all flights operated under BA flight codes (BA6800–6999 were allocated exclusively for GB Airways flights).

> GB Airways' aircraft . . . [were] painted in the standard BA livery while BA seats and colour schemes are to be found inside the passenger cabins. [The] cabin crew [wore] BA uniforms and the airline delivers the full BA Club Europe and Euro Traveller service. The arrangement also [gave] GB Airways affiliate membership of the oneworld global airline alliance, allowing passengers easier international travel between leading airlines.[28]

The franchise agreement covered flights to Spain, including the Canaries and Balearics, Malta, North Africa, Cyprus and France.[29] The terms and conditions of the BA–GB Airways franchise agreement were nearly identical to those found in agreements with BMED, Comair, Logan Air and Sun-Air.

From a consumer's perspective, successful airline franchises, in theory, are likely to offer a 'seamless', consistent (or identical) product or service. Consumers will typically know what to expect, and feel confident with the franchised company, based on the brand and reputation of the franchiser. On the other hand, in the absence of adequate disclosure as to the actual operating carrier, consumers may feel that the franchisee is passing itself off as the franchiser. If, for instance, under the former agreement a passenger was booked to fly from London Gatwick to Faro, Portugal on flight 'BA6881', a GB Airways-operated service, and GB Airways had just been named in the newspaper the day before the flight as having a poor

---

24 BA Archives and Museum Collection. Online Available HTTP: <http://www.bamuseum.com/1996.html> (accessed 12 July 2011).

25 Ibid.

26 EasyJet bought GB Airways after the UK's Office of Fair Trading cleared the merger in 2007. *See* R. Marshall 'Ryanair Holdings PLC – EasyJet to Buy GB Airways', *Reuters* (23 January 2008). Online. Available HTTP: <http://www.reuters.com/article/pressRelease/idUS137554+23-Jan-2008+RNS20080123> (accessed 19 August 2011).

27 Airlines of Britain Group (ABH) was formed to act as a holding company for British Midland and British Midland Aviation Services, and became de-merged British Midland (BMI) in 1997.

28 GB Airways, About Us. Online. <http://www.gbairways.co.uk/company-details/about-us/?PHPSESSID=ed0fd477ca3b2306ed1b68f22fbb46dd> (No longer available; accessed 21 January 2006).

29 Airline Business 'Analysis and OAG Scheduled Data' *Airline Business* 21 (9), September 2005, 64.

maintenance inspection, the consumer may have been wary of flying GB Airways. It is not until the consumer, with BA ticket in hand and confidence with that airline's safety record, would board the aircraft that he would notice that the service was in fact operated by GB Airways.

From the perspective of BA, the hypothetical scenario above would have likely resulted in a negative repercussion on their image and reputation. This is perhaps the greatest risk to a franchiser under such an agreement: condemnation by association. Although there are elements of service-level agreements in the vast majority of franchise agreements, the potential for a breach of such an agreement is, though perhaps avoidable by stringent micromanagement of the franchisee, highly likely. In this scenario, BA might have suffered some financial loss, which might have been passed on to the franchisee, GB Airways, in the form of a penalty for incompetence.

GB Airways, on the other hand, would suffer damage twice over. Immediately, the press statement would affect its own brand and image, and consequently any impending action taken by BA. This may range from no action to serving a penalty and probationary measures, to termination of the franchise agreement.

In an effort to avoid any uncertainties and to mitigate loss in the event of a chance event, franchise agreements should be as detailed as possible. It is the franchiser who is responsible for drafting the franchise contract, and therefore the onus is on him to ensure clarity. If an ambiguity arises, the English court is likely to interpret the ambiguity in favour of the franchisee. Owing to the fact that, in most cases, a franchiser will stand to benefit from a position of greater power in hiring the 'contractor', and therefore in a bargaining position, the *contra proferentum* rule is likely to hold in jurisdictions outside the UK, too. These include Member States of the EU and the US. The franchise agreement also benefits from the fact that no international jurisdictional or legal element is involved. Therefore, no legal problems arise from the choice of forum and conflict of laws.

The franchise contract can be seen as an investment by the franchisee, and as such, is sometimes entirely dependent on its existence. In the event that the contract is terminated, which may occur relatively swiftly and with little notice by the franchiser, the franchisee stands in a position to lose a great deal. Although the franchise agreement would appear to recognize franchisees as an integral part of the family, with no preferences given to individual 'members', it must be remembered that goodwill and contract are two very different concepts. In this case, the contract will remain in force, while any sense of goodwill will unfortunately not outlive the contract itself.

There are always implied risks associated with franchise agreements, as with any other contract-based commercial venture. In order to minimize these risks and the probability of being caught off-guard, the best course of action is to clearly identify them in the franchise agreement. However, it is inevitable that new risks will come to light, particularly with the advent of new technologies, and these will only be protected against with an amendment to the franchise agreement. Due diligence, from the time of negotiation of terms and seeking of counsel, is key.

When GB Airways was sold to easyJet in October 2008, BA CEO said: 'UK franchises have outlived their purpose. EasyJet has made an offer to buy GB Airways and this has enabled us to end the franchise agreement early'.[30] In the US and Australia,[31] however, the franchise agreement remains a popular partnering strategy.

Block space agreement (wet lease)

The 'block space arrangement', or 'wet lease', is a commercial agreement in joint venture involving the allocation of seats or cargo space on one airline to another on all or some of its flights. Under this type of arrangement, an airline gains access to capacity and markets that are otherwise restricted or prohibited owing to, in the majority of cases, government regulations.

By strict definition, a wet lease is any leasing arrangement, or charter, whereby a company agrees to provide an aircraft and at least one pilot to another company.[32] Variations on the wet lease include the 'codeshare arrangement' and 'blocked-seat agreement'. Conversely, a 'dry lease' refers to leasing only the aircraft. For the purposes of this book, a wet lease includes the leasing of space, in the form of passenger seats and in the aircraft cargo holds.

In the past, an airline would resort to a wet lease arrangement in order to maintain scheduled passenger or cargo services in the event of an unforeseen disruption. The practice has become more commonplace in the industry over the past decade or so with carriers focusing, according to Endres,

> entirely or almost entirely on providing a full wet lease service, including aircraft, crews, maintenance and insurance (ACMI). All but one has come into existence since 1990 and according to ACMI specialist Air Atlanta Icelandic, traffic carried by wet lease providers since then has been growing by 18 per cent a year.[33]

The rationale behind the popularity of this business practice is often that '[a]irlines can no longer afford to invest in high-capacity aircraft, staff and infrastructure, when the expected returns are uncertain, or at best minimal'.[34] When an airline looks to start a new route, for instance, ACMI wet lease is the preferred enterprise to minimize risk and ensure lower short-term costs. It should be noted that although a block space agreement is a form of wet lease, an ACMI wet lease is the most comprehensive format for this agreement. Under a block space agreement, some space is reserved and purchased whereas under an ACMI wet lease, an entire airplane and crew are

---

30 The agreement was due to end in 2010. (M. Caswell, 'BA Sells GB Franchise to EasyJet (correction)', *Business Traveller*, 30 October 2007. Online. Available HTTP: <http://www.businesstraveller.com/news/ba-sells-gb-franchise-to-easyjet> (accessed 14 June 2011).

31 RegionalLink and AirNorth are prime examples of strong franchise agreements with Qantas Airlines in Australia. *See* online. Available HTTP: <http://www.regionallink.com.au> and <http://www.airnorth.com.au> (both accessed 12 September 2011).

32 §207.1 of title 14, Code of Federal Regulations.

33 G. Endres, 'Surrogate Supply', *Airline Business (Factiva)*, 27 June 2006.

34 Ibid.

contracted. It is interesting to note that under the UK Emissions Trading Scheme, the environmental costs of emissions are to be borne by the airline leasing aircraft regardless of whether this is done on the basis of wet or dry lease.[35] This may raise questions over who the 'contracting carrier' and who the 'actual carrier' is, in respect of the emissions trading in conjunction with route charges, i.e. by Eurocontrol.

The key legal implications for block space agreements are those associated with tax, licensing and maintenance. A lessee may incur tax liability, in most cases when operating under a wet lease rather than a dry lease.[36] Since an aircraft has the 'domicile' of the country in which it has been registered, there may beramifications if this is different from the country in which it is leased, intended to be used, or both. Depending on whether the 'other' country requires that a foreign-registered aircraft be licensed in order to be used within its jurisdiction, which is highly likely in most cases, this will add cost and time before the aircraft is brought into service. Finally, at the conclusion of the lease, the lessee will be required to return the aircraft – and crew, if a wet lease – to the lessor in good order, subject to an agreed margin for 'reasonable' wear and tear as expected. There will be a clause in the lease agreement stipulating the terms of maintenance and with whom the relevant responsibility lays.

Wet leases have implications when conducted internationally, where for instance a US carrier leases an aircraft registered in the UK. Regulations in the US currently prohibit this, and the trade unions federation the AFL–CIO supports the government's position to protect its pilot and cabin crewmembers. This issue is added to the list of pressures by the EU for the US to revise its aviation policy to open up market access to EU carriers. In general, wet leases in the EU are *prima facie* valid and for the most part encouraged, with provisions for expanding opportunities for wet leasing beyond the EU, in the first instance including Morocco.[37]

Under US law,[38] certain types of agreements[39] must be submitted to the US DoT 30 days before their proposed effective date. The US DoT then reserves the right to extend the waiting period while the agreement is reviewed. The review process involves issuing a determination of whether the proposed agreement presents competitive issues that might require further investigation, independent and secondary to the antitrust laws as defined in the first section of the Clayton Act.[40] In practice,

---

35 'European Commission MRV Guidance for aviation in the EU ETS – Draft Technical Report', Entec UK Ltd, issued September 2008. Online. Available HTTP: <http://ec.europa.eu/environment/climat/pdf/aviation/Annual%20Emissions%20Report.pdf> (accessed 12 August 2011).

36 *See generally* R.C. Speciale, *Aircraft Ownership: A Legal and Tax Guide* (New York: McGraw-Hill, 2003).

37 Press Release IP/06/582 'South East Europe flying towards the EU: first steps taken for extending the Single Aviation Market', *Europa* (05 May 2006).

38 49 U.S.C. §41720(a)(1).

39 This includes joint ventures and for the air transport sector, tactical and strategic alliances; however, while applications for antitrust immunity (ATI) must be reviewed and approved before the appliance is implemented, there is no requirement to apply for ATI. 'As is the case in many other industries, airlines have the option of proceeding with commercial cooperation *at their own risk* and subject to traditional antitrust enforcement by the DOJ and other agencies. Airlines can, and often do, form alliances with varying degrees of integration absent a grant of ATI' (ECDOT, *Transatlantic Airline Alliances*, p. 17, *emphasis added*).

40 15 U.S.C. §12.

the US DoT tends to rely on the terms of the agreement, data provided by the airlines upon request, and 'acceptance of restrictions imposed by the US DoJ that are intended to limit the possibility of anti-competitive conduct.'[41]

However, the statute does not require that parties to domestic block space, codeshare and frequent flyer reciprocity agreements obtain approval from the US DoT before they implement the agreement.

> Blocking [the parties] from implementing their agreement would normally require our issuance of an order[42] in a formal enforcement proceeding that determined that the agreement's implementation would be an unfair method of competition and thus a violation of that section. Our review of all agreements submitted under 49 U.S.C. 41720 has been informal. It is analogous to the review of major mergers and acquisitions conducted by the Justice Department and the Federal Trade Commission under the Hart–Scott–Rodino Act[43] since we consider whether we should institute a formal proceeding for determining whether an agreement would violate section 41712.[44]

However, international airline alliances must seek prior approval[45] or exemption[46] from the US DoT.[47] The outcome of such review is independent and secondary to the antitrust laws as defined in the first section of the Clayton Act,[48] and the respective authority of the Attorney General. The US DoT will grant authority if the arrangement is in the public interest, which includes questioning the level of safety of the codeshare service and regular audits of the arrangement.[49]

In Canada, China Airlines Ltd applied for and was granted the necessary exemption authority to operate a scheduled international service between Taipei, Taiwan and Vancouver, British Columbia *vis-à-vis* a commercial agreement in joint venture including a block space arrangement with Canadian Airlines International Ltd in 2001.[50] Under the order, the Canadian Transportation Agency required China Airlines Ltd to

> apply its own tariffs in respect of its allotted capacity, as if each flight were to be operated with its own aircraft . . . [and] issue tickets for flights carried out by Canadian Airlines International, in the name of China Airlines Ltd.[51]

41 US Department of Transportation (Office of the Secretary) Press Release *Review under 49 U.S.C. 41720 of United/US Airways Agreements*, Washington, 2 October 2002.

42 Under 49 U.S.C. §41712 (formerly section 411 of the Federal Aviation Act).

43 15 U.S.C. §18a.

44 US Department of Transportation (Office of the Secretary) Press Release *Review under 49 U.S.C. 41720 of United/US Airways Agreements*, Washington, 2 October 2002.

45 49 U.S.C. §41308.

46 Ibid.

47 Under 49 U.S.C. §41309, the DoT has the authority to approve agreements that are not adverse to the public interest and do not substantially reduce/eliminate competition.

48 15 U.S.C. §12.

49 Codeshare Safety Program Guidelines, Federal Aviation Association. Online. Available HTTP: <http://www.intl.faa.gov/restrictions/code1.pdf> (accessed 12 September 2011).

50 Canadian Transportation Agency, Rulings, Order 1990-A-716. Online. Available HTTP: <http://www.cta-otc.gc.ca/rulings-decisions/orders/1990/A/1990-A-716_e.html> (accessed 12 July 2011).

51 Order 1990-A-716, subsections 5 and 7.

Under these provisions, the two airlines remain autonomous as regards the 'business' operation of the route. The Canadian government apparently intends to ensure that China International will not be regarded as a Canadian entity, thereby limiting the potential for distortion of competition on this particular market. Thus, each airline carries on trading with a portion of the market share and separate demand-based fare/cost calculations may be made.

This stands out against the codeshare and marketing agreement Delta (DL) signed with Virgin Atlantic (VS) in 1994, which was approved by the US DoT in 1995. DL ended the codeshare in 1997, citing its anticipation of the EU–US Air Transport Agreement and hopeful that it would soon see its own aircraft flying to LHR. VS signed a similar agreement with Continental Airlines (CO) in 1997, under which CO regularly purchases block space on all VS-operated transatlantic flights, giving CO access to the VS flight network and *vice versa*. Thus, while CO had no traffic rights under the Bermuda II Agreement, it was able to market flights between EWR and LHR airports.

Hanlon notes that 'Under the present system of traffic rights, negotiated in terms of freedom of air and with restrictions on cabotage, each country/region tends to be an individual market'.[52] As demonstrated by these case studies, block space arrangements thus extend the possibility of access to otherwise restricted markets. Although the relevant authorities must first clear this type of commercial agreement, it may be argued that block spacing arrangements are slowly replacing bilateral ASAs, and that future prospects are looking good. In keeping with Hanlon, 'BSAs are likely to increase in the years ahead, as more and more airlines seek to break out of the conditions attaching to bilateral ASAs negotiated by national governments'.[53]

Block space agreements permit airlines to expand their route network, especially if the sole operation of a regular or seasonal service in the market would not be profitable. There is an element of reciprocity involved, for as one partner to a block space agreement gains access to a new market or increased frequency on a market already supplied, the other will negotiate a similar arrangement on services operated on the same or other markets operated by its partner. The block space enterprise is not only cost efficient and useful to marketing more destinations, it also enables airlines to gain access to markets otherwise prohibited by competition or antitrust regulations. Many trade barriers exist in respect of entry to a new market, whether it is a government or industry-influenced intention to protect a market or ensure fair competition for national businesses (carriers).

Whilst block-space agreements are in theory a very low-risk, low-cost and potentially highly profitable venture, it is necessary to mention that such arrangements must normally be authorized if they are international in nature as we have seen. Expanding business relationships across borders, which may impact on one or more domestic markets, raises concern with national governments and criticism by competitors of the domestic carrier making the application to 'partner up'. Nevertheless, the appropriate

---

52 Hanlon, *Global Airlines*, p. 96.

53 Ibid., p. 101; Based on more recent trends, increased multilateralism is forecasted. *See for instance* Williams's view on 'prospects for global deregulation' (G. Williams, *Airline Competition: Deregulation's Mixed Legacy* (Aldershot: Ashgate, 2002), pp.159–166).

transport and/or competition authorities are in most cases likely to investigate and assess the potential for any anti-competitive effects of the relationship on the relevant markets before delivering a determination on the matter. Whether granted an approval or exemption from the rules, the partners to a block space agreement are bound to realize their goals and, in theory, offer competitive, fair tariffs to consumers.

'Codeshare' agreement

In 2005, Air Malta signed an agreement with Qantas Airlines. Under the agreement, the two airlines 'share' airline codes (codeshare) on flights operated between Malta and Australia. For instance, all flights from Sydney (SYD) and Melbourne (MEL) to LHR on Qantas Airlines carry an Air Malta airline designator code (AM). Passengers wishing to travel 'seamlessly' from Australia to Malta may do so by flying Qantas from Australia to London before connecting to Air Malta to Catania, Malta. The effect of this is that tickets may be sold by Air Malta from Australia to Malta and on the return journey. Air Malta gains 'access' to the Australian market even though they do not offer direct services to Australia.[54]

Codesharing refers to an increasingly common 'commercial agreement between two airlines under which an airline operating a service allows another to offer that service to the travelling public under its flight designator code, even though it does not operate the service'.[55] Codeshare agreements typically include provisions for revenue/profit sharing, baggage handling, and often combine block space arrangements and franchising agreements to form partnerships or realize global alliances.

Perhaps the prime feature of these agreements is the joint marketing of connecting flights and flight routes on which both airlines fly. For the former, cooperating airlines synchronize their flight schedules to minimize connecting times for consumers, while the latter gives the 'appearance' of an increased frequency of services. For example, BA might offer six daily flights between London and New York, while AA offers five daily flights in the opposite direction. When these two airlines form a codeshare agreement, they may each market to their customers (or on the market as a whole) 11 daily (return) flights between the city-pair. Thus, whereas a BA customer would have the choice of six daily flights, they would now have 11 choices, all with BA flight numbers and frequent flyer benefits. This codeshare is not hypothetical, but does in fact exist within the scope of the oneworld Alliance, of which both airlines are a member, and which extends an element of seamless 'level of service' too. Beyond New York, a BA customer will also benefit from BA flight numbers, boarding passes, checked-through luggage, to say, Phoenix, Arizona aboard an AA-operated aircraft.

'The motive behind many [joint] marketing agreements stems from the belief that the airlines that will be in the best position to compete in the future will be those who can offer the most extensive global networks'.[56] From a business perspective, an air-

54 *See* the Australian government International Air Services Commission's Determination for renewal of Determination [2003] IASC 120 allocating capacity on the Singapore route to Qantas ([2007] IASC 116).

55 Hanlon, *Global Airlines*, p. 101.

56 Ibid., p. 210.

line that can offer the most destinations globally clearly has a competitive advantage over its competitors. Joint marketing allows the participating airlines to sell seats on a more widely distributed network, thereby capturing otherwise lost market-share on routes it cannot, for financial or regulatory reasons, operate. In addition, from a consumer's perspective, the effects of the joint marketing give the appearance of airlines with a truly global character.

As early as 1992, it was recorded that 'no less than 96 per cent of passengers in the US flew on codesharing alliances'.[57] Nonetheless, it should be noted that there has been much criticism levelled against codesharing by consumer organizations and national departments of trade, with claims that this type of tactical alliance is confusing to passengers and stifling to competition, but there have been no successful actions brought in the EU or US to date.

Criticisms arise from the belief that anti-competitive effects on the industry are a result of codeshare agreements. Although the disapproval of codeshare agreements is not conceivably tenable, the antipathy towards them may be inferred by conduct in the sector. For instance, the US DoT refused to allow BD to codeshare with UA on routes from LHR to the US, owing to 'the current state of US–UK aviation relations',[58] meaning of course the Bermuda II Agreement,[59] which explicitly outlines the authority of services in that market. Shortly after this decision, British Midland called for the UK government to take retaliatory action against the codeshare agreement between Virgin Atlantic and Continental Airlines on the LHR–US markets.

According to the US DoJ:

> The term 'codesharing' can mean as little as one airline allowing another airline to use its computer reservations system codes to sell seats on its planes on routes in which the second airline cannot compete, or as much as comprehensive integration of market and operations that involves joint decisions on price, capacity, schedules, and other competitively sensitive matters.[60]

This relatively broad definition steps away from the literal meaning and intention of the codeshare agreement and expands its scope to any 'sharing'.[61]

---

57 Chambers 1993, as cited in Hanlon, *Global Airlines*, p. 101.

58 IAAE, 'International Airport Report' Vol 9, Num 2 (February 2001). Online. Available HTTP: <http://www.iaae.org/publications/pdf/iaae_2001_02.pdf> (accessed 12 August 2011).

59 Bermuda II was formerly the 'traditional' bilateral air service agreement in place between the US and UK prior to the EU–US Air Transport Agreement, which was provisionally implemented in March 2008. Signed in 1977, the Bermuda II amended the previous 1946 Bermuda I agreement. Highly restrictive, the agreement outlined which airlines were permitted to fly, for instance, to London's Heathrow *versus* Gatwick airports from designated US cities.

60 US DoJ *Antitrust Division Statement, International Aviation Alliances: Market Turmoil and the Future of Airline Competition* (2001), p. 6. Online. Available <http://www.usdoj.gov/atr/public/testimony/9508. htm> (accessed 5 October 2011).

61 *See* US Department of Transportation (Office of the Secretary) Press Release *Review under 49 U.S.C. 41720 of United/US Airways Agreements*, Washington, 2 October 2002.

In 2002, the US DoJ took the following position:

> On July 25 United and US Airways submitted code-share and frequent flyer program reciprocity agreements to us for review under 49 U.S.C. 41720. After informally reviewing the agreements, we find that no formal investigation of the agreements is warranted at this time, and we have determined that we should end the waiting period. The two airlines have agreed to restrictions proposed by the Justice Department that are intended to limit the possibility of anti-competitive behaviour, and each airline has represented to us that it will continue to compete independently on fares and service levels. To ensure that they abide by those representations, we will monitor closely their conduct in implementing the agreements.

Procedurally, codeshare agreements do not generally allow the parties to discuss pricing and schedule plans with one another, but while keeping two separate schedules, they may add the flight number and other details, and for this reason they are usually approved by the US DoJ.[62] However, the US DoJ's approach is flexible in weighing up, in the public interest,[63] whether a proposed codesharing agreement 'promotes or enhances competition in the affected markets, rather than the narrower issue of whether the parties would violate the antitrust laws if they engaged in the joint activities contemplated by the proposed agreement'.[64] Rather than setting out a predefined set of circumstances to describe a typical codeshare agreement and subsequent law to allow or prohibit it, the US approach considers each agreement on a case-by-case basis.

The EU leaves initial regulation of cooperative agreements such as codesharing to the parties themselves in the form of 'self-regulation'. Airlines must ensure that the terms of their agreements fit within the ambit of EU competition law. However, 'alliances between major US carriers, as distinct from alliances between hub carriers and commuter carriers that serve those hubs are a relatively recent phenomenon'.[65] The former is most commonly associated with franchise agreements (e.g. United Airlines and Sky West), whereas the latter is an actual alliance between carriers (e.g. United Airlines and US Airways). Air Wisconsin pioneered the concept of codesharing with United Express and rapidly became the nation's largest regional airline in the 1980s. Although Air Wisconsin's agreement with UA ceased in April 2006, it remains a member of US Airways Express.

In the US, 'United Express' is a name under which nine regional airlines operate over 2,000 daily 'feeder' flights for UA.[66] The regional airlines include Air Wisconsin

62 'Airlines' code-sharing plan challenged', CNN (22 January 2003). Online. Available HTTP: <http://edition.cnn.com/2003/TRAVEL/01/21/airlines.codeshare/index.html> (accessed 28 July 2011).
63 49 U.S.C. §40109.
64 *American Airlines Inc and TACA Group Code-Share Services Proceeding*, Docket OST-96-1700, US Department of Transportation. Online. Available HTTP: <http://www.usdoj.gov/atr/public/comments/1779.htm> (accessed 12 July 2011).
65 US DoJ, *Antitrust Division Statement, International Aviation Alliances: Market Turmoil and the Future of Airline Competition*.
66 United Airlines, About United, Products and Services, United Express. Online. Available HTTP: <http://www.united.com/page/middlepage/0,6823,1315,00.html> (accessed 12 August 2011).

Airlines Corp (AWAC), Chautauqua Airlines, Colgan Air, GoJet Airlines, Mesa Airlines, Republic Airlines, Shuttle America, SkyWest and Trans States Airlines, and are considered as 'members' of United Express. Although the aircraft are painted in UA colours, they are separate companies with different crews and management.

America West Airlines Inc. (AWA) and Mesa Airlines Inc. (Mesa) entered into their first codeshare and revenue sharing agreement in 1998, which they amended in 2001. The impetus for the new agreement remained the same, 'in order to provide scheduled air transportation services as America West Express and to share in revenue and cost of such services'.[67] Under this agreement, Mesa's rights, responsibilities and obligations include operation of America West Express air transportation services using a specified fleet of aircraft to and from cities as scheduled by AWA. The schedule may be changed at any time by AWA by means of a so-called 'Schedule Notice' to Mesa, which is required to implement all changes within 60 days of the notice. In addition, Mesa and its affiliates agree to provide services to and from Phoenix, Arizona exclusively for AWA. When creating a schedule, AWA agrees to consider Mesa's maintenance requirements, and for the aircraft specified, provide that maintenance independently; accommodate 'turn times'[68] appropriate to airport and aircraft demands; give at least 45-days notice of any holiday cancellations; and permit Mesa to set flight crew schedules 'consistent with industry operational practices'. In the event that Mesa subcontracts for its services, such as with Air Midwest (AM), the agreement specifically outlines the rules for this.

In its sole discretion and at its own cost, AWA agrees to market, advertise and sell tickets on all flights[69] operated by Mesa. AWA will pay Mesa's actual costs and expenses incurred in connection with performing flight services and other services, including hull and liability insurance premiums, property taxes, de-icing expenses, fuel costs, landing fees, security and other passenger and ground handling fees incurred at stations not maintained by AWA. Mesa is required to remit tickets pulled back to AWA on a daily basis, the 'segment revenue' that, after being processed, will be paid to Mesa as revenue. The contract sufficiently clarifies the points of liability and indemnities and reiterates the agreed definition on codesharing. 'Nothing contained in this Agreement will be deemed to create any agency or partnership or similar relationship between AWA and Mesa'.[70]

Codeshare agreements with complementary industries

Importantly, codeshare agreements also exist between airlines and railway lines. The two most prominent examples are with the *Deutsche Bahn AG* (DB German Rail) in

67 AWA Codeshare and Revenue Sharing Agreement, p.1. Online. Available HTTP: <http://contracts.corporate.findlaw.com/agreements/americawest/mesa.share.2001.02.01.html> (accessed 22 August 2011).
68 Ibid., p. 2.
69 To clarify, this refers to the amount of time between arrival at gate and next departure of designated aircraft for those flights agreed and authorized by AWA. The length of time depends upon the size of aircraft (for deplaning, boarding, cleaning, catering, maintenance and refuelling) and usually ranges between 20 and 120 minutes.
70 AWA, p. 27.

Germany and the *Société Nationale des Chemins de fer Français* (SNCF French National Railway) in France.

At present, DB has three different cooperative arrangements with domestic and international airlines. The first of these agreements is called 'AIRail'[71] and involves cooperation between DB, LH and Fraport AG, the Frankfurt am Main International Airport (FRA) management company. Under this agreement, certain high-speed Intercity-Express (ICE) trains between Frankfurt Airport south to Stuttgart and north to Cologne, Germany, are designated with LH flight numbers and dedicated LH check-in counters and baggage handling. In other words, a passenger who checks in for a flight in central Cologne, including checked-in luggage, to New York, will be issued two flight coupons, one for Cologne–Frankfurt on DB, and the other for Frankfurt–New York on LH. Baggage is checked through to New York, and passengers may accrue LH frequent flyer mileage.

The second is called 'Fly&Rail – Rail&Fly'[72] and involves issuing a rail ticket integrated into a passenger's airline ticket book, for an onward or originating journey to and from over 5,600 railway stations in Germany and Amsterdam-Schipol airport in the Netherlands. In April 2007, Qantas Airlines announced its first ever fly-rail codeshare outside of Australia with Lufthansa. Flights arrive early in the morning in Frankfurt, Germany from Sydney, Melbourne and Perth, Australia and passengers are connected with DB's ICE trains to Cologne, Dusseldorf, Hamburg, Hanover, Munich and Stuttgart.[73] Under this scheme, DB has some 91 partners, including AA, IB, LH, TP and US Airways.

The second arrangement involves cooperative codesharing agreements with four international airlines: AA, NH, China Airlines and TP.[74] Under these agreements, certain originating or onward rail journeys within Germany may be issued as an airline ticket on any of these airlines' ticket stock, with the same airline's code and flight number. On AA, passengers may even accrue frequent flyer mileage credit for the rail journey travelled. Similar cooperative agreements exist between SNCF (*Société Nationale des Chemins de fer français* [National Corporation of French Railways]) and CO, AA, Qatar Airways (QR), Cathay Pacific (CX), Air Austral[75], AF, UA and Air Tahiti Nui, under the 'TGVair' programme.[76]

SNCF's agreement with CO provides for 'seamless plane and high-speed TGV train connections as well as the ability to earn frequent flyer miles. Through an air/

71 DB Website. Available HTTP: <http://www.bahn.de/p/view/service/flug/rail_und_fly.shtml> (accessed 20 August 2011).

72 Which name is chosen depends on whether the travel is originating by air or rail, respectively. DB Website, International Guests, Travel Agent, FlyandRail – RailandFly. Online. Available HTTP: <http://www.db.de> (accessed 22 September 2011).

73 'New Qantas Rail Codeshare Link to Seven German Cities', *Air Transport News* (19 April 2007). Online. Available HTTP: <http://www.airtransportnews.aero/article.pl?id−3167&keys−nuremberg> (accessed 10 July 2011).

74 Deutsche Bahn website, International Guests, TravelAgent, Codeshare cooperative ventures

75 For additional information on this agreement, *see* Air Austral – TGV website. Available HTTP: <http://www.air-austral.com/partenaire.php?id_rubrique=11> (accessed 25 September 2011).

76 TGVair Website. Available HTTP: <http://www.tgv.com/EN/apropos/air/air.htm> (accessed 16 August 2011).

rail codeshare, SNCF provides connecting service on TGV trains'.[77] Passengers may transfer at Paris CDG Airport between CO transatlantic flights and 14 SNCF TGV destinations throughout France. There also exists an agreement[78] with AA similar to that with DB. Selected SNCF trains share AA flight codes and therefore allow for an AA ticket to be exchanged for an SNCF rail journey along with the respective accrual of frequent flyer mileage for the entire journey.

QR entered into its codeshare agreement with SNCF in late 2004, covering 15 cities across France.[79] With terms in the QR–SNCF agreement nearly identical to those in the agreement with AA, the QR flight code is applied on selected SNCF rail services 'ensuring travellers have a seamless journey between Doha and the French regions'.[80] According to Eric Didier, QR Area Finance Manager for France: 'Our Paris flights have proved extremely popular which is why we recently increased frequency to a daily service. With this bi-modal agreement with SNCF, we will now be able to meet increasing demand from our customers in the regions'. Mireille Faugère, Voyages France Europe Director at SNCF, said: 'This new agreement reinforces the development of TGV AIR connections and the promotion of TGV at an international level. By the end of 2004, almost 100,000 passengers will have used the TGV AIR product via SNCF partner airlines'.

CX's agreement provides codesharing between Paris CDG and ten other cities in France, while the AF agreement[81] includes six destinations in France by TGV and Brussels, Belgium by Thalys International rail services. 'United Ground Link' offers a rail service between 12 cities in France and Paris, under an agreement between UA and SNCF. 'Train services are assigned an UA flight number. Fares to these cities from North America are generally the same as those offered to Paris'.[82] And finally, Air Tahiti Nui currently sells tickets on SNCF rail to 16 destinations in France.[83]

Global airline alliances

For the purposes of this study, airline alliances should perhaps first be distinguished from the general (non-airline) concept of 'strategic alliances' in that they comprise a number of elements from various cooperative 'partnering' strategies. Perhaps best defined as cooperative agreement between two or more airlines, an airline alliance is usually created with short-term vision: a way to extend and optimize flight networks, reduce costs and offer greater benefits to the travelling consumer.

---

77 CO Website, About Continental, Global Alliances, SNCF – French National Railway. Available HTTP: <http://www.continentalairlines.com> (accessed 30 September 2011).

78 AA Website: http://www.aa.com.

79 Qatar Airways website: http://www.qatarairways.com

80 Ibid.

81 Air France website: http://www.airfrance.com.

82 UA website, United Ground Link. Online. Available HTTP: <http://www.united.com/page/article/0,6722,1125,00.html> (accessed 13 August 2011).

83 Air Tahiti Nui website. Available HTTP: <www.airtahitinui.com/news.asp?id=78> (accessed 12 September 2011).

The level of cooperation between partners to an airline alliance varies according to the extent of integration: from sharing frequent flyer programmes or airport lounges to minimum standards for crew uniforms, seat comfort and in-flight services, a 'stock investment by one airline in its partner',[84] to merger-like integration.[85] Many alliances began as codeshare agreements aimed at extending existing flight networks and have subsequently developed into regional or global alliances.

Alliances involving codeshare agreements may have the potential for both pro-competitive and anti-competitive effects.

> On the pro-competitive side, they can create new service, improve existing service, lower costs, and increase efficiency, all to the benefit of consumers. On the anti-competitive side, they can result in market allocation, capacity limitations, higher fares, or foreclosure of rivals from markets, all to the injury of consumers.[86]

Perhaps the most important development in recent years has been the emergence of a grouping of major carriers in the form of deeper and more complex alliances[87] extending to all aspects of the airline business.[88] To provide a better understanding of alliances, the focus may be turned to the three largest alliances: Star Alliance, SkyTeam and oneworld, which if combined, fly 54 per cent of all passengers travelling each year.[89]

AC, LH, SK, TG and UA established the largest of these three at present, Star Alliance, in 1997. Star has its roots in a codeshare agreement between AC and UA in 1992, which led to a comprehensive marketing and codeshare agreement between LH and UA in 1993. The second-largest is the SkyTeam Airline alliance, founded in 2000, The third-largest is the oneworld Alliance, established in 1999, and includes AA, AY, BA, CX, EI, IB, LA, QF and a number of affiliates Cost reduction is achieved though sharing of facilities, such as sales offices, maintenance facilities, catering and computer systems, ground handling staff, check-in and gate agents, and in some cases, investments and purchases.[90]

In 1998, AC applied to the Canadian Transportation Agency for permission to operate an A340 aircraft bearing the livery of Star Alliance. The CTA granted exemption from paragraph 80(1) (c) of the *Canada Transportation Act*,[91] which states that 'the

---

84 US DoJ, *Antitrust Division Statement, International Aviation Alliances: Market Turmoil and the Future of Airline Competition*.

85 ECDOT, *Transatlantic Airline Alliances*, p. 5.

86 Ibid., p. 6.

87 *See Table 5.1*.

88 For a look at the position of the non-allied airlines as against the global alliances, *see* B. Kleymann and H. Seristö, 'Competing with the Alliance: Strategy Options of Independents', in Kleymann and Seristö, *Managing Strategic Airline Alliances*, pp. 95–112.

89 As of June 2005, according to IATA 2005 Annual Report. Online. Available HTTP. <www.iata.org/iata/Sites/agm/file/2005/file/Annual_report_2005.pdf>. (accessed 12 August 2011).

90 Star Alliance requires that 2 per cent of each member's aircraft be painted in Star Alliance livery, including all alliance member logos. Generally, the first logo to appear at the cockpit is the airline which actually operates that particular aircraft; *See* B. Kleymann, and H. Seristö, 'Marketing Airline Alliances: The Branded Airline', in Kleymann and Seristö, *Managing Strategic Airline Alliances*, pp. 113–128.

91 S.C., 1996, c. 10.

Table 5.1 Alliance network comparison[a]

Alliance	Members	Total destinations	Duplicates	Countries served	Frequencies (thousands)	Capacity (ASK)[b] (billions)	Transatlantic passengers carried in 2009 (millions)[c]	Market share of transatlantic market in 2009[d]
Star Alliance	26	1,135	460	181	146	33.5	8.85	37.6 %
SkyTeam	13	832	229	169	84	2.9	6.66	28.3 %
oneworld	11	712	182	182	57	18.2	5.36	22.7 %

a Unless otherwise indicated, all information in this table is compiled with permission from S. Mills, 'Alliance Network Comparison: Weekly Global Operations Summer 2011', Flightglobal Data Research and Flightglobal Insight, *Airline Business* 27(9), 2011, 32–47. Unless indicated above, data in the table are taken from this source under permission from the copyright holder.

b ASK = available seat kilometre (1 mile = 1.609 kilometres).

c European Commission and US Department of Transport (ECDOT), *Transatlantic Airline Alliances: Competitive Issues and Regulatory Approaches*, A report by the European Commission and the United States Department of Transportation (16 November 2010), p. 6. Online. Available HTTP: <http://ec.europa.eu/competition/sectors/transport/reports/joint_alliance_report.pdf> (accessed 2 August 2011).

d Ibid.

licensee shall not operate an international air service, or represent by advertisement or otherwise the licensee operating such air service, under a name other than that specified in the license', allowing AC to operate one such aircraft.[92]

Consumer benefits may include lower prices, owing to lowered operational costs on a given route; more departure times to choose from; more destinations; shorter travel times, owing to optimized transfers; faster mileage rewards, by earning on a single airline's account rather than on several different ones; and round-the-world tickets, at a relatively low price. On the other hand, consumers might be disadvantaged owing to higher prices, where competition is erased or distorted on a certain route; less frequent flights on certain routes where, prior to alliance, each of the two airlines flew three times daily but now the alliance flies only four times daily in total.

The first large alliance still in existence today was formed in 1989 as a large-scale codeshare agreement between NW[93] and KL. In October 1992, the Netherlands signed the first-ever 'Open Skies'[94] agreement with the US, despite objections by

92 CTA, Order No. 1998-A-250. Online. Available HTTP: <http://www.cta-otc.gc.ca/rulings-decisions/orders/1998/A/1998-A-250_e.html> (accessed 12 August 2011).

93 NW and DL merged in 2008.

94 This agreement was negotiated in line with a US DoT initiative (*See* Final Order, In the Matter of Defining 'Open Skies', Docket 48130, 05.08.1992) and in keeping with its international aviation policy (*See* Statement of United States International Air Transportation Policy, Docket 49844, *Federal Register*, 60 FR 21841, 03.05.1995). The 'open skies' form of agreement is not to be confused with the 'Treaty on Open Skies' negotiated between 1992 and 2005 in the context of national defence observation flights (*See* the US Defence Threat Reduction Agency, Public Affairs website. Available HTTP: <http://www.dtra.mil/press_resources/fact_sheets/print/index.cfm?factsheet=os.cfm> (accessed 16 August 2011).

the EU, and gave both countries unrestricted landing rights in the two countries. In conjunction with the first 'Open Skies' Agreement, the US granted the NW–KL alliance antitrust immunity. This case was paramount, as until today, similar alliances have or continue to struggle to overcome transnational barriers.

According to the US Department of State, 'open skies' agreements create a

> free market for aviation services and provide substantial benefits for travellers, shippers, and communities as well as for the economy of each country. Bilateral 'Open Skies' agreements give the airlines of both countries the right to operate air services from any point in the country to any point in the other, as well as to and from third countries. These rights enable airlines to network using strategic points across the globe.[95]

The US DoT retains authority over 'whether to approve proposed international air-line alliances and to decide whether to grant antitrust immunity for all or part of any such alliance' under 49 U.S.C. Sections 41309 and 41308, respectively.

Where no antitrust immunity is expressly granted, US antitrust laws apply to domestic and international airline alliances alike. By conducting a case-by-case analysis of the terms of the agreements between proposed alliances, the Division assesses its potential effect on competition. This process begins with the defining and measure of the relevant market, its participants and concentrations. 'Generally, the greatest threat to competition comes when two of very few airlines that compete in a market enter into a codeshare agreement in that market'.[96] One main feature of 'open skies' agreements is authorization to enter into codesharing or leasing agreements with other airlines, and an optional provision for codesharing between airlines and surface transportation companies.[97]

On the other hand, the US DoJ in 2001 stated:

> [W]hen a codeshare is proposed to link a city-pair market served by one carrier with a city-pair market served by the other, rather than to cover a city-pair market in which both carriers are actual or potential competitors, the proposed codeshare would create what is referred to as an 'end-to-end efficiency', which is generally pro-competitive.[98]

If both codeshare partners plan to operate flights in the specified market, then the Division looks to whether the structure of the agreement is such that each partner independently sets and controls its capacity, scheduling and pricing. If this is the case, carriers, in theory, will have more incentive to market and sell seats on flights they themselves operate, rather than on their partners'.

95 US Department of State website (Office of Transportation Affairs, Bureau of Economic and Business Affairs). Online. Available HTTP: <http://www.state.gov/e/eb/tra/c661.htm> (accessed 1 September 2011).

96 US DoJ, *Antitrust Division Statement, International Aviation Alliances: Market Turmoil and the Future of Airline Competition.*

97 US Department of State website, Office of Aviation Negotiations (31 January 2001). Avaialable HTTP: <http://www.state.gov.uk/e/eb/rls/fs/208.htm> (accessed 1 October 2011).

98 US DoJ, *Antitrust Division Statement, International Aviation Alliances: Market Turmoil and the Future of Airline Competition.*

Rather than fully integrating to 'joint' sales and marketing on shared flights, some airlines construct codeshare agreements that adopt the blocked space, or block-seat feature 'to preserve some independence in pricing and marketing of seats on the shared flights . . . where the non-operating carrier purchases a fixed number of seats and bears the risk of loss if those seats are not sold'.[99] This way, airlines are not bound to develop additional budgets or share resources on a joint sales project. Codeshare agreements with blocked space provisions are simply space purchase agreements and the buyer bears the risk if they are unable to sell the space on to passengers. If independent operations by the two proposed codeshare partners are neither planned nor likely, the Division will analyze whether new competitors would be likely to enter into the markets if the agreement were approved. If likely, the proposed alliance will be allowed; if unlikely, it will be blocked.

In the case of an international codeshare, which means new entry into the international market, the question first raised by the Division is whether that market would be covered by an 'open skies' or 'traditional' bilateral air service agreement. 'Where new entry is legally constrained by a restrictive bilateral agreement, the threat to competition of a codeshare on that city-pair could be substantial, particularly if the codeshare partners were the only two carriers authorized under the bilateral agreement'.[100] However, if the market is covered by an 'open skies' agreement, new entry is legally possible, save for an investigation of 'how likely such entry would be in the event codeshare partners attempt to raise fares or reduce service'.[101] In Williams' study on the extent and impact of deregulation, he observes:

> [It is] . . . an interesting exercise to compare the ten largest domestic routes in the world with their international equivalents. Whilst the respective domestic markets have been deregulated, the international routes [in 2000] are still constrained by the terms contained in bilateral agreements.[102]

In 2001, two applications were made to the US DoJ for approval and antitrust immunity for alliance agreements under 49 U.S.C. 41308-09. The first application was made by AA and BA: the '*AA–BA transaction*'; and the second was made by BD, Lauda Air Luftfahrt AG (Lauda), LH, OS, SK and UA: the '*UA–BMI transaction*'. These two applications concerned capacity and pricing in US–UK markets, which remains 'severely restricted and distorted'[103] under the previous Bermuda II bilateral aviation agreement.[104] Four

---

99 Ibid., p. 8.
100 Ibid., p. 9.
101 Ibid.
102 Williams, *Airline Competition*, pp. 12, 15–22.
103 US DoJ, *Antitrust Division Statement, International Aviation Alliances: Market Turmoil and the Future of Airline Competition*.
104 The EU–US Air Transport Agreement, has replaced this agreement. Under the Bermuda II agreement, only four airlines from the UK and US were permitted to operate from LHR: BA, VS, AA and UA. In addition, carriers could only fly to a short list of US cities. However, airlines not based in the UK or US were not subject to the agreement, for instance Kuwait Airlines, Air New Zealand and Air India, who flew from LHR to the US with little restriction.

notable European decisions previously raised the question of substitutability of LHR and LGW: *KLM–Alitalia*,[105] *Eurostar*,[106] *KLM–Air UK*[107] and *BA–CityFlyer*.[108]

Cargo alliances

Many of the concepts and principles of tactical and strategic alliances discussed thus far apply equally to the cargo sector of the industry. 'Having first focused on passengers, airline alliances now are tackling cargo issues and initiating new services that often include, but also, worry their freight-forwarder partners'.[109] Virtually all passenger aircraft carry cargo in their holds, and the freight to be earned on some of these and all-cargo operations is quite significant. In Doganis's view:

> There are routes where the enormous payload of wide-bodied aircraft in all-cargo configuration is too large for the potential freight demand, while belly-hold capacity may be insufficient or unable to cope with bulky consignments. In such circumstances, the wide-bodied combo-aircraft, on which passengers and freight are carried on the main deck, may prove a commercially attractive proposition.[110]

There are three main types of cargo airlines: integrated airlines, such as those which have both passenger and cargo operations like BA; all-cargo airlines, such as United Parcel Services (UPS); and charter cargo airlines, which are unscheduled or leased, such as Cargolux. Cargo alliances are not restricted to airlines, however, and many cooperative agreements include freight forwarders or other logistics companies. In Nall's view:

> Whatever form an alliance takes, the impetus is the same as in other sectors – keeping pace with the demands of the global marketplace. For air cargo carriers, that means filling geographic gaps in their networks and empty space in their cargo bays – efficiencies that translate into better service and lower cost for customers.[111]

In 2001, three integrated airlines, Lufthansa Cargo (td.Flash), SAS Cargo (SAS Priority) and Singapore Airlines Cargo (Swiftrider), combined efforts to create a single functioning 'express' product. The resulting relationship became known as the WOW alliance (WOW). The harmonization developed to incorporate all cargo products in 2002, when

105 Case No. COMP/JV.19 (11 August 1999).
106 Case No. IV/M.1305 (19 December 1998).
107 Case No. IV/M.967 (22 September 1997).
108 UK Competition Commission, British Airways Plc and CityFlyer Express Ltd (1999).
109 S. Nall, 'Air Cargo Alliances Take Tentative First Steps Into Cargo Arena in Global Logistics and Supply Chain Strategies' *Keller Publishing*, 1998. Online. Available HTTP: <http://www.supplychainbrain.com> (accessed 12 August 2011).
110 R. Doganis, *Flying Off Course; Airline Economics and Marketing*, 4th ed. (London: Routledge, 2010), p. 206.
111 Nall, 'Air Cargo Alliances'.

JL Cargo became a member.[112] WOW once offered a worldwide network of 523 destinations in 103 countries with a fleet of 44 freighters and cargo holds of more than 760 passenger planes,[113] but now only two members remain: SAS and Singapore.

In a majority of cases, two or more partners in a global alliance share freight handling facilities or perform up to 100 per cent of the handling (customs clearances, dangerous goods acceptance, storage, loading and unloading) for partners, where two separate or joint operations would not be profitable. For instance, Lufthansa handles Star Alliance partner Air New Zealand's cargo at Los Angeles (LAX) Airport, while they share their facilities with partner United Airlines at FRA. In a statement, Mel Torre, a spokesman for Lufthansa Cargo AG, said:

> It's not as easy on the cargo side as it is on the passenger side . . . it takes more coordination and planning. We [Star Alliance members] got together to talk about developing joint activities involving four to five areas. First, we will develop a global network for air cargo, then we will work on the ground services.[114]

Other global (airline) cargo alliances include SkyTeam Cargo and oneworld.

Joint ventures

A joint venture, or joint operation, may be defined as 'a situation where an airline operates on a route or route network on the basis of a joint cost and revenue-sharing agreement with a counterpart airline'.[115] Again, this type of agreement has been the subject of much criticism and debate within the European Commission. Under Regulation 1617/93, the Commission may grant block exemptions for joint operations that meet certain requirements. The Commission has shaped its policy mainly following *12 joint operation agreements between airlines*[116] notified between May and September 1988.[117]

> Although all agreements were similar in content, the attitude of the Commission in relation to them varied according to the nature of the route and size of the parties involved. Three of them, between British Airways and Air France (Paris–Manchester and Nice–Manchester) and British Airways and Alitalia (London–Genoa), were terminated after discussions with the Commission.[118]

112 WOW Alliance website: <http://www.wowtheworld.com>.
113 'WOW Wins Award for Best Air Freight Alliance',WOW Website. Available HTTP: <http://www.wowtheworld.com/news_press9.html> (accessed 23 July 2011).
114 Nall, 'Air Cargo Alliances'.
115 J.Child, D. Faulkner and S.Tallman, *Cooperative Strategy: Managing Alliances, Networks, and Joint Ventures*, 2nd ed. (Oxford: Oxford University Press, 2005), p. 39.
116 *Air France and NFD Luftverkehrs AG* [1989] OJ C 204/3; *Air France and Iberia* [1989] OJ C 204/4; *Air France and Iberia* [1989] OJ C 204/4; *Air France and Alitalia* [1989] OJ C 204/5; *Air France and Brymon* [1989] OJ C 204/6; *Air France and Sabena* [1989] OJ C 204/7, 8 and 10; *Aer Lingus and Sabena* [1989] OJ C204/11; *London City Airways and Sabena* [1989] OJ C 204/12.
117 The Commission's XIXth Report on Competition Policy (1990) at point 25.
118 Sir Leon Brittan's response to the European Parliament Written Question No. 580/89, [1990] OJ C 97/6, [1990] 4 CMLR 432.

It is needful to discuss the difference between a joint venture with contractual integration and a joint venture company. In some cases, two or more parties to a joint venture may 'expand' its product lines or services through a series of contracts, as we have seen. In other cases, however, the parties may decide to form a new joint venture company to manage this new enterprise. In the former case, while there is no company with legal personality, there must subsist some sort of joint venture management, as agreed and governed by the joint venture contracts. A joint venture with contractual integration, which does not establish of a joint venture company and may therefore be perceived as simply a contract to cooperate, will likely be handled just as if it were a joint venture company. This was the case in the now defunct *KLM–Alitalia*[119] alliance, where their joint operation was held a joint venture for the purposes of applying the ECMR.[120] The ECMR was also applied in the cases of *Lufthansa–SAS*,[121] *Finnair–Maersk Air*[122] and *Austrian Airlines–Lufthansa*[123] in treating the joint operations as pure joint ventures with approval subject to the fulfilment of some conditions including divesture of slots at hub airports.

In *United Airlines v Mesa Airlines*,[124] United and Mesa had entered into an exclusive service agreement and codeshare agreement, whereby Mesa would operate United's commuter services from a number of smaller regional airports to United's hubs. Mesa purchased a number of larger planes from Untied to accommodate this. Some time later, United entered into a separate agreement with SkyWest to perform a similar service. In short, Mesa was unhappy with this and refused to perform on the contract owing to what they alleged was a breach of contract on the part of United. United cancelled Mesa's contract and replaced it entirely with SkyWest, upon which Mesa brought an action against United for breach of contract. Mesa contended that the 'relationship' between themselves and United was one characteristic of more than a mere contract. Mesa alleged that they and United were 'partners', and that United fraudulently induced them to purchase additional aircraft to perform under the contract.

The issue before the court was to determine whether the relationship between United and Mesa was something more than a contract for services. They sought to distinguish between 'independent contractor' and 'partner' in the context of a partnership.[125] The court referred to a similar case, *Vaugh v General Foods Corp*, where it was held that 'businesses often refer to suppliers, customers, and producers of complementary products colloquially as 'partners' without summoning up fiduciary duties'.[126] Looking at the nature of the relationship and contract suggested that this was a contractual supplier (agent–distributor) relationship and thus the two airlines were 'partners' in the sense of working together, rather than 'partners' in a *legal* partnership.

---

119 Comp/JV.19, This application was appealed by SAS (T-241/01, *SAS v Community*).
120 The provisions of the ECMR are detailed above at point 4.4.2.5 'Concentrations under the ECMR'.
121 *See* [1996] OJ L 54/28, [1996] 4 CMLR 845, *see also* (1998) 19 ECLR 116.
122 *See* The Commission's XXVIIIthReport on Competition Policy (1998), pp. 146–147.
123 [2002] OJ L 242/25, [2003] 4 CMLR 252.
124 *United Airlines, Inc v Mesa Airlines, Inc and WestAir Commuter Airlines, Inc v SkyWest Airlines, Inc* 219 F.3d 605; 2000 U.S. LEXIS 15522.
125 Ibid., para. 610.
126 797 F.2d 1403 (7thCir 1986).

Stock investment

As discussed earlier, alliances may be formed with short-term objectives in sight. They are, however, likely to be established to create long-term cooperative relationships 'when the partners invest substantially in them'.[127] Clearly, the most prevalent risks associated with stock investment, especially between partners located in two different countries, are the transaction–cost and corporate governance risks as discussed earlier.

Parke's research on 111 inter-firm alliances tested propositions drawn from transaction–cost economics and 'found that alliances buttressed by non-recoverable mutual investments are more likely to be high performers, and this supports the argument that the incorporation of deterrence against opportunism is beneficial in partnerships'.[128]

As part of any of the above business strategies, cooperating airlines may seek to take additional steps to strengthen their relationship and commitment to one another through investment in one another's stock. Prior cases of this type of financial investment include BA–US Airways and KL–NW.

In 1993, BA purchased stock in US Airways (then called USAir) under an investment–alliance plan, which entailed US Airways relinquishing its London route authority. After changing its name in 1996 to US Airways, the airline challenged its relationship with BA in an attempt to regain rights to London[129] and asked that BA dispose of its stock, which occurred a few months later.[130] The US DoJ Antitrust Division brought its first civil action[131] under the Clayton Antitrust Act[132] against the investment between BA and US Airways, 'after concluding that the transaction threatened competition in gateway city pairs and connecting city pairs – in particular, service between Northeast and Mid-Atlantic cities and London'.[133] Section 7 of the Act prohibits mergers and acquisitions where the effect may substantially lessen competition.

Within the former Wings part-alliance between AZ, KL and NW, now part of the SkyTeam alliance, acquired a 25 per cent stake in NW along with AF, DL, KL, the former Belgian flag carrier Sabena and LX, which demonstrates a 'virtual locking together of their networks'.[134] This investment came after the two airlines were given

---

127 Child, Faulkner and Tallman, *Cooperative Strategy*, p. 7.

128 A. Parke, 'Strategic Alliance Structuring: A Game Theoretic and Transaction–cost Examination of Interfirm Cooperation', *Academy of Management Review* 36, 1993, 227–268, as cited ibid., p. 21; *See also* 'Multilateral Airline Alliances: The Fallacy of the Alliances to Mergers Proposition', in J.F. O'Connell and G. Williams (eds), *Air Transport in the 21st Century: Key Strategic Developments*, (Farnham: Ashgate), pp. 171–183.

129 In fact, US sought rights to LHR from four US gateway cities: PIT, PHL, CLT and BOS, whereas prior to 1993, it had rights only to LGW under the terms of the US/UK Bermuda bilateral agreement.

130 Liegl, P. 'US Airways History' in *US Airways: Fleet and Network Analysis*. Online. Available HTTP: <http://www.erau.edu/research/BA590/USAIR/chapters/ch1.htm> (accessed 12 August 2011).

131 In 1991, at the outset of the BA/US negotiations.

132 Clayton Antitrust Act of 1914, 15 U.S.C. §§12–27, §7.

133 US DoJ, *Antitrust Division Statement, International Aviation Alliances: Market Turmoil and the Future of Airline Competition*.

134 OECD, *Deregulation and Airline Competition: Organisation for Economic Cooperation and Development* (Washington, DC: OECD Publications,1998).

antitrust immunity from US antitrust laws under the 'open skies' (in this case also bilateral) air service agreement between the US and the Netherlands.[135]

Mergers

A merger is the combination of two companies into one larger company. Proposed mergers almost always raise some concern for potential effects on competition. Mergers may have further implications for antitrust in cases where each of the two companies is established in a different legal jurisdiction.[136]

A good example of a cross-border European merger is AF with KL. After five years of informal talks, the French and Dutch airlines merged in May 2005, when Jean-Cyril Spinetta, CEO of AF–KL and Leo van Wijk, former CEO of KL jointly reported:

> Air France and KLM have decided to join their forces and destinies to build a new entity on a par with the great European Single Market. Today we share a single ambition, which is to be one of the few airlines that are powerful enough to play a leading role in the future of global alliances that will structure the airline industry. In other words, to be big enough to be a key player on the world stage, in order to improve our profitability, offer the best service possible to our customers and protect our jobs over the long-term.[137]

Prior to this merger, KL had planned to deepen its relationship with AZ, to the extent that their entire management would be unified, in what some have called 'a merger in everything but name'.[138] Under the terms of the proposed KL-led 'virtual merger', the two airlines would combine sales and marketing operations, jointly buy aircraft and share profits.[139] KL decided to drop the venture amidst concerns over the 'privatisation of the state-owned carrier and disagreements over the role of its main hub at Milan's MXP airport'.[140]

In its 2001 statement, *International Aviation Alliances: Market Turmoil and the Future of Airline Competition*[141] before the US Senate Subcommittee on Antitrust, Competition, and Business Rights, the US DoJ discusses the position and analytical approach of its Antitrust Division (the Division) on the subject.

---

135 The Netherlands were the first EU country to be granted antitrust immunity in the US, with Belgium and Germany as the second and third.

136 The EU is an exception to this rule, under freedom of establishment . . . although comp authorities will still scrutinize potential for anti-competitive behaviour or abuse of dominant position in under concentration of affected markets.

137 '5 May 2004: Air France – KLM, A Global Airline Market Leader', Air France Press Releases, www. airfrance.com.

138 OECD, *Deregulation and Airline Competition*.

139 Ibid.

140 'KLM/Alitalia' (2000), *CNN Money*, http://money.cnn.com/2000/05/02/europe/klm_alitalia/.

141 US DoJ, *Antitrust Division Statement, International Aviation Alliances: Market Turmoil and the Future of Airline Competition*.

Until 1989, the US DoT had authority over airline mergers in the US, but acted at the recommendation of the Division to disapprove two mergers, TW–OZ and NW–RW. These two proposed mergers, if they had been approved, would have led to the merging of the only two hub carriers[142] at St Louis and Minneapolis international airports respectively. In 1998, the Division filed suit to block NW from buying a controlling stake in CO, the fourth- and fifth-largest US airlines at the time, which was dropped when NW agreed to sell the shares back to CO that would have given it a 'voting trust', retaining only a 5 per cent share.[143]

The Division also challenged the UA–US Airways proposed merger in mid-2001, the second- and sixth-largest US airlines at the time, 'after concluding that the merger would reduce competition, raise fares, and harm consumers on routes throughout the US and on a number of international routes, including giving UA a monopoly or duopoly on non-stop service on over 30 routes'.[144] After the challenge announcement, the airlines abandoned their merger plans. This may be circumvented if the relevant competition authority grants antitrust immunity, such as the EU–US Air Transport Agreement discussed earlier. In the absence or at the refusal of the requisite permission, international airlines typically resort to one of the aforementioned business strategies for forming an alliance. While the terms of such multilateral cooperative agreements between carriers are heavily scrutinized by the respective competition authorities and transportation agencies, entry into a foreign market may be achieved, albeit it sometimes in a roundabout, yet 'lawful' way.

For competition authorities, the concern is that alliances are moving increasingly beyond codeshare and joint marketing agreements, in some cases amounting to what they would call a 'virtual (cross-border) merger', despite national rules forbidding foreign ownership.[145] The OECD's general position on this is provided in their 2001 paper, *Airline Mergers and Alliances*:

> Although agreements and alliances between international air carriers have long been a feature of the airline industry, the last few years has seen a rapid expansion in the number of such alliances and, more importantly, a deepening of their scope and depth, raising fundamental questions about their effect on international air services competition.[146]

Some argue[147] that the tendency in the airline industry is towards deeper alliances. 'In effect, these super-alliances are coming as close to actual mergers as aviation's

---

142 The proposed merging carriers were the only airlines providing non-stop service between the hub city and smaller cities in the surrounding region. (US DoJ, *Antitrust Division Statement, International Aviation Alliances: Market Turmoil and the Future of Airline Competition*).

143 Ibid.

144 Ibid.

145 OECD, *Deregulation and Airline Competition*.

146 Ibid.

147 The European Air Law Association and the OECD argue this. *See also* B. Agusdinata and W. de Klein, 'The Dynamics of Airline Alliances', *Journal of Air Transport Management*, 8, 2002, 201–211; T.H. Oum, and A. Zhang, 'Key Aspects of Global Strategic Alliances and the Impacts on the Future of Canadian Airline Industry', *Journal of Air Transport Management* 7, 2001, 287–301.

Byzantine regulations allow'.[148] Others have gone a step further to allege that the airline industry is moving from 'one extreme, of regulation and state ownership, to another, of global consolidation – with little or no exposure to competition in between'.[149]

The proliferation of alliances between carriers around the globe is now more appropriately matched with growing willingness of governments to negotiate the opening of domestic aviation markets on a multilateral basis. The momentum of the seemingly efficient global airline networks has encouraged governments both to recognize the force of globalization and in cases like Singapore, the United Arab Emirates, Australia and Thailand to name a few, to enjoy the benefits of previously-shunned cabotage rights.[150]

Whilst airline alliances are as exclusionary as any organization offering membership, the high quality, service and safety standards for instance required on admission fly in the face of arguments claiming their detriment to consumer benefits and competition, particularly where public service obligations will be ever-present.

Loyalty programmes

Loyalty programmes, such as frequent flyer programmes (FFPs), travel agent commission schemes and, albeit indirectly, computerized reservation systems, raise concern as regards their impact on the competitiveness of the air transport sector. It has been argued that in the absence of such programmes, the nature of competition would shift towards route-by-route rather than network-by-network competition.[151] This is a key area of criticism owing to the biases towards consumer (e.g. online travel websites) and business (e.g. travel agents) preferences that are gained through frequently imperfect information. The advent of imperfect competition in any market means highly subjective decision-making, which, with a lack of supervision or control on the part of an impartial third party, may not necessarily be in the best interests of the consumer.

Links between airline FFPs are common features of cooperative agreements such as codeshares and alliances. Designed to operate as a volume discount, they offer more free travel and benefits to consumers the more they fly. Likely unbeknownst to them, consumers ultimately pay for free travel in higher prices for paid travel, whereas the frequent flyer 'bonus is a kickback to the purchasing agent, the business-travelling employee'.[152]

Exclusive loyalty discounts

Loyalty or fidelity discounts are generally given to a customer as a reward for exclusive loyalty to the supplier, rather the requirement that a certain quota of 'purchases' must first be met. There will be an infringement on Article 102 if it is a dominant under-

---

148 OECD, *Deregulation and Airline Competition*.
149 Ibid., footnote 22.
150 Vasigh, Fleming and Tacker (*Introduction to Air Transport Economics*, p. 138) note that, 'Perhaps, open skies in lieu of cabotage will eventually become routine and allow a true flourishing of the air travel industry.'
151 OECD, *Deregulation and Airline Competition*, p. 50.
152 Ibid.

taking that is granting loyalty rebates, as this would tie together the dominant undertaking and the customer and create an unfair, exclusionary effect on competitors. The CJEU and EC have handed down a number of decisions on the discriminatory practice of granting loyalty rebates. The first occasion on which loyalty rebates were considered contrary to Article 102 was in the *Suiker Unie*[153] case, and confirmed in the *Hoffmann–La Roche*[154] case (both under ex. Article 82 TEC).

In the case *Hoffmann–La Roche*, the European Commission found that Hoffmann–La Roche had granted 22 large customers loyalty rebates, which owing to their dominant position, was in effect an abuse of a that position. The CJEU clarified the issue:

> The fidelity rebate, unlike quantity rebates exclusively linked with the volume of purchases from the producer concerned, is designed through the grant of a financial advantage to prevent customers from obtaining their supplies from competing producers.[155]

It was held, and is thus the European position, that the granting of loyalty rebates

> by an undertaking in a dominant position and especially on an expanding market [as was the case here] tend to consolidate this position by means of a form of competition, which is not based on the transactions effected and is therefore distorted.[156]

Target discounts

Target discounts are awarded when a customer reaches a previously agreed quota. A customer will receive a discount on all purchases made over a certain time period if the quota is reached. Under this scheme, customers are usually pressured, albeit absent of an 'exclusivity agreement' to purchase from a single supplier, much like with loyalty rebates. This could prove even more problematic for the customer whose quotas will likely increase over time. If the supplier is in a dominant position, there may be implications for an infringement of Article 102, again, much as with loyalty rebates.[157]

Short of an outright prohibition of loyalty programmes, an alternative would be to require dominant airlines to allow rivals to participate in its loyalty schemes, eliminating any competitive advantage to the dominant incumbent.[158] In alliances, for instance, FFPs

---

153 Case 40/73, *Suiker Unie v EC Commission* [1975] ECR 1663, [1976] 1 CMLR 295. It was held in this case that a rebate allowed abuse of a dominant position as the customer feared buying from other suppliers would lead to forced repayment of rebate or risk of withdrawal.

154 Case 85/76, *Hoffmann-La Roche v Commission* [1979] ECR 461, [1979] 3 CMLR 211.

155 Ibid., p. 540.

156 Ibid.

157 *See for instance* Case 322/81, *Nederlandsche Banden-Industrie Michelin v Commission* [1983] ECR 3461, [1985] 1 CMLR 282.

158 OECD, *Deregulation and Airline Competition*.

must be kept separate, essentially restricting the attractiveness of both schemes, as was the principle applied in both the *LH–SK–UA*[159] and *BA–AA* cases discussed above.

Although the impact of computerized reservation systems (CRSs) may not be immediately apparent, it may be argued that the 'loyalty' benefits or detriments are even greater than travel agent commissions or FFPs. In order to book airline tickets, consumers, including businesses (either directly on the Internet, indirectly by telephone or through a travel agent) must encounter some form of CRS. In the earlier days of CRSs, each airline owned and operated their own system; AA owned Sabre and UA owned Apollo. In more recent years, perhaps in response to the influence of 'mega-alliances', these systems have been updated and merged. For instance, the CRS conglomerate Amadeus now sells tickets for five oneworld, eight Star and two SkyTeam alliance airlines.[160]

In order to access an airline's CRS, you must contract to subscribe. This potentially creates yet another 'distortion' to competition through the incorporation of exclusive use clauses in the service contracts. For example, 'Sabre and Apollo have been accused of attempting to lock travel agents into exclusive use of their systems through various contract requirements'.[161] Clearly, if a travel agent is forced to use a specific CRS it is yet more 'out of their control' than with the travel agent commission schemes where a choice of reaching a quota may involve at least some independent decision-making.

In the past, airlines who owned their own CRSs would seek wherever possible to promote their airlines, or in the case of alliances, their partner airlines before all others. This would perhaps not be such an issue if it did not, again, impact confusingly on the mind of the travel agent. To overcome some of the associated interference with the competitive process, the US Civil Aeronautics Board in 1984 outlawed 'screen bias'. This involved showing, in a listing of flight options, those operated by the airline that owned the CRS first, regardless of minimum flight time, connections, and pricing parameters. In 1991, ICAO went a step further and established a code of conduct governing standards of information display and access on CRSs.

Airline alliances: abuse and relevant market

This section discusses how the concepts of abuse and dominance might apply to the specifics of commercial manoeuvring in the air transport sector whether unilateral, bilateral or multilateral in nature.

In his paper, *Airline Alliances and Mergers – The Emerging Commission Policy*,[162] J. Stragier details the Commission's procedural and substantive approach to evaluating the

159 *See* Commission Notice concerning the alliance between Lufthansa, SAS and United Airlines (cases COMP/D-2/36.201, 36.076, 36.078 – procedure under Article 105 TFEU (ex. Article 85 TEC), [2002] OJ C 181/2, 30 July 2002. The three airlines agreed to make slots available at FRA to other airlines as well as access to the incumbents' FFPs and interlining opportunities. In addition, the three were not to participate in those particular IATA fare conferences.

160 Amadeus website. Available HTTP: <www.amadeus.com/x8451> (accessed 2 August 2011).

161 S. Borenstein, 'The Evolution of U.S. Airline Competition', *Journal of Economic Perspectives*,6(2), Spring 1992, 63–64.

162 J. Stragier, 'Airline Alliances and Mergers – The Emerging Commission Policy', Paper presented at the 13th Annual Conference of the European Air Law Association, Zurich (9 November 2001). Online.

relevant market in the application of the EU competition rules to the air transport sector.

Stragier explains how the Commission defines the relevant market by looking at five main areas: origin and destination city pairs, time-sensitive and non-time-sensitive passengers, direct and indirect services, airport substitution and substitution between different transport services. The primary distinction to be made in this sector is between scheduled and charter air services.[163] For the purposes of the present study, the analysis will focus on scheduled air services.

In four important air transport cases, *Swissair–Sabena*,[164] *British Airways–Air Liberté*,[165] *Marine-Wendel–SairGroup–AOM*[166] and *Ahmed Saeed*,[167] the relevant markets were defined on the basis of a 'route' or 'bundle of routes'.

In the *KLM–Alitalia*[168] merger decision, the Commission clarified the market definition in air transport focusing on demand substitutability. In particular, it concluded that each point-of-origin/point-of-destination pair constitutes a relevant market, and that such market includes a route or bundle of routes comprising:

- the non-stop flights between the two airports;
- non-stop flights between the airports whose respective catchment areas significantly overlap with the catchment area of the airports concerned;
- indirect flights between the airports concerned to the extent that these flights are substitutable for the non-stop flight.[169]

It should be reiterated that other transport services supplied by coach, train or ferry may be substituted for flights, subject of course to whether the service is reasonably interchangeable with the flight. Next, the Commission makes a distinction between 'time-sensitive' and 'non-time-sensitive' travellers in analyzing potential anti-competitive effects in relevant markets. The distinction correlates to time constraints as a factor for business travellers in determining their choices of airlines. Stragier summarizes the classification:

> In general these passengers typically are less willing to substitute for alternative (longer) times or paths than non time-sensitive passengers . . . time- sensitive-passengers generally require flexibility to change routings and flight times and they are therefore ready to pay higher priced unrestricted first, business or economy tickets.[170]

Available HTTP: <http://www.eu.int/comm/competition/speeches/text/sp2001_040_en.pdf> (accessed 15 March 2002).

163 *See* Commission Decision of 16.1.1996, Case IV/25.545 – *Lufthansa/SAS* [1996] OJ L 54, 5.3.1996.
164 Commission Decision of 20 July 1995, Case IV/M.616, para. 19.
165 Commission Decision of 28 February 1997, Case IV/M.857, para. 15.
166 Commission Decision of 3 August 1999, Case IV/M.1494.
167 Case 66/86, *Ahmed Saeed Flugreisen* [1989] ECR 803.
168 Commission Decision of 11 August 1999, Case M/JV-19.
169 Stragier, 'Airline Alliances and Mergers – The Emerging Commission Policy'.
170 Ibid., p. 4.

As regards the relevant origin and destination city pairs, the Commission considers the potential for indirect flights between the two respective airports in a market to serve as substitutions for the direct service. The substitutability of short-haul indirect flights is, however, lower than on long-haul indirect flights as was found in *KLM–Alitalia*,[171] and therefore at a greater disadvantage as compared primarily with the total duration of the 'direct' journey. On long-haul routes, however, the substitutability might be significantly higher, owing to the fact that long-haul journey times are greater. This was the view of the Commission in *United Airlines–US Airways*.[172]

> The Commission concluded that certain indirect flights which are marketed as connecting flights on the city-pair concerned, and which only cause a limited extension of the trip duration . . . [and] found that for indirect services to be competitive they should have an in-flight duration comparable with that of the non-stop service, and their connection time should be no longer than 150 minutes.[173]

It is important to next define the geographic market to assess the relevant overlap between catchment areas of two or more airports concerned. The question the Commission asks itself is whether the airports are substitutable. To answer this, they will look to the nature of the services offered from each of the airports: 'In particular for time-sensitive business travellers, the choice of airport will also be determined by the number of frequencies, schedule, connectivity and overall quality of airport service'.[174] Some examples of disputes arising over defining the relevant market follow.

In *KLM–Alitalia*,[175] the Commission determined that the catchment areas of Brussels, Dusseldorf and Amsterdam airports do not significantly overlap in terms of short-haul flights between Amsterdam and Milan–Rome: 'In particular, a passenger will accept to travel (for example, by car) a longer distance to the departure airport to catch a long-haul flight than to catch a short-haul flight, because of the minor impact that additional travel by car on the total travel time'.[176]

In *Lufthansa–SAS–BMI British Midland*,[177] the Commission held that for non-time-sensitive travellers between London and Frankfurt, the five London airports: London City (LCY), LGW, LHR, Luton (LTN) and STN in the UK and FRA and Frankfurt-Hahn (HHN) airports in Germany can be considered substitutable. For time-sensitive travellers in the same market, the Commission decided that flights in the STN–HHN market were not substitutable, and therefore did not belong to the (time-sensitive)

---

171 Commission Decision of 11 August 1999, Case M/JV-19.
172 Commission Decision of 12 January 2001, Case COMP/M.2041.
173 Stragier, 'Airline Alliances and Mergers', p. 5.
174 Ibid.
175 Commission Decision of 11 August 1999, Case M/JV-19.
176 Stragier, 'Airline Alliances and Mergers', p. 5.
177 Case COMP/38.712 (The three airlines concluded a tripartite joint venture agreement on 9.11.1999, which was granted an exemption from Article 81 TEC under Article 5 of Regulation (EEC) No 3975/87, *see* [2001] OJ C 83/03.

LON–FRA market. Furthermore, it should be noted that smaller regional airports which offer less frequencies, connections and destinations than the larger 'hubs' are not suitable alternatives for one another. Take for instance, Stuttgart (regional), FRA (hub) and Munich (MUC) (hub).

When defining the relevant market, it is also important to consider the substitutability of different transport services, such as coach, ferry or train. In *British Midland v Aer Lingus*,[178] the Commission held that there is considerable demand for fast, flexible and convenient travel in the LON–Dublin (DUB) market, and there are no other modes of transport that can, at present, provide a sufficient substitute in relation to that demand. However, the codeshare agreements mentioned earlier between German Rail and airlines offers an argument for rail as a form of transport complimentary to air transport.

Similarly, in *British Airways–Air Liberté*,[179] the Commission found that although there are air and rail transport services available in the Paris–Toulouse market, the two modes of transport are unable to substitute each other since the rail journey is significantly longer and less frequent than journeys by air. However, in *British Airways–TAT (II)*[180] and *Lufthansa–SAS*,[181] the Commission concluded that high-speed trains offer an alternative to air transport over medium distances. In the London–Paris market, for instance, Eurostar operates between both cities' centres in less than three hours. While the duration of the 'in-flight' journey on a direct flight between the suburbs of the two cities may only last 45 minutes, the overall journey time from the city centre of London to the city centre of Paris may take well over four hours by air transport.

Unilateral manoeuvring

Airlines have also developed alliances with airports; regions and governments; ground handling companies; catering services and other complementary forms of public transport. Through unilateral manoeuvring,[182] airlines seek to invest in an array of industries complementary to air transport to reap benefits such as reduced costs and an increase in market power. This is an area of aviation and competition law that finds itself increasingly under the watchful eye of regulators, airlines, airports and the media, owing to the typical nature of the 'airport' serving the 'public utility'.

Air transport requires a number of complementary services to operate effectively. Airports, air traffic control and maintenance are among the most obvious examples of these services, but it is important that the ancillary services are not omitted, such as slot allocation, gates, handling facilities, baggage, refuelling, cleaning and catering.

178 Commission Decision of 26 February 1992, Case IV/33.544, [1992] OJ L 96, 10 April 1992, p. 34.
179 Commission Decision of 28 February 1997, Case IV/M.857.
180 Commission Decision of 26 August 1996, Case IV/M.806.
181 Case COMP/38.712.
182 Although unilateral manoeuvring is outside the scope of this book, it is useful to note that airlines' cooperative strategies extend beyond the immediate air transport industry. It is likely that this (relatively domestic) trend will continue as airlines face difficulty in cross-border consolidation. This subject serves as a parallel stream for future research.

Complementary and ancillary service providers are generally owned and operated by government or independent firms. In recent years, however, some of these providers have taken a more cooperative approach to integration with airlines. From an airline's perspective, vertical integration with service providers offers to lower transaction costs and the opportunity to provide the 'seamless end-to-end' service desired by travellers.[183] The features of the integration may vary between joint marketing campaigns, investment, and outright ownership. In the US, for instance, 'the majority of gates and ticket counters are closely held by the individual airlines either through lease agreements with the airport or under full ownership . . . and at hub airport airline may own facilities'.[184] This appears to be evidence of yet another form of strategic commercial manoeuvring sought by both service firms and airlines to gain a competitive advantage and achieve efficiencies.

The basic concern raised by competition authorities with respect to such unilateral manoeuvring is that where an airline integrates vertically with a complementary or ancillary service provider, 'the incumbent [service provider] may use that dominant position to prevent the growth of competition'.[185] For instance, a service provider that has an existing dominant position in slots at a particular airport has the power to distort competition on any number of routes from that airport. Furthermore, 'firms which provide services in one or more of these markets may reduce competition and potentially distort competition in the industry'.[186] In addition, there are often regulatory or security requirements, or physical limitations on space restricting the number of firms that can provide complementary or ancillary services.

An example of unilateral manoeuvring and vertical integration is EasyJet (U2) and LTN. U2 incorporated in March 1995 to offer low-cost scheduled air services within Europe. Its first call centre 'EasyLand' was based at LTN, from which the airline's first bookings were taken. Later that year, the LCC began flying from LTN to Edinburgh and Glasgow, Scotland.[187] By April 2007, easyJet operated 289 routes between 74 key European airports across the UK and Europe, of which 33 were from LTN.[188]

Prior to the Airports Act 1986, the Luton Borough Council owned and managed the airport. The Act required, however, that local authorities establish the airports as companies with an executive board to manage the business. In 1987, a limited-liability company was formed in the name of 'Luton International Airport' with Luton Borough Council as sole shareholder.[189] The airport's name was changed in 1990 to 'London Luton Airport', most likely to represent its proximity to London and position as a viable competitor to London's four other airports: LHR, LGW, STN and LCY.

183 OECD, *Deregulation and Airline Competition*.
184 Vasigh, Fleming and Tacker, *Introduction to Air Transport Economics*, p. 190.
185 Ibid.
186 Ibid.
187 EasyJet website. Available HTTP: <http://www.easyjet.com/EN/About/Information/infopack_keyevents.html> (accessed 2 August 2011).
188 London Luton Airport's Annual Monitoring Report 2006. Online. Available HTTP: <http://www.london-luton.co.uk/en/content/4/1070/annual-monitoring-report.html> (accessed 6 August 2011).
189 Ibid.

In 1986, Monarch Airlines began scheduled flights to Spain and Irish airline Ryanair launched services to Ireland. In 1991, Ryanair moved most of their business to STN, which had a severe impact on LTN.[190] Nevertheless, the scheduled services account for 92 per cent of LTN's business volume.[191] With the exception of BA, scheduled services from LTN are operated by LCCs, which coupled with the availability of slots and airport services makes the airport popular to start-ups or new entrants to the London air services market. LTN claims to have 'helped pioneer an entirely new concept in Europe – 'low cost' or 'no frills' flying – by becoming the first UK base for EasyJet in late 1995.[192] This is a very positive experience of vertical integration: cooperation between an airline and government–airport, which efficiently creates, and utilities (market) capacities within the Greater London catchment area.

Conclusions

The benefits of tactical and strategic alliances are many, hence their attractiveness, especially in recent years. The most notable of these advantages are product or service innovation; the combination of complementary skills and assets, technology transfer[193]; economies of scale[194]; expansion into new domestic markets; entry to foreign markets; building industry credibility and brand awareness; the provision of added value to consumers[195]; and the establishment of higher technological standards for the industry.

As new products or services are developed and introduced in a market, there will be a certain level of risk that comes with any learning process. However, as risk increases in this instance, so does the quantum of reward potential from the new action. Product and service innovation means developing new ideas to accommodate the needs or simply demands of the consumer. If the risk can be shared between members of a tactical alliance, then the attractiveness of such an innovation increases, serving the interests of all parties involved, including consumers.

In the process of this cooperation, partners will likely seek to combine complementary skills and assets to pursue their common goals. This may have the positive knock-on effect of technology transfer between players in the industry, and in the long-term, build greater industry credibility and brand awareness. Clearly, any changes made within the industry internally to encourage efficiency and reduce costs will provide an added value to consumers. Introducing new products or services in a market in the airline industry means doing so in conjunction with the implementation

---

190 *See* D. Starkie, *Aviation Markets: Studies in Competition and Regulatory Reform* (Farnham: Ashgate, 2008), pp. 89–110; S.D. Barrett, *Deregulation and the Airline Business in Europe: Selected Readings* (London: Routledge, 2009), pp. 120–157.

191 Ibid.

192 Ibid.

193 Technology transfer here refers to the relatively unrestricted access to knowledge and expertise beyond company borders.

194 Put simply, the concept of economies of scale is analogous with the phrase 'bigger is better'. Here, it is meant to describe an increase of scale of operations, production mass and momentum.

195 This point is subjective, and as such sparks intense debate on the regulatory balancing of consumer welfare and benefits of tactical and strategic alliances.

and adaptation of new technologies, thereby raising the bar on technological standards for the industry.

It has been argued that 'alliances are a means to an end, and consequently they are not necessarily formed with a long-term cooperative relationship in mind'.[196] For instance, a firm may enter into an alliance 'as a means of appropriating competencies and knowledge from a partner, which it continues to regard as an actual or potential competitor'[197] or to enter into 'an unfamiliar national market'[198] where a degree of uncertainty and with it, high financial and other risks may exist.

According to Porter:

> Alliances are a tool for extending or reinforcing competitive advantage, but rarely a sustainable means for creating it . . . [but they are] . . . frequently transitional devices . . . [which] proliferate in industries undergoing structural change or escalating competition, where managers fear that they cannot cope. They are a response to uncertainty, and provide comfort that the firm is taking action.[199]

This suggests that an alliance is a type of coping mechanism for businesses, with managers 'resorting' to cooperation at this level in order to 'survive'. In the case of the airline industry, it can be argued that alliances have become such a common trade practice that they have an independent brand image and as such can create a competitive advantage for an airline. Thus alliances are not necessarily only used as transitional devices, although it could be argued that the industry has been undergoing significant change and subjected to escalating competition over the past two decades.

This chapter has identified each type of autonomous action airlines devise and take in the deregulated US and liberalized European air transport sectors. These multilateral, contractual 'commercial manoeuvres' range from franchising to codesharing agreements to alliances to mergers at the structural level and links between frequent flyer programmes, joint ventures in catering, ground handling and aircraft maintenance at the operational level. They exist either within the framework or beyond the perceived impediments of the current regulatory framework for the sector, including state airspace sovereignty, foreign ownership restrictions, competition rules and antitrust law.

The Chicago Conference attempted to reach a multilateral solution to international air transport as regards the industry's safety, sustainability and economic efficiency in its 1944 Convention, hosted by the US President Franklin D. Roosevelt 'was pushing for . . . a true open skies agreement, whereby there would be few, if any, restrictions, on international flying. Unfortunately, few of the 54 delegates attending the Chicago Convention actually backed him on his goal for open skies'.[200]

---

196 Child, Faulkner and Tallman, *Cooperative Strategy*, p. 7.
197 Ibid.
198 Ibid.
199 R. Doganis, *The Airline Business*, 2nded. (London: Routledge, 2006), p. 74, citing M.E. Porter, *The Competitive Advantage of Nations* (New York: Free Press, 1990).
200 Vasigh, Fleming and Tacker, *Introduction to Air Transport Economics*, p. 155, citing D. Phillips, 'Open Skies' Reality Still Proves Elusive', *International Herald Tribune* (4 June 2006). Online. Available HTTP: <http://www.iht.com/bin/print_ipub.php?file=/articles/2006/06/04/new/ravsky.php>.

It proposed to create a system for those involved in the industry to collaborate to achieve these ends. Although IATA was created to ensure the safety and reliability of the industry, route planning and networks remained dependent upon bilateral agreements between governments. Sustainability and economic efficiency were put in the charge, for the first time, of the airlines themselves. Industry cooperation and collaboration is now an option, if not a necessity. On top of this, the air transport industry, by its very nature, encourages cooperation. A key characteristic of the industry is multilateral interline traffic agreements coordinated by IATA, which exist between virtually all carriers: one may accept the other's tickets and air way bills on a reciprocal basis in exchange for transport. This defining feature of the airline network serves as the foundation upon which additional cooperative arrangements are assembled.

Globally, aviation is experiencing a strong trend towards more complex agreements between airlines, which take the form of increasingly integrated, global strategic alliances.[201] In some instances, these alliances push the limits of contractual agreements to the edge of regulators' merger definitions, creating a quasi-'virtual merger'. Whereas a merger might be illegal owing to foreign ownership restrictions or the threat to 'fair' competition, an agreement to cooperate might fit well within the competition rules. Parties to a 'virtual merger' enjoy the benefits of a merger in everything but name (e.g. joint marketing, sales, management and operations), which raises the question: is this industry innovation or collusion? Classification is integral to the issue because whereas regulators encourage innovation, law prohibits collusion. From the perspective of 'joint venturing', there appears to exist a fine line between cooperation and collaboration, when, from a regulatory perspective, there should be a great difference between cooperation and collusion.

Innovation, from R&D to restructuring and cost-cutting, is examined in the context of a firm's motivations for forming a tactical alliance. There are elements to alliance-forming which exist beyond regulations, such as corporate governance, contract theory in assessing a good partner, negotiating terms, and other drivers for forming an alliance, which interact at a number of junctures from negotiation to operation within or along the edges of the law.

The categories of horizontal alliances in the air transport sector vary in integration and intimacy between firms. The franchise agreement, a highly successful form of contract-based alliance in many industries, most commonly involves regional or feeder–franchisee airlines, operating as the trunk carrier. The block-space agreement involves reserving a stipulated amount of space on an aircraft to be sold by another carrier, a practice often employed where an airline may not for 'legal' or financial reasons be able to gain access to a particular market. A codeshare agreement, the most prevalent form of tactical alliance in the air transport sector since interlining, allows one airline similar benefits to the block space agreement plus the ability to market the space on another carrier's aircraft as its own operation, under its own flight designator code.

---

201 Within the largest three existing global alliances, 'increased breadth and increased depth in cooperation between members' is evidenced. Breadth implies network reach and to expand this, 'Alliances recruit new members to fill so-called "white spots" in their networks, where an alliances does not yet have coverage'. Depth in cooperation means expanded cooperation towards 'merger-like integration' (ECDOT, *Transatlantic Airline Alliances*, p. 9).

Global airline and cargo alliances are currently the most intimate, highly-integrated, complex form of strategic alliance in the air transport sector. These alliances are unique in that they are centrally managed much like joint ventures, yet involve a number of parties cooperating on a multilateral, reciprocal basis. Features of global alliances are its strong linkages between frequent flyer programmes, common lounges, and minimum standards for crew uniforms, levels of service, seat configuration/type/comfort and in-flight services. The reach of global alliances' route networks is significant: last year more than half of air passengers were carried by the three largest global alliances: Star Alliance, oneworld and SkyTeam.

Global alliances are compared with recent examples of airline mergers to evaluate to what extent they might constitute a 'virtual' merger. The long-term objectives for joining a global alliance go beyond simple cost-cutting and expanding flight networks to include cross-border stock investment, developing joint identities and liberalized multilateral air service agreements such as 'Open Skies'. The implications for strategic alliances and their interaction with and impact on competition (relevant market, market power, abuse of a dominant position) are considered in the light of relevant European and US competition rules and case law.

In a recent joint report, the European Commission and US DoT concluded:

> The global alliance strategy is rooted in the fundamentals of network economics and a global economy. Post deregulation, the legacy carrier business model on both sides of the Atlantic predicated on a 'from anywhere to everywhere' consumer proposition. However, no airline is able to efficiently serve every destination its customers require with its own aircraft. Additionally, few city-pairs can generate sufficient demand on a daily basis to sustain non-stop service. To meet the demands of customers, carriers must seek commercial partners that can help them provide greater network coverage and increased service options.[202]

The research in this chapter has identified the ways in which airlines are responding to competition in the current regulatory environment, and the pros and cons of these actions. It has been argued that the airline industry is, thanks to its 'interline' nature, a cooperative business. The phenomenon is that whereas in other industries competitors would not seek to interact with one another on such a fundamental level, airlines do. This serves as the basis for further industry-wide cooperation in the form of contracts.

The rationale for this cooperative spirit may be the current, seemingly difficult regulatory climate prohibiting mergers, the foreign ownership of airlines and restrictions on cabotage; the 'invisible hand' of the airline industry's economic self-interested motivation to survive and profit; or the result of natural industrial evolution. The tentative conclusion here is that the impetus for the multilateral commercial manoeuvring by European and US airlines is a combination of the current structure of the industry, as influenced by the respective regulatory regimes, and the creative adaptation of the law to business ventures, wedged into the confines of the current regulations.

---

202 ECDOT, *Transatlantic Airline Alliances*, p. 3.

Irrespective of how market deregulation and liberalization is perceived to have impacted on airlines and the industry *vis-à-vis* the current regulatory regimes in the EU and US, the measures devised and taken by airlines within the liberalized and deregulated environments demonstrate the achievement of economic efficiency, and thus the fundamental goals of the economic principles, as evidenced by the level of intense cooperative manoeuvring such as growing instances of tactical alliances, increasing airline memberships in strategic alliances and continued sector consolidation.

6   Final thoughts

Puppets and strings

The economic objectives underpinning the deregulation and liberalization of markets are identical: increased efficiency. It is clear that market deregulation suggests the removal of unilateral state regulation of an industry. The newly deregulated sector will be exposed to free market conditions under re-regulation whereby firms are protected to some extent from unfair practices, which might negatively affect the competitiveness of the sector. Thus, the reregulation requires the maintenance of government's interventionist character. Much like any form of 'regulation', the level of governmental intervention is subject to much socio-economic and socio-political debate.

In basic form the two economic principles have encouraged policymakers to tailor sector-specific antitrust in the US and competition policies in Europe. Because the objectives of market deregulation and liberalization are vague, regulators retain a significant degree of discretion and interpretation. The resulting policies have inspired the construction of relevant antitrust and competition rules, but the policies are not 'purely' deregulatory or liberal, in the economic sense.

Antitrust and competition rules have had an impact on the structure and economic operation of the air transport sector. The observed innovative character of the air transport industry cannot be rightly attributed to antitrust or competition policy approaches. In the case of air transport, there is a weaker than expected association between law and policy, and the industry responses.

Firms in a deregulated market engender autonomy. Autonomous actions taken within the deregulated space has most cases produced innovative, cooperative strategies. In an industry that is undeniably complex – even chaotic, well beyond the economic, and to some extent socio-political perspectives this book has investigated – it is no surprise that the lack of clarity of the economic principles of market deregulation and liberalization have contributed to deep-seated confusion over the regulatory environment. Whilst it is argued that the intended outcome of market deregulation and liberalization – economic efficiency – is achieved, the path followed is not that which one would anticipate where dialogue between regulators and the air transport industry, both in the EU and US, would bear out a more policy-influenced response, policed by antitrust and competition rules, with the regulator pulling the strings. The cooperative agreements between airlines do at times run a foul of the rules, however economic efficiency as a driving force outweighs regulatory policy objectives. The entrepreneurial nature and cooperative spirit of airlines should thus be recognized to suggest that whether through autonomous action or lobbying regulators, and despite what is perceived as a complex and confused regulatory environment that makes workable competition – and therefore economic efficiency – a difficult ambition, incumbent airlines do at times pull the strings.

There is certainly a relationship between the strategies airlines have developed and the current state of the law. Airlines have adapted to the situational factors, and it could be said therefore that the innovative strategies taken in an autonomous space are contingent upon the confines of the regulatory environment. It is submitted in this book that these are hybrid strategies, which draw on both organic and inorganic interpretations of organizational, group-forming behaviour. Airlines devise competitive strategies, and at times they are adopted out of necessity.

If the analysis is taken a step further, one could make the case that regulators are the puppets. It is accepted that both EU and US airlines have regard for their respective countries' laws in their current state, but through different conduits. Antitrust 'catches' breaches, *ex post*, whereas competition law 'forces' compliance through self-regulation. Thus, the American experience shows that regulators can be more puppet-like, with the industry objectives holding relatively high authority in the deregulated environment since the antitrust regulator reacts at a much later point.

The European approach, on the other hand, reveals that regulators can be less puppet-like, setting the ground rules for fair, workable competition, whilst airlines are free to manoeuvre within that lineated, liberalized space of *ex ante* rules. Thus liberalization confers less autonomy than deregulation, and thus cooperation is an inherent feature of the EU regulatory environment. Cooperation, albeit with respect for rivals through forced self-regulation, is accepted as 'workable' competition under the European definition. A third perspective would be in a regulated industry, where regulators pull all the strings all the time, without room for innovation or unprompted industry-seeking economic efficiency.

Even without presupposing the puppet-strings perspective, deregulation and liberalization have still played the most fundamental role in creating the airlines' strategies by untying the hands of directors and managers. The extent to which these hands are truly 'free' depends on the stage – European or American – and the tautness of the strings – competition policies and rules, or antitrust.

At times, airlines pull 'the strings' with respect to regulatory capture, interest groups and their autonomy, mostly in the US. At other times, regulators are perceived to be pulling the strings through market regulation determining the market and industry structure through strict rules, particularly in the EU.

Conclusions

Airlines operate within what is perceived as a complex and confused regulatory environment. Despite the difficult competitive atmosphere, US and European airlines have remained economically efficient, in the broadest sense of the phrase. The remarkable level of innovative strategies devised and adopted by airlines, particularly through multilateral cooperation within the air transport sector and with firms in sectors complementary to air transport, is supporting evidence of this.

Although the legal and economic aspects of air transport have been extensively studied in the past, particularly over recent decades since deregulation of the US and liberalization of the European sectors, the link between the regulatory environment and cooperative agreements within air transport has remained relatively unexplored. In this book, the relationship between seemingly vague market deregulation and liberalization principles, the antitrust and competition policies which are devised on certain aspects of these principles and influence in greater part respective rules for 'workable competition',[1] and the industry outcomes have been presented and discussed in detail.

Preliminary analysis on the current state of the global air transport sector revealed the trend of a growing number of airlines entering into cooperative arrangements including franchising, codeshare agreements, alliances, and in some cases mergers, with other airlines or groups of airlines. The first step in developing the study's objectives was to identify the factual elements of this movement, namely the airlines involved and the impetus for these strategies. The majority of the airlines identified as leading the change carry US and European designations.

Research has revealed the current state of the air transport sector, including the operational and structural intricacies, progress in the changing system of bilateral to multilateral regulation, and the extent of cooperation within the sector, but also demanded a closer look at the US and European approaches to regulating their respective air transport markets. EU competition rules and US antitrust legislation, relevant court precedents, economic theories on regulation and in particular market deregulation, and influences on inter-firm cooperation, assisted in identifying the regulatory environments in which the airlines operate in order to evaluate whether the commercial activities undertaken by airlines demonstrate a commercial, economically efficient advantage for airlines in spite of the perceived impediment of the regulatory regimes.

This study takes into consideration a number of diverse subject areas on both the public and private sides of law and commerce, including deregulation, liberalization, competition and antitrust law, the political and social perspectives of 'public utility', contract, organizational behaviour, network theories and economic theories on efficiency. In terms of chronology, the study takes the years leading up to deregulation of the US air transport market as the starting point. A detailed examination of the impetuses for deregulation and intentions of regulators *vis-à-vis* regulation theory is not required for this study.

The early, tentative conclusion was that the rationale for this cooperative spirit amongst airlines was a combination of the restrictive nature of bilateral air service

1   The various levels of 'workable' competition measure economic efficiency. In the US this is guided by neoclassical economics, which through allocative efficiency encourages vigorous competition, whereas in the EU the system calls for cooperation and self-regulation-based competition. The allocative efficiency model suggests that a limited number of resources are allocated according to the desires of consumers under a system of supply and demand.

agreements (BSAs) and the current, seemingly difficult regulatory climate prohibiting mergers, foreign ownership of airlines, and placing restrictions on cabotage; the 'invisible hand' of the airline industry's economic self-interest in success or in any case survival; the current structure of the industry, as influenced by the respective regulatory regimes; and the creative adaptation of the law to business ventures, wedged into the confines of the current regulations.

The question 'how have airlines profited or survived in what is perceived as a complex and confused regulatory environment?' gives rise to three secondary questions: (1) what is the perceived impetus for airlines to innovate and cooperate; (2) how does airline sector deregulation impact on and implicate airlines in the context of 'workable competition'; and (3) does the 'industry innovation' demonstrate a workable business strategy in the context of economic efficiency and the law?

The perceived impetus is that airlines are finding a way to 'cope' in the difficult regulatory environment, but the actual impetus is a result of the combination of the current structure of the industry as influenced by the respective regulatory regimes and the creative adaptation of the law to these business strategies wedged within the confines of the current regulations.

The implication, taking the orthodox Chicago School[2] view, is that market regulation *vis-à-vis* public ordering should produce workable competition. Despite the uncertainties of liberalization and deregulation, the advent of market and non-market strategies has yielded a successful sector.

An analysis of the system of BSAs and the EU and US regulatory environments reveals confusion owing to different approaches and rules, which in addition to a number of separate theories that generally support cooperation, further encourages private ordering through integrated business strategies. As a result, airlines are able to in effect utilize the law on liberalization and deregulation to achieve a competitive advantage, following Porter,[3] although this may be short-lived as competitors innovate or competition and antitrust rules intervene.

The degree of presence of regulatory capture varies between the EU and US. The effects of this are that the European regulator focuses on the market, is far more interventionist and can therefore better predict outcomes, whereas the American regulator is motivated by the benefits to consumers *vis-à-vis* what is in the best interest of the firms, and is far more protectionist. This leads to a confused state of affairs, but the level of regulatory capture is later observed as playing an integral role in determining the effects of the two regulatory environments on airlines.

US antitrust regulators are at risk of protecting firms, whilst their European counterparts appear to be focused on protecting the market. The short-term orientated, static American approach is highly responsive, immediate, and reactionary, compared to the EU approach, which is more long-term orientated, proactive and dynamic.

---

2 This refers to the Chicago school of thought on economics and the economists associated with it such as Pigou, Posner, Peltzman and Stigler, referenced above.

3 *See* M.E. Porter, *Competitive Strategy: Techniques for Analyzing Industries and Competitors* (New York: Free Press, 1980); M.E. Porter, *On Competition* (Cambridge, MA: Harvard University Business Review Series, 1996).

For instance, there are limits on the extraterritorial effect of antitrust as seen in *Travel Agencies*,[4] *Sisal*[5] and the US Foreign Trade Improvements Act.[6] Generally speaking, antitrust looks to the direct, substantial and reasonably foreseeable anti-competitive effect on US commerce to give rise to an antitrust claim under the Sherman Act.[7] In the EU, behaviour that is incompatible with common market principles gives rise to an investigation into potential breach of competition rules.

The European Community Merger Regulation (ECMR) treats codeshare agreements as joint ventures, whereas in the US, in *United Airlines v Mesa*,[8] decided on the basis of *Vaugh v General Foods*,[9] the two airlines were treated as 'partners' but this definition fell just short of 'joint venture'. This resulted in a reduction of United's liability towards Mesa.

Also, the EU competition regulators dislike loyalty discounts as evidenced in *Suiker Unie*,[10] *Hoffmann–La Roche*[11] and Virgin Atlantic's 'predatory foreclosure' case against British Airways,[12] whereas in the US, the requirement for an action is evidence of an actual injury sustained, as found in the US private action brought by Virgin Atlantic against British Airways.[13]

Market regulation impacts on structure of market along a continuum. At one end is the explicit rules-based regulation where market principles are forced upon firms and thereby define the structure of the market. The conclusion in this book is that this is best characterized by the 'interventionist' EU system and its *ex ante* approach. At the other end of the spectrum is 'soft regulation', that is to say self-regulation and space for autonomous action, wherein airlines act independently. The conclusion in this book is that this typifies the 'reactionist' US system and its rather *ex post* approach. Somewhere in the middle is law-through-policy regulation that guides the structure and affords airlines an opportunity to respond. This book argues that the regulators should work towards this optimal point.

Because European liberalization of air transport began over a decade after American deregulation and was completed nearly two decades later, it comes as no surprise that the American experience had a demonstrative effect in Europe. The latest experience, however, is that of reverse demonstrative effect of the European system on the American counterpart.

4 *Travel Agencies* 303 F.3d 293, 2002 US App LEXIS 18467; 2002–2 Trade Cas (CCH) P73, 795; 1 ALR Fed 2d 719.
5 *United States v Sisal Sales Corp*, 274 U.S. 268, 275–76, 71 L. Ed. 1042, 47 S. Ct. 592 (1927).
6 Pub. L. No. 97–290, 96 Stat. 1234, Title IV, *codified at* 15 U.S.C. §§ 6a and 45(a)(3).
7 15 U.S.C. §1, 1890.
8 *United Airlines, Inc. v Mesa Airlines, Inc. and WestAir Commuter Airlines, Inc. v SkyWest Airlines, Inc.* 219 F.3d 605; 2000 U.S. Appl. LEXIS 15522.
9 *Vaugh v General Foods Corp*797 F.2d 1403 (7th Cir 1986).
10 Case 40/73, *Suiker Unie v EC Commission* [1975] ECR 1663, [1976] 1 CMLR 295.
11 Case 85/76, *Hoffmann-La Roche v Commission* [1979] ECR 461, [1979] 3 CMLR 211.
12 The European Commission found in its decision 2000/74 of 14.4.1999 in *Virgin/British Airways*, OJ L30/1, 4 February 2004, that British Airways abused its dominance on the UK market for the purchase of travel agent services by rewarding loyalty. In its judgement in Case T-219/99 *British Airways v Commission*, of 17 December 2003, the CFI dismissed an appeal against this decision.
13 257 F.3d 256 (2nd Cir. 2001).

The link between private ordering and both corporate governance and game theory, as applied to the industry-led development of new internal rules of the game, predominantly visible in the increasingly leading role of LCCs in determining common industry-standard business practices, supports the argument for an industry remarkably self-sufficient through self-regulation, especially in the EU. If Porter's theory on competitive advantage[14] is applied to the air transport sector where profitability is low, it is apparent that individual companies, particularly LCCs, have been able to make a return in excess of the industry average by applying unique business models. Additional reasons for tactical alliances between airlines and with firms in industries complementary to air transport are economies of scale, shared-learning and the expansion of assets and manpower.[15]

The Commission's regulations and to some extent the CJEU's decisions discussed above are evidence of liberalizing the air transport sector towards EC 'antitrust' and away from Chicago School where practices were 'forbidden unless expressly allowed'. Applying Williamson's theory on antitrust economics,[16] it is argued that this was merely a policy reaction to counteract the growth and strong competitive strategies of US megacarriers. For instance, the previous prohibition of EU larger incumbent carriers from merging in the early 1990s has been reversed, as seen in the acquisitions by *Lufthansa*, and the *Air France–KLM* and *BA–Iberia* mergers.

Following Schwarcz's theory on private ordering, quasi-self-regulation is evident in the air transport sector.[17] It is evidenced that the air transport sector is to some extent capable of self-regulation, for instance by the degree to which airlines have corrected failures of lawmakers and avoided using interest groups to assert pressure. There is good reason to agree that this is a more efficient process. Furthermore, the points have been classified along the aforementioned market regulation continuum according to private ordering as self-regulation, 'enforced self-regulation' and 'command regulation with discretionary punishment'.[18] The optimum is in the middle at enforced self-regulation.

Deregulation and liberalization policy approaches as viewed through responses of the airlines to competition rules and antitrust demonstrate a workable strategy for competition, but are not evidence of the objectives of these policies as an element of the extra-legal – likely a combination of private ordering, industry-led innovation and economics – also exists. This book has demonstrated that the current law on deregulation and liberalization has not driven these industry responses; more exactly, airlines should be given the credit.

The state of industry cooperation and apparent innovation are welcome, rational outcomes to what was envisaged by the expressed ideals of deregulation and liberalization,

---

14 *See* Porter, *Competitive Strategy*; Porter, *On Competition*.

15 *See* M.E. Porter and M.B. Fuller, 'Coalitions and Global Strategy', in M.E. Porter (ed.), *Competition in Global Industries* (Boston, MA: Harvard Business School Press, 1986).

16 *See* O.E. Williamson, *Markets and Hierarchies: Analysis and Antitrust Implications* (New York: The Free Press, 1975); O.E. Williamson, *The Economic Institutions of Capitalism* (New York: The Free Press, 1985); *and* O.E. Williamson, *Antitrust Economics: Mergers, Contracting, and Strategic Behaviour* (Oxford: Basil Blackwell, 1987).

17 S.L. Schwarcz, 'Private Ordering', *Northwestern University Law Review*, 97, Fall 2002, 319–350.

18 J. Braithwaite and P. Drahos, *Global Business Regulation* (Cambridge: Cambridge University Press, 2000). *See also* I. Ayres and J. Braithwaite, *Responsive Regulation: Transcending the Deregulation Debate* (Oxford: Oxford University Press, 1992).

but they are not exactly the expressed outcomes. The industry responses represent a 'rationalization' strategy by airlines, on the balance of very different approaches to market regulation in the EU and US, yet towards a more optimal point subject to industry–regulator dialogue. In other words, there is a correlation between sector deregulation, liberalization and the observed business strategies. The normal question line would go: 'do the business strategies achieve the objectives of deregulation and liberalization?' The answer is 'yes' but not conventionally and therefore simply because they are achieved does not mean any of this is necessarily evidence of good regulatory policy.

Confusion over unclear objectives has led to transport and competition policies, which should encourage innovation and economic efficiency, but instead 'confuse' the already complexly competitive environment so much so that airlines instead utilize private ordering and to an extent self-regulation as a means to move forwards. The objectives of the deregulation and liberalization ideals are thus achieved, but it follows that if regulators were more concerned with outcomes, they would seek a more symbiotic and interdependent dialogue with private orderings and only then would their approaches be evidence of 'good regulatory policy'.

Thus lessons learnt from the 'airline experience' should guide future regulators towards drafting clearer policies, taking into account the significance of the market environment,[19] to achieve a policy–industry equilibrium: one that is more linear and causal. Otherwise, policymakers in a deregulated or liberalized air transport sector will have little impact on the state of market innovation and level of economic efficiency, much like puppets in chaos.

Recently, there has been significant development in the transatlantic regulatory space: the EU–US Air Transport Agreement.[20] It has been argued earlier that the turning point in the EU regulatory landscape was between 2002, following EU competency on negotiating multilateral agreements, and 2004, when the European Commission obtained jurisdiction on competition matters.[21] 'Special treatment' of airlines

---

19   The uniqueness of the air transport market refers for instance to the discussion above in Chapters 2–4 on the different EU and US industry evolution, regulatory approaches to liberalization and deregulation, the industry–regulator discourse and private ordering, the methods employed to regulate the markets in the EU and US though competition and antitrust rules, and the role of IATA.

20   *See* Decision 2007/337/EC of the Council and the Representatives of the Governments of the Member States of the European Union, meeting within the Council of 25 April 2007, on the signature and provisional application of the Air Transport Agreement between the European Community and its Member States and the United States of America, OJ L134/1, 25 May 2007; *See also* Protocol to Amend the Air Transport Agreement between the United States of America and the European Community and its Member States, signed on 25 and 30 April 2007. Online. Available HTTP: <http://ec.europa.eu/transport/air/international_aviation/country_index/doc/2010_03_25_us_protocol_attach_b.pdf> (accessed 10 October 2011). The Second Stage Agreement (Protocol amending the First Stage Agreement) was adopted by the Council of Transport Ministers on 24 June 2010.

21   The turning point in the legal framework came following Regulation (EC) No 847/2004 of the European Parliament and of the Council of 29 April 2004, on the negotiation and implementation of air service agreements between Member States and third countries, OJ L157/7, 30 April 2004; Council Decision of 5 June 2003, on authorizing the Commission to open negotiations with third countries on the replacement of certain provisions in existing bilateral agreements with a Community agreement; and Council Decision of 5 June 2003, on authorising the Commission to open negotiations with the United States in the field of air transport.

in the EU is now a thing of the past, the continued regulatory exception survives today in the US. Despite this, it should be remembered that the US system enjoys some advantage insofar as the US DoT is also the country's transport policymaking organ.

A report by the European Commission and US DoT found that:

> with fewer regulatory barriers in place for transatlantic air services, more commercial opportunities are created, including those allowing airlines to restructure and adapt to dynamic industry changes . . . LCCs may expand their networks or adjust their business models to take advantage of new possibilities, such as the right to operate transatlantic services from any EU city to any US city.[22]

The report also found that, in terms of improved regulator–regulator cooperation, 'the tremendous value and need for non-case specific cooperation, which both enhances understanding of alliances and informs the assessment of specific cases, facilitating a more compatible approach to antitrust regulation and enforcement'.[23] The involvement of airlines in the inquiry as stakeholders in the regulatory process is a major success that will, once some time passes, create more commercial opportunities for airlines and more appropriate regulations and remedies.

Only two years ago the conclusion to this book would have been along the lines of suggesting increased dialogue between industry and regulators as advantageous to all concerned. Now, as evidenced by the recent intensification of the open dialogue between industry and regulators, more mutually beneficial outcomes are *certain* to come in future. Transatlantic cooperation between airlines has been extended to include regulatory authorities, as formalized by the EU–US Air Transport Agreement, in addition to the already 'long-standing and productive cooperation with US DoJ'.[24] For now one must wait, several years perhaps, for the market to adjust to these recent regulatory changes to give airlines time to restructure and adapt, and regulators time to devise more tailored remedies.

---

22 European Commission and US Department of Transportation (ECDOT), (2010) 'Transatlantic Airline Alliances: Competitive Issues and Regulatory Approaches', p. 13. Online. Available HTTP: <http://ec.europa.eu/competition/sectors/transport/reports/joint_alliance_report.pdf> (accessed 7 October 2010).
23 Ibid., p. 25.
24 Ibid., p. 12.

References

Abeyratne, R. *Aviation Trends in the New Millennium* (Aldershot: Ashgate, 2001).

—— 'Competition and Predation: Legal Aspects', in P. Forsyth, D. Gillen, O.G. Mayer and H. Niemeier (eds), *Competition versus Predation in Aviation Markets: A Survey of Experience in North America, Europe and Australia* (Aldershot: Ashgate, 2005).

Adkins, B. *Air Transport and E.C. Competition Law* (London: Sweet and Maxwell (European Competition Law Monographs), 2001).

Agusdinata, B. and de Klein, W. 'The Dynamics of Airline Alliances', *Journal of Air Transport Management*, 8, 2002, 201–211.

'Air France Cancel London – LA from 26 October 2008', *Airline Route*. Online. Available HTTP: <http://airlineroute.net/2008/10/08/air-france-cancel-london-la-from-26oct08/> (accessed 5 July 2011).

Airline Business 'Analysis and OAG Scheduled Data', *Airline Business*, 21(9), September 2005, 64.

Alford, E. and Champley, R. 'The Impact of the 2007 US–EU Open Skies Air Transport Agreement', *International Trade Administration: US Department of Commerce,* ITA Occasional Paper no. 07–001(2007).

'Antitrust: British Airways, American Airlines and Iberia Commitments to Ensure Competition on Transatlantic Passenger Air Transport Markets Made Legally Binding – Frequently Asked Questions', *Europa Press Release Rapid* (MEMO /10/330, Brussels, 14 July 2010). Online. Available HTTP: <http://europa.eu/rapid/pressReleasesAction.do?reference=MEMO/10/330&format=HTML&aged=0&language=EN&guiLanguage=en> (accessed 16 July 2011).

Armstrong, M. and Sappington, D. 'Recent Developments in the Theory of Regulation', in M. Armstrong and R.H. Porter (eds) *Handbook of Industrial Organization* (Oxford: North-Holland, 2007).

Ayres, I. and Braithwaite, J. *Responsive Regulation: Transcending the Deregulation Debate* (Oxford: Oxford University Press, 1992).

'BAA Airports Market Investigation: A Report on the Supply of Airport Services by the BAA in the UK', UK Competition Commission, 19 March 2009 (final). Online. Available HTTP: <http://www.competition-commission.org.uk/rep pub/reports/2009/fulltext/545.pdf> (accessed 12 July 2011).

Baker, C. 'The Global Groupings', *Airline Business,* July 2001.

—— 'Back to the Table', *Airline Business,* September 2006.

Baldwin, R. and Cave, M. *Understanding Regulation: Theory, Strategy, and Practice* (Oxford: Oxford University Press, 1990).

—— Cave, M. and Lodge, M. 'Introduction: Regulation – The Field and the Developing

Agenda', in R. Baldwin, M. Cave and M. Lodge, *The Oxford Handbook of Regulation* (Oxford: Oxford University Press, 2010).

Barrett, S.D. 'Ryanair and the Low-Cost Revolution', in J.F. O'Connell and G. Williams (eds), *Air Transport in the 21st Century: Key Strategic Developments* (Farnham: Ashgate, 2011).

—— *Deregulation and the Airline Business in Europe: Selected Readings* (London: Routledge, 2009).

Barwise J. (ed.) *Situation Theory and Its Applications* (Stanford, CA: Center for the Study of Language and Information, 1991).

Baumol, W.J. *Economic Theory and Operations Analysis* (Englewood Cliffs, NJ: Prentice-Hall, 1965).

Beckman, C.M., Haunschild, P.R. and Phillips, D.J. 'Friends or Strangers? Firm-Specific Uncertainty, Market Uncertainty, and Network Partner Selection', *Organization Science*, 15, 2004, 259–275.

Berenstein, A. *Grounded: Frank Lorenzo and the Destruction of Eastern Airlines* (Washington, DC: Beard Books, 1999).

Berg, S.V. 'Sustainable Regulatory Systems: Laws, Resources and Values' *Utilities Policy*, 9(4), 2000, 159–170.

Bernstein, H.M. *Regulating Business by Independent Commission* (Princeton, NJ: Princeton University Press, 1955).

Bilotkach, V. and Huschelrath, K. 'Antitrust Immunity for Airline Alliances', *Journal of Competition Law and Economics*, 7(2), 2011, 335–380.

Birger, J. 'The Bailout Bounty', *Fortune* 155(4), 2007, 24–26.

Black, J. 'Regulatory Conversations', *Journal of Law and Society*, 29(1), 2002, 163–196.

Blair, R.D. and Lafontaine, F. *The Economics of Franchising* (Cambridge: Cambridge University Press, 2005).

'BMI Being Taken Over by Lufthansa', *BBC News* (29 October 2008). Online. Available HTTP: <http://news.bbc.co.uk/1/hi/business/7697261.stm> (accessed 10 June 2011).

Bolton, P.A. and Dewatripont, M.A. *Contract Theory* (Cambridge, MA: MIT Press, 2005).

Borenstein, S. 'Airline Mergers, Airport Dominance, and Market Power', *American Economic Review*, 80(2), 1990, 400–404.

—— 'The Evolution of U.S. Airline Competition', *Journal of Economic Perspectives*, 6(2), Spring 1992, 63–64.

Bradshaw, B. and Patel, B. 'Final Descent? The Future of Antitrust Immunity in International Aviation', *GCP: ANTITRUST CHRON* 1, 2010, 1–8.

Braithwaite, J. and Drahos, P. *Global Business Regulation* (Cambridge: Cambridge University Press, 2000).

Breyer, S.G. 'Analyzing Regulatory Failure: Mismatches, Less Restrictive Alternatives, and Reform', *Harvard Law Review*, 92, 1979, 549–609.

——*Regulation and Its Reform* (Cambridge, MA: Harvard University Press, 1982).

—— 'Antitrust, Deregulation, and the Newly Liberated Marketplace', *California Law Review*, 75(3), May 1987, 1005–1047.

—— 'Regulation and Deregulation in the United States: Airlines, Telecommunications and Antitrust', in G. Majone (ed.), *Deregulation or Re-Regulation: Regulatory Reform in Europe and the United States* (New York: St. Martins, 1990).

'British Airways to Pay Record £121.5m Penalty in Price Fixing Investigation' *OFT*. Online. Available HTTP <www.oft.gov.uk/news/press/2007/113–07> (accessed 10 March 2011).

Brueckner, J. 'Network Structure and Airline Scheduling', *Journal of Industrial Economics*, 52(2), 2004, 291–312.

Button, K. and Swann, D. 'European Community Airlines – Deregulation and Its Problems', *Journal of Common Market Studies*, 27(4), 1989, 259–282.

Carter, J. 'Speech: *International Air Transportation Competition Act Statement on Signing S. 1300 Into Law*', *15.2.1980*, University of California at Santa Barbara Presidency Project. Online. Available HTTP: <http://www.presidency.ucsb.edu/ws/index.php?pid=32939#> (accessed 10 March 2011).

Caswell, M. 'BA Sells GB Franchise to EasyJet (correction)', *Business Traveller*, 30 October 2007. Online. Available HTTP: <http://www.businesstraveller.com/news/ba-sells-gb-franchise-to-easyjet> (accessed 14 June 2011).

Child, J., Faulkner, D. and Tallman, S. *Cooperative Strategy: Managing Alliances, Networks, and Joint Ventures*, 2nd ed. (Oxford: Oxford University Press, 2005).

Clark, A. 'EasyJet Lines Up Merger with Go: Shake-Up of Budget Airlines Could Mean Higher Fares', *Guardian*, 04 May 2002, 2.

Clark, J.M. 'Toward a Concept of Workable Competition', *American Economic Review*, 30(2), 1940, 241–256.

Coase, R.H. 'The Problem of Social Cost', *JL & Econ*, 3, 1960.

Coglianese, C. and Mendelson, E. 'Meta-Regulation and Self-Regulation', in R. Baldwin, M. Cave and M. Lodge (eds), *The Oxford Handbook of Regulation*, (Oxford: Oxford University Press, 2010).

'Commission Sets Out Limits for State Aid to Regional Airports', *EU News and Policy Positions* (6 September 2005). Online. Available HTTP: <http://www.euractiv.com/en/transport/commission-sets-limits-state-aid-regional-airports/article-143875> (accessed 10 August 2011).

'Convention on International Civil Aviation, 9th ed., Doc. 7300/9, 2006' (Chicago Convention 1944). Online. Available HTTP: <www.icao.int/icaonet/arch/doc/7300/7300_9ed.pdf> (accessed 12 May 2011).

Cooper, M. 'Freeing Public Policy from the Deregulation Debate: The Airline Industry Comes of Age (and Should Be Held Accountable for Its Anti-Competitive Behaviour)', Consumer Federation of America Paper, 1999, p. 2. Online. Available HTTP: <http://www.consumerfed.org/pdfs/abaair1.pdf> (accessed 2 June 2011).

Cowan, R., Jonard, N. and Zimmermann, J.B. 'Bilateral Collaboration and the Emergence of Innovation Networks', *Management Science*, 57(7), 2007, 1051–1067.

Cunningham, N. 'Enforcement and Compliance Strategies', in R. Baldwin, M. Cave and M. Lodge (eds), *The Oxford Handbook of Regulation*, (Oxford: Oxford University Press, 2010).

Dal Bó, E. 'Regulatory Capture: A Review', *Oxford Review of Economic Policy*, 22(2), 2006, 204.

Daley, B. and Thomas, C. 'Challenges to Growth: Environmental Issues and the Development of the Air Transport Industry', in J.F. O'Connell and G. Williams (eds), *Air Transport in the 21st Century: Key Strategic Developments* (Farnham: Ashgate, 2011).

Dempsey, P.S. 'Antitrust Law and Policy in Transportation: Monopoly I$ the Name of the Game', *Ga. L. Rev.*, 21(505), 1987.

—— *The Social and Economic Consequences of Deregulation* (New York: Quorum Books, 1989).

—— and Goetz, A.R. *Airlines Deregulation and Laissez-Faire Mythology* (London: Quorum Books, 1992).

Denzau, A. and Munger, M. 'Legislators and Interest Groups: How Unorganized Interests Get Represented', *American Political Science Review*, 80, 1986, 89–106.

Department of Trade and Industry, *Productivity and Enterprise: A World Class Competition Regime White Paper*, Cm 5233 (2001).

Devlin, K. *Logic and Information* (Cambridge: Cambridge University Press, 1991).

Dobson, A. *Globalization and Regional Integration* (London: Routledge, 2007).

Doganis, R. *The Airline Business in the 21st Century* (London: Routledge, 2001).

—— *The Airline Business in the 21st Century*, 2nd ed. (London: Routledge, 2006).

—— *Flying Off Course: The Economics of International Airlines*, 4th ed. (London: Routledge, 2010).

—— 'An Inherently Unstable Industry: Airlines Have Themselves to Blame', in J.F. O'Connell and G. Williams (eds), *Air Transport in the 21st Century: Key Strategic Developments* (Farnham: Ashgate, 2011).

Douglas, G.W. 'The Importance of Entry Conditions: Texas Air's Acquisition of Eastern Airlines', in J.E. Kwolka, Jr and L.J. White (eds), *The Antitrust Revolution: Economics, Competition, and Policy* (Oxford: Oxford University Press, 1986).

Dunn, G. 'KLM Launches Low Cost Airline – Named "Buzz"', *Air Transport Intelligence News*, 22 September 1999.

Easterbrook, F.H. 'Vertical Arrangements and the Rule of Reason', 53 *Antitrust LJ*, 1985, 135–174.

Ehlermann, E.D. 'The Contribution of EC Competition Policy to the Single Market', *CML Rev*, 29, 1992, 257.

Ellerman, A.D. and Buchner, B.K. 'The European Union Emissions Trading Scheme: Origins, Allocation, and Early Results', *Rev Environ Econ Policy*, 1(1), 2007, 66.

Endres, G. 'Surrogate Supply', *Airline Business (Factiva)*, 27 June 2006.

European Commission and US Department of Transportation (ECDOT), 'Transatlantic Airline Alliances: Competitive Issues and Regulatory Approaches' (2010), p. 2. Online. Available HTTP: <http://ec.europa.eu/competition/sectors/transport/reports/joint_alliance_report.pdf> (accessed 23 July 2011).

Farantouris, N. 'Firms in Difficulty and State Aids: A Compatibility Analysis', *ECLR* 30(10), 2009, 494–504.

Feintuck, M. 'Regulatory Rationales Beyond the Economic: In Search of the Public Interest', R. Baldwin, M. Cave and M. Lodge (eds), *The Oxford Handbook of Regulation,* (Oxford: Oxford University Press, 2010).

Findlay, C. and Round, D. 'The "Three Pillars of Stagnation": Challenges for Air Transport Reform', *World Trade Review*, 5(2), 2006, 251–270.

Fiorina, M. and Noll, R. 'Voters, Bureaucrats and Legislators: A Rational Choice Perspective on the Growth of Bureaucracy', *Journal of Public Economics*, 9, 1978, 239–254.

Fisher, F.M. 'Pan American to United: The Pacific Division Transfer Case', *RAND Journal of Economics*, 18(4), Winter 1987, 492–508.

Flint, P. 'The Leopard Changes Its Spots', *Air Transport World*, 33(11), 1996, 51–54.

Forsyth P., Gillen, D., Mayer, O.G. and Niemeier, H. (eds), *Competition versus Predation in Aviation Markets: A Survey of Experience in North America, Europe and Australia* (Aldershot: Ashgate, 2005).

Fox, E.F. 'Monopolization, Abuse of Dominance, and the Indeterminacy of Economics: The U.S./E.U. Divide', *Utah Law Review*, 2006, 739.

Francis, L. 'Singapore–China "Open Skies" Has Restriction on LCCs', *Air Transport Intelligence News*, February 2005, as cited in B. Vasigh, K. Fleming and T. Tacker, *Introduction to Air Transport Economics* (Farnham: Ashgate, 2008), p. 165.

Franke, M. 'Innovation: The Winning Formula to Regain Profitability in Aviation?' *Journal of Air Transport Management*, 13, 2007, 23–30.

Friedman, J. *Oligopoly Theory* (Cambridge: Cambridge University Press, 1983).

Fundenberg, D. and Tirole, J. *Game Theory* (Boston, MA: MIT Press, 1991).

Gersemann, O. 'Cowboy Capitalism: European Myths, American Reality', CATO Institute, 2004, as cited in J.B. McDonald, 'Section 2 and Article 82: Cowboys and Gentlemen', paper presented to the College of Europe, Brussels (16 June 2005). Online. Available HTTP: <http://www.justice.gov/atr/public/speeches/210873.htm> (accessed 13 September 2011).

Gillespie, W. and Richard, O.M. *Antitrust Immunity and International Airline Alliances*, Economic Analysis Group Discussion Paper, Antitrust Division, U.S. Department of Justice, Washington D.C., EAG 11–1, February 2011.

Gilroy, B.M., Lukas, E. and Volpert, T. 'The European 'No-Frills'-Aviation Market: Current and Future Developments', in P. Forsyth, D. Gillen, O.G. Mayer and H. Niemeier (eds), *Competition versus Predation in Aviation Markets: A Survey of Experience in North America, Europe and Australia* (Aldershot: Ashgate, 2005).

Gilson, S.C. *Creating Value through Corporate Restructuring: Case Studies in Bankruptcies, Buyouts and Breakups* (New York: Wiley 2001).

Goetz, A.R. and Dempsey, P.S. 'Airline Deregulation Ten Years After: Something Foul in the Air', *Journal of Air Law and Commerce* 54, 1989, 927.

Gogbashian, A. and Lawton, T. 'Airline Strategy: Keeping the Legacy Carrier Competitive. How Can Mature Airlines Stay Ahead in the Low-fare Airline Era?', in J.F. O'Connell and G. Williams (eds), *Air Transport in the 21st Century: Key Strategic Developments* (Farnham: Ashgate, 2011).

Goh, J. *European Air Transport Law and Competition* (Chichester: John Wiley & Sons, 1997).

Goldsmith, C. 'British Airways Launches No-Frills Unit – Move May Risk Diluting Brand Name, Some Say', *Wall Street Journal*, 22 May 1998, 5.

Hagedoorn, J. 'Understanding the Rationale of Strategic Technology Partnering: Interorganizational modes of Cooperation and Sectoral Differences', *Strategic Management Journal*, 14, 1993, 371–385.

Hall, M. 'House Rejects Foreign Ownership of US Airlines – But the Fight Isn't Over', *AFL-CIO* (15 June 2006). Online. Available HTTP: <http://blog.aflcio.org/2006/06/15/house-rejects-foreign-ownership-of-us-airlines%E2%80%94but-the-fight-isn%E2%80%99t-over/>.

Hanlon, J.P. *Global Airlines: Competition in a Transnational Industry*, (Oxford: Butterworth-Heinemann, 1996).

Hargreaves Heap, S. and Varoufakis, Y. *Game Theory*, 2nd ed. (London: Routledge, 2004).

Havel, B.F. *Beyond Open Skies: A New Regime for International Aviation* (The Netherlands: Kluwer Law International, 2009).

HMSO, *British Air Transport in the Seventies*, Report of the Committee of Inquiry into Civil Air Transport (London, 1969).

Holloway, S. *Straight and Level: Practical Airline Economics,* 3rd ed. (Aldershot: Ashgate, 2008), Part 1.

Horwitz, R. 'Deregulation as a Political Process', Unpublished. Online. Available HTTP: <http://www.connect-world.com/Articles/14Deregulation.html>(accessed 10 July 2011).

Hugon, P. 'Global Public Goods and the Transnational Level of Regulation', *Issues in Regulation Theory* 1–3, 48, April 2004. Online. Available HTTP: <http://web.upmf-grenoble.fr/regulation/Issue_Regulation_theory/LR48english.pdf> (accessed 25 March 2011).

Hymer, S.H. *The International Operations of National Firms: A Study of Direct Foreign Investment* (Cambridge, MA: MIT Press, 1976)

Immers, L. and Stada, J. 'Basics of Transport Economics', *Faculty of Engineering, Katholieke Universiteit Leuven*, Belgium (2004), p. 6. Online. Available HTTP: <http://www.kuleuven.be/traffic/stats/download.php?id=65> (accessed 5 March 2011).

Inglada, V., Rey, B., Rodríguez-Alvarez, A. and Coto-Millan, P. 'Liberalization and Efficiency in International Air Transport', *Transportation Research Part A*, 40, 2006, 95–105.

Johnson, P.S. *The Structure of British Industry,* (London: Routledge, 1988).

Jones, A. and Sufrin, B. *EC Competition Law: Texts, Cases and Materials*, 4th ed. (Oxford: Oxford University Press, 2010).

Kagan, R. 'Regulatory Enforcement', in D. Rosenbloom and R. Schwartz, (eds), *Handbook of Regulation and Administrative Law* (New York: Dekker, 1994).

Kahn, A.E. 'Airline Deregulation', *The Concise Encyclopaedia of Economics,* Library of Economics and Liberty. Online. Available HTTP: website at <http://www.econlib.org/library/Enc/AirlineDeregulation.html> (accessed 11 September 2011).

—— 'The Changing Environment of International Air Commerce,' *Air Law*, (Netherlands Journal), Vol. 3, No. 3, 1978a.

—— 'Deregulation of Air Transportation – Getting from Here to There,' *Regulating Business: The Search for an Optimum* (San Francisco, CA: Institute for Contemporary Studies, 1978b).

—— 'Statement of A.E. Kahn before the Aviation Subcommittee of the House Public Works and Transportation Committee on H.R. 11145, 95th Cong. 2d Sess. 8' (6 March 1978); Aviation Regulatory Reform, Hearings before the Subcommittee on Aviation of the House Committee on Public Works and Transportation, 95th Cong. 2d Sess. 124 (1978c).

—— 'Surprises from Deregulation', *AEA Papers and Proceedings*, 78, 1988.

Kau, J. and Rubin, P. 'Self-Interest, Ideology and Logrolling in Congressional Voting', *Journal of Law and Economics*, 22, 1979, 365–384.

Keeley, M.C. *A Social-Contract Theory of Organizations* (Notre Dame, IN: University of Notre Dame Press, 1988).

Kelman, S. 'Public Choice and Public Spirit', *Public Interest*, 87, 1987, 80–94.

Ketokivi, M.A. and Schroeder, R.G. 'Strategic, Structural Contingency and Institutional Explanations in the Adoption of Innovative Manufacturing Practices', *Journal of Operations Management*, 22, 2004, 63–89.

Khemani, R.S. and Shapiro, D.M. (eds), *Glossary of Industrial Organisation Economics and Competition Law*, commissioned by the Directorate for Financial, Fiscal and Enterprise Affairs, OECD, 1993. Online. Available HTTP: <http://www.oecd.org/dataoecd/8/61/2376087.pdf> (accessed 25 June 2011).

Kleymann, B. and Seristö, H. *Managing Strategic Airline Alliances* (Aldershot: Ashgate, 2004).

—— 'Challenges to Federation Governance', in B. Kleymann and H. Seristö, *Managing Strategic Airline Alliances* (Aldershot: Ashgate, 2004).

—— 'Competing with the Alliance: Strategy Options of Independents', in B. Kleymann and H. Seristö, *Managing Strategic Airline Alliances* (Aldershot: Ashgate, 2004).

—— 'Marketing Airline Alliances: The Branded Airline', in B. Kleymann and H. Seristö, *Managing Strategic Airline Alliances* (Aldershot: Ashgate, 2004).

Knorr, A. and Arndt, A. 'Most Low-Cost Airlines Fail (ed): Why Did Southwest Airlines Prosper?' in P. Forsyth, D. Gillen, O.G. Mayer and H. Niemeier (eds), *Competition versus Predation in Aviation Markets: A Survey of Experience in North America, Europe and Australia* (Aldershot: Ashgate, 2005).

Kole, S.R. and Lehn, K. 'Workforce Integration and the Dissipation of Value in Mergers: The Case of US Air's Acquisition of Piedmont Aviation', in S.N. Kaplan (ed.), *Mergers and Productivity: NBER Conference Report Series* (London: University of Chicago Press, 2000).

Korah, V. *An Introductory Guide to EC Competition Law and Practice*, 9th ed. (Oxford: Hart Publishing, 2007).

Koza, M.P. and Lewin, A.Y. 'The Co-Evolution of Strategic Alliances', *Organization Science*, 9, 1998, 99–117.

Küschelrath, K. 'Strategic Behaviour of Incumbents: Rationality, Welfare and Antitrust Policy', in P. Forsyth, D.W. Gillen, O.E. Mayer and H-M. Niemeier (eds), *Competition versus Predation in Aviation Markets: A Survey of Experience in North America, Europe and Australia* (Aldershot: Ashgate, 2005).

Lall, A. 'Predatory Pricing: Still a Rare Occurrence?', in P. Forsyth, D.W. Gillen, O.E. Mayer and H-M. Niemeier (eds), *Competition versus Predation in Aviation Markets: A Survey of Experience in North America, Europe and Australia* (Aldershot: Ashgate, 2005).

Lavie, D. and Rosenkopf, L. 'Balancing Exploration and Exploitation in Alliance Formation', *Academy of Management Journal*, 49(4), 2006, 797–818.

Levine, M.E. 'Revisionism Revised? Airline Deregulation and the Public Interest', *Law and Contemporary Problems*, 44, 1981, 179–195.

—— and Forrence, J.L. 'Regulatory Capture, Public Interest, and the Public Agenda: Toward a Synthesis', *Journal of Law, Economics, and Organization*, 6(168), 1990.

Levinthal, D.A. and March, J.G. 'The Myopia of Learning', *Strategic Management Journal*, 14, 1993, 105.

Levy, B. and Spiller, P.T. 'The Institutional Foundations of Regulatory Commitment: A Comparative Analysis of Telecommunications Regulation', *Journal of Law, Economics and Organization*, 10(2), 1994, 201–246.

Liegl, P. 'US Airways History', *US Airways: Fleet and Network Analysis*. Online. Available HTTP: <http://www.erau.edu/research/BA590/USAIR/chapters/ch1.htm> (accessed 12 August 2011).

Lufthansa German Airlines, 'Green light for Lufthansa and Brussels Airlines: the European Commission has approved the merger of the two airlines'. Online. Available HTTP: <http://www.lufthansa.com/ph/en/Lufthansa-and-Brussels-Airlines> (accessed 23 September 2011).

Marshall, R. 'Ryanair Holdings PLC – Easy Jet to Buy GB Airways', *Reuters*, 23 January 2008. Online. Available HTTP: <http://www.reuters.com/article/pressRelease/idUS137554+23–Jan-2008+RNS20080123> (accessed 19 August 2011).

Meier, K.I. *The Political Economy of Regulation* (New York: State University of New York Press, 1988).

Mikva, A. 'Forward, Symposium on the Theory of Public Choice', *Virginia Law Review*, 71, 1988, 167–177.

Miller, R. and Chua, J. (eds), *Airlines – 2006 World Wide Competition Law Review*, A Civil Aviation Authority (CAA) policy document. Online. Available HTTP: <www.caa.co.uk/default.aspx?catid=5&pagetype=90&pageid=6264> (accessed 18 July 2011).

Mills, S. 'Alliance Network Comparison: Weekly global operations Summer 2011', Flight global Data Research and Flight global Insight, *Airline Business* 27(9), 2011, 32–47.

Mintzberg, H. *The Rise and Fall of Strategic Planning* (Hemel Hempstead: Prentice Hall, 1994).

Monasso, T. and Van Leijden, F. 'Telecommunication Regulation as a Game: Deepening Theoretical Understanding', *SSRN Working Paper Series*, 14. December 2007.

Morrison, S. and Winston, C. *The Economic Effects of Airline Deregulation* (Washington: Brookings Institution Press, 1986).

—— 'The Remaining Role for Government Policy in the Deregulated Airline Industry', in S. Peltzman and C. Winston (eds), *Deregulation of Network Industries: What's Next?* (Washington: Brookings Institution Press, 2000).

Murphy, J.G. and Coleman, J.L. (eds) *Philosophy of Law: An Introduction to Jurisprudence* (Boulder, CO: Westview Press, 1990).

Nall, S. 'Air Cargo Alliances Take Tentative First Steps Into Cargo Arena in Global Logistics and Supply Chain Strategies' *Keller Publishing*, 1998. Online. Available HTTP: <http://www.supplychainbrain.com> (accessed 12 August 2011).

'New Qantas Rail Codeshare Link to Seven German Cities', *Air Transport News* (19 April 2007).

Online. Available HTTP: <http://www.airtransportnews.aero/article.pl?id=3167&keys=n uremberg> (accessed 10 July 2011).

O'Connell, J.F. 'Airlines: An Inherently Turbulent Industry', in J.F. O'Connell and G. Williams (eds), *Air Transport in the 21st Century: Key Strategic Developments* (Farnham: Ashgate, 2011).

—— 'Ancillary Revenues: The New Trend in Strategic Airline Marketing', in J.F. O'Connell and G. Williams (eds), *Air Transport in the 21st Century: Key Strategic Developments* (Farnham: Ashgate, 2011).

—— 'IT Innovations in Passenger Services', in J.F. O'Connell and G. Williams (eds), *Air Transport in the 21st Century: Key Strategic Developments* (Farnham: Ashgate, 2011).

OECD Annual Report (2003), Online. Available HTTP: <http://www.oecd.org/datao-ecd/45/28/2506789.pdf> (accessed 11 March 2011).

Olson, M. *The Logic of Collective Action* (Cambridge, MA: Harvard University Press, 1965).

Organisation for Economic Cooperation and Development (OECD), *Deregulation and Airline Competition* (Washington, DC: OECD Publications, 1988) p. 3.

Oum, T.H., Park, J.H. and Zhang, A. *Globalization and Strategic Alliances: The Case of the Airline Industry* (Oxford: Elsevier, 2000).

—— and Yamaguchi, K. 'Asia's tangled skies', *Far Eastern Economic Review*, January-February 2006, as cited in B. Vasigh, K. Fleming and T. Tacker, *Introduction to Air Transport Economics* (Farnham: Ashgate, 2008), p. 164.

—— and Zhang, A. 'Key Aspects of Global Strategic Alliances and the Impacts on the Future of Canadian Airline Industry', *Journal of Air Transport Management* 7, 2001, 287–301.

Pape, W. 'Socio-Cultural Differences and International Competition Law', *European Legal Journal*, 5, 1999, 444–445.

Parke, A. 'Strategic Alliance Structuring: A Game Theoretic and Transaction–Cost Examination of Interfirm Cooperation', *Academy of Management Review* 36, 1993, 227–268, as cited in J. Child, D. Faulkner and S. Tallman, *Cooperative Strategy: Managing Alliances, Networks, and Joint Ventures*, 2nd ed. (Oxford: Oxford University Press, 2005), p. 21.

Peltzman, S. and Winstron, C. *Deregulation of Network Industries* (Washington, DC: Brookings Institution Press, 2000).

Peritz, R.J.R. *Competition Policy in America: History, Rhetoric, Law*, Rev. Ed. (Oxford: Oxford University Press, 1996).

Peterson, K. 'A United-US Airways Merger Could Restrict Competition', *International Herald Tribune*, 2008. Online. Available HTTP: <www.iht.com/articles/2008/05/04/business/rtrdeal05.php> (accessed 12 May 2011).

Pilarski, A.M. *Why Can't We Make Money in Aviation?* (Aldershot: Ashgate, 2007).

Pitofsky, R. 'Competition Policy in Communications Industries: New Antitrust Approaches', *US Federal Trade Commission Speeches* (1997). Online. Available HTTP: <http://www.ftc.gov/speeches/pitofsky/newcomm.shtm> (accessed 8 August 2011).

Poole Jr, R.E. and Butler, V. 'Airline Deregulation: The Unfinished Revolution', *Regulation*, 22(1), 1999, 44.

Porter, M.E. *Competitive Strategy: Techniques for Analyzing Industries and Competitors* (New York: Free Press, 1980).

—— *The Competitive Advantage of Nations* (New York: Free Press, 1990).

—— *On Competition* (Cambridge, MA: Harvard University Business Review Series, 1996).

—— and Fuller, M.B. 'Coalitions and Global Strategy', in M.E. Porter (ed.), *Competition in Global Industries* (Boston, MA: Harvard Business School Press, 1986).

Posner, R.A. 'Theories of Economic Regulation', NBER Working Papers 0041, National Bureau of Economic Research Inc (US), 1974. Online. Available HTTP: <http://ideas.repec.org/p/nbr/nberwo/0041.html> (accessed 12 June 2011).

—— 'The Rule of Reason and the Economic Approach: Reflections on the *Sylvania* Decision', *The University of Chicago Law Review*, 45(1), Fall 1977, 1–20.

—— *Economic Analysis of Law*, 7th ed., (Austin, TX: Wolters-Kluwer, 2007).

Quinn, J.B. *Strategies for Change: Logical Incrementalism* (Homewood, IL: Irwin, 1980).

Reisinger, M. 'Why do Low Cost Carriers Arise and How can they Survive the Competitive Responses of Established Airlines? A Theoretical Explanation', in P.P. Forsyth, D.W. Gillen, O.E. Mayer and H-M. Niemeier (eds), *Competition versus Predation in Aviation Markets: A Survey of Experience in North America, Europe and Australia* (Aldershot: Ashgate, 2005).

'Responses to "Ash Crisis" for Air Transport Outlined', *EU Focus*, 272, 2010, 34–35.

Rhoades, D.L. *Evolution of International Aviation: Phoenix Rising*, 2nd ed. (Aldershot: Ashgate, 2008).

—— 'State of US Aviation: Clinging to Old Ways in a New Century', in J.F. O'Connell and G. Williams (eds), *Air Transport in the 21st Century: Key Strategic Developments* (Farnham: Ashgate, 2011).

Robertson, D. 'BA-Iberia merger would create biggest airline in Europe', *Times Online* (30 July 2008). Online. Available HTTP: <http://business.timesonline.co.uk/tol/business/industry_sectors/transport/article4426034.ece>(accessed 4 August 2008).

Robson, J.E. 'Airline Deregulation: Twenty Years of Success and Counting', *Regulation*, Spring 1988, 17.

Rose-Ackerman, S. 'Progressive Law and Economics – and the New Administrative Law', *Yale Law Journal*, 98, 1988, 341–368.

Rowley, T., Behrens, D. and Krackhardt, D. 'Redundant Governance Structures: An Analysis of Structural and Relational Embeddedness in the Steel and Semi-Conductor Industries', *Strategic Management Journal*, 21, 2000, 369–386.

'Ryanair Under Fire at Charleroi', *EIRO*. Online. Available HTTP: <www.eiro.eurofound.eu.int/2003/12/inbrief/be0312302n.html> (accessed 5 May 2011).

Schelling, T.C. *The Strategy of Conflict* (Cambridge, MA: Harvard University Press, 2007).

Scherer, F.M. *Competition Policies for an Integrated World Economy* (Washington, DC: Brookings Institution, 1994).

Schwarcz, S.L. 'Private Ordering', *Northwestern University Law Review*, 97, Fall 2002, 319–350.

Scott, C. 'Analysing Regulatory Space: Fragmented Resources and Institutional Design', *Public Law*, 2001, 329–353.

Semberya, D. 'Kikwete Advises on Air Transport Investment', *East African Business Week*, 5 September 2011. Online. Available HTTP: <http://www.busiweek.com/11/news/tanzania?start=5> (accessed 13 September 2011).

Smith, S. 'The Strategies and Effects of Low-Cost Carriers', *Steer Davies Gleave*, 2005 (available at www.icea.co.uk/archive.htm), as cited in B. Vasigh, K. Fleming and T. Tacker, *Introduction to Air Transport Economics* (Farnham: Ashgate, 2008).

Smith, S.A. *Contract Theory* (Oxford: Oxford University Press, 2004).

Snow, J. 'Advanced in Transport Aircraft and Engines', in J.F. O'Connell and G. Williams (eds), *Air Transport in the 21st Century: Key Strategic Developments* (Farnham: Ashgate, 2011).

Speciale, R.C. *Aircraft Ownership: A Legal and Tax Guide* (New York: McGraw-Hill, 2003).

Stragier, J. 'Airline Alliances and Mergers – The Emerging Commission Policy', Paper presented at the 13th Annual Conference of the European Air Law Association, Zurich (9 November 2001). Online. Available HTTP: <http://www.eu.int/comm/competition/speeches/text/sp2001_040_en.pdf>(accessed 15 March 2002).

Starkie, D. *Airports and Airlines and the Role of Competition and Regulation Aviation Markets. Studies in Competition and Regulatory* (Aldershot: Ashgate, 2008).

—— *Aviation Markets: Studies in Competition and Regulatory Reform* (Farnham: Ashgate, 2008).

Stigler, G.J. 'The Theory of Economic Regulation', *Bell Journal of Economics and Management Science*, 2, 1971, 3.

—— *The Theory of Price*, 2nd ed., (New York: Macmillan, 1987).

—— and Irwin, D. *Production and Distribution Theories* (London: Transaction Publishers, 1994).

Trebilcock, M.J. *The Limits of Freedom of Contract* (Cambridge, MA: Harvard University Press, 1997).

Trier Academy of European Union Law, 'Deregulation and Regulation of the European "Airscape"', Vol. 23, Cologne (Germany): *Bundesanzeiger Verlags*, 1997.

Truxal, S. 'Competitive Distortions, Carbon Emissions Efficiencies or the Green Ultimatum?' *International Trade Law and Regulation*, 14(4), 2008, 77–79.

—— 'EU Transport Emissions Compliance Catch-up', *International Trade Law and Regulation*, 14(6), 2008, 117–121.

—— 'At the Sidelines of Implementing the EU ETS: Objections to "Validity"', *International Trade Law and Regulation*, 16(4), 2010, 111–119.

UK Department of Trade and Industry, *Productivity and Enterprise: A World Class Competition Regime White Paper*, Cm 5233 (2001).

Utton, M. 'Going European: Britain's New Competition Law', Working Paper – University of Reading. Online. Available HTTP: <http://www.rdg.ac.uk/Econ/Econ/workingpapers/emdp403.pdf> (accessed 12 August 2011).

Uzzi, B. and Sprio, J. 'Collaboration and Creativity: The Small World Problem', *American Journal of Sociology*, 111, 2005, 447–504.

Vasigh, B., Fleming, K. and Tacker, T. *Introduction to Air Transport Economics* (Farnham: Ashgate, 2008).

Veljanovski, C.G. 'The Coase Theorems and the Economic Theory of Markets and Law', *Kyklos*, 35, 1982, 53–74.

—— 'EC Merger Policy after GE/Honeywell and Airtours', *Antitrust Bulletin*, 49, 2004, 153–193.

—— 'Economic Approaches to Regulation', in R. Baldwin, M. Cave and M. Lodge (eds), *The Oxford Handbook of Regulation* (Oxford: Oxford University Press, 2010).

—— 'Strategic Use of Regulation', in R. Baldwin, M. Cave and M. Lodge (eds), *The Oxford Handbook of Regulation,* (Oxford: Oxford University Press, 2010).

Völcker, S. 'Start-Up Aid for Low Cost Carriers – A Policy Perspective', *Competition Law Insight* (Informa Professional) 4.6(3), 2005.

Weingast, B. 'Regulation, Reregulation and Deregulation: The Foundation of Agency-Clientele Relationships', *Law and Contemporary Problems*, 44, 1981, 147–177.

Wensveen, J.G. *Air Transport: A Management Perspective,* 6th ed., (Aldershot: Ashgate: 2007).

Werden, G.J., Joskow, A.S. and Johnson, R.L. 'The Effects of Mergers on Price and Output: Two Case Studies from the Airline Industry', *Managerial and Decision Economics*, 12(5), 1991, 341–352.

Whish, R. *Competition Law* (Oxford: Oxford University Press, 2009).

Whitaker, M. 'Liberalized Airline Ownership and Control: Good for Consumers, Airlines and the United States', Seminar paper for AT Conf/5, 2003, ICAO Worldwide Air Transport Conference, 22–23 March 2003.

Williams, G. *The Airline Industry and the Impact of Deregulation* (Aldershot: Ashgate, 1993).

—— *Airline Competition: Deregulation's Mixed Legacy* (Aldershot: Ashgate, 2002).

—— 'Comparing the Economic and Operating Characteristics of Charter and Low-cost Scheduled Airlines', in J.F. O'Connell and G. Williams (eds), *Air Transport in the 21st Century: Key Strategic Developments* (Farnham: Ashgate, 2011).

Williamson, O.E. *Markets and Hierarchies: Analysis and Antitrust Implications* (New York: The Free Press, 1975).

—— *The Economic Institutions of Capitalism* (New York: The Free Press, 1985).

—— *Antitrust Economics: Mergers, Contracting, and Strategic Behaviour* (Oxford: Basil Blackwell, 1987).

Wong, J. 'International Airline to Allow Cell Phone Chatter on Planes' (*CNN*, 2006). Online. Available HTTP: <http://www.cnn.com/2006/TECH/12/21/wired.airline/index.html> (accessed 6 January 2007).

Wright, M., Marsden, S. and Antonelli, A. *Building an Evidence Base for the Health and Safety Commission Strategy to 2010 and Beyond: A Literature Review of Interventions to Improve Health and Safety Compliance* (Norwich: HSE Books, 2004).

Zwaniecki, A. 'House Approves Moratorium on Airline Foreign Ownership Rule', 2006, American Information Web website, HTTP: <http://usinfo.org/wf-archive/2006/060317/epf507.htm> (accessed 12 August 2011).

Index

An environmentally friendly book printed and bound in England by www.printondemand-worldwide.com

#0302 - 230614 - C0 - 234/156/11 - PB